Swt (o)
12/93

Background to Dylan Thomas
and
Other Explorations

BACKGROUND TO DYLAN THOMAS

and Other Explorations

GWYN JONES

Oxford   New York

OXFORD UNIVERSITY PRESS

1992

Oxford University Press. Walton Street. Oxford OX2 6DP

Oxford New York Toronto
Delhi Bombay Calcutta Madras Karachi
Petaling Jaya Singapore Hong Kong Tokyo
Nairobi Dar es Salaam Cape Town
Melbourne Auckland

and associated companies in
Berlin Ibadan

Oxford is a trade mark of Oxford University Press

British Library Cataloguing in Publication Data
Data available

Library of Congress Cataloging in Publication Data
Jones, Gwyn, 1907-
Background to Dylan Thomas, and other explorations / Gwyn Jones.
p. cm.
1. Wales—Civilization. 2. Thomas, Dylan, 1914-1953.
3. Literature—History and criticism. 4. Vikings. I. Title.
DA711.5.J64 1992 942.9—dc20 91-27346
ISBN 0-19-811283-1

Typeset by Colset Private Limited, Singapore
Printed in Great Britain by
Bookcraft (Bath) Ltd.
Midsomer Norton, Avon

FOREWORD

'Everything an author writes is part of an autobiography, by his own hand taken down, and may be used in evidence against him.' The words (I am told) are my own, taken down in 1974, but the thought is at least as old as the Bible's 'O that mine enemy would write a book!' Acting on the theory that a man's worst enemy, like a man's best friend, is himself, this I have done—written a book, many a book, and many a kind of book: fiction, history, literary criticism, folktale-legend-myth, translations, books for children, and editions of other men's work. But *Background to Dylan Thomas and Other Explorations* is distinct from its predecessors in that it is the only one which I have not merely written down, but also uttered forth. For as a man who for sixty years or more has been by definition a teacher, lecturer, professor, and communicator-at-large, in classrooms, lecture-halls, museums, learned institutions, broadcasting studios, demoted chapels and other such auditoria in the British Isles, Northern Europe, Canada, and the United States of America, to all kinds of audiences captive or free, normally on my feet but latterly on my seat—all my adult life I have been deploying what some style the oratorical arts, and others the South Wales gift of the gab.

My twelve lectures, essays, addresses (and sometimes essays become addresses, and addresses turned essays) will, I trust, yet again speak for themselves without an apparatus of footnotes and directives. But having said that, I at once feel the need to add that a lecture delivered on an expanding subject may, just like a book, require emendation in the light of increased knowledge and improved judgement. The address with which my volume opens, and which supplies its title, is a case in point. It began life as five or six short pieces in newspapers and journals, before becoming 'The First Forty Years' (itself the first W. D. Thomas Memorial Lecture, 1957). Its subject—the writings of contemporary Welsh authors in the English language—was for political and social reasons a compelling one, and fecund of dispute, and not surprisingly I dealt with it again in 1972 in my BBC Wales Annual Radio Lecture, 'Being and Belonging', and then yet again in 'Babel and the Dragon's Tongue' (the last Gwilym James Memorial Lecture, 1983). Except in Wales or a close Welsh context (and occasionally there too) the lecture's title made unashamed use of the compelling magic of Dylan Thomas's name, for the very good reason that Northern Europe and North America would have no other. So whatever the name of the rose, Anglo-Welsh literature had a good airing in some twenty-five Universities and Learned Societies from Copenhagen to Vancouver and, on a more southerly arc, from London to San Francisco.

Other notable palimpsests are 'Here Be Dragons' and my latest and last discourse on 'the best-hated man in Wales', Caradoc Evans, but rather than chase the Minute Particulars, I turn with pleasure and gratitude to list my Acknowledgements of permissions given and favours granted. They are in the main of three kinds.

To publishers and Institutions for permission to reproduce copyright or otherwise restricted material: the British Academy, for No. 3, 'Three Poetical Prayer-Makers of the Island of Britain'; the Honourable Society of Cymmrodorion, for No. 1, 'Background to Dylan Thomas' and No. 2 'The Golden Cockerel *Mabinogion*'; Edinburgh University Press, for four stanzas from *The Gododdin* by Kenneth Hurlestone Jackson, 1969, reproduced in No. 9, 'Here Be Dragons', pp. 145–52; Messrs Faber and Faber, for the passage from *Epoch and Artist*, by David Jones, 1959, reproduced in No. 1, pp. 14–15; Glasgow University Publications, for No. 10, 'The Legendary History of Olaf Tryggvason'; the National Library of Wales, for No. 7, 'On First Planting a Library'; the *Times Literary Supplement*, for contributions to No. 2, 'The Golden Cockerel *Mabinogion*' and No. 4, 'A Mighty Man in Sion'; the University College of Wales, Aberystwyth, for No. 9, 'Here Be Dragons'; the *Welsh Review*, March 1945, for contributions to No. 4, 'A Mighty Man in Sion' and for No. 6, 'Son of the Late Earl Rivers'.

To friends who have allowed me the free use of published and

unpublished material in their private ownership: Professor
Joseph P. Clancy, New York, now of Aberystwyth, for his
translations of Cynddelw and J. Kitchener Davies in No. 3,
pp. 52–71, and of Cynddelw, Hywel ab Owain Gwynedd,
and Gwalchmai in No. 9, pp. 153–4, from *The Earliest Welsh
Poetry* (Macmillan, 1970), and *Twentieth Century Welsh Poems*
(Macmillan, 1982); Professor Gwyn Thomas, University
College of North Wales, Bangor, for his translations of Saunders
Lewis in No. 3, pp. 68–71; the late Mrs Lyn Thomas for the
classic passage from her husband Gwyn's work in No. 1, p. 8;
Monica Dunbar, for the unfettered use of her papers and
personal reminiscence of the Caradoc Evans; Elaine Attias of
Los Angeles for her photograph of the author at Laugharne;
Mrs Megan Tudur of Aberystwyth for confirming me in my use
of her father J. Kitchener Davies's poem No. 3.

To a wide circle of friends, colleagues, and fellow-workers
in those fields of study and delight traversed or reconnoitred in
this volume. First, five names from the University College of
Wales, Aberystwyth: Professor Walford Davies, Extra-Mural
Studies; Dr Geraint Gruffydd, Director of the Centre for
Advanced Welsh and Celtic Studies; Dr John Harris, the Welsh
College of Librarianship; Dr Brynley F. Roberts, our National
Librarian; Professor Desmond Slay, Former Head of the
English Department. Second, four names from away: Professor
Ólafur Halldórsson of Stofnun Árna Magnússonar, Reykjavík,
Iceland; Dr Glyn Jones, Cardiff; Dr Thomas H. McGovern,
Hunter College, New York; Professor Dai Smith, Cardiff.
Contemplating the learning, judgement, and professional skill
of the members of this benevolent comitatus, yet wishing to
avoid a solemnity they would deplore, what can I do but echo
the heartfelt sentiment of the Tea-on-Sunday Preacher-Guest
who when invited—nay, pressed—to take a piece of bread-and-
butter from an as yet unpunished plateful, replied unselfishly,
'No, no, the apple tart is good enough for me.'

One name remains—'Foremost of those I would hear
praised.' It can be found on page 207 below, by my own hand
taken down on 24 May 1987, and may be used, as evidence of
intent, against me. It is the name of my wife, Mair. And it is

TO MAIR, in happy fulfilment of that intent, and with a rich sense of privilege, that on this renewed anniversary date, 24 May 1991, I dedicate my twelve-parted book, in whose making and uttering forth she has been so fully participant.

Gwyn Jones
1991

CONTENTS

Background to Dylan Thomas

Anglo-Welsh Literature, 1934–1946:
A Personal View

In the nature of things it is not often that a speaker can open his address with a reminder—be it threat or promise—that he has been part of his subject for a full half-century. But I can, literally, go one better than that: I have been part of mine for a full fifty years and a full year over. And as the poet sang of old: 'It don't seem a year too long'. In a sentence, it was in 1936 that *Times Like These* fell, as they say, from the press, my novel about a South Wales mining valley during the Great Depression; and ever since an unbroken sequence of lectures and articles, broadcasts and reviews, eulogies and diatribes, rejoinders and explications, punctuated by editings and editorials, novels and short stories—all these have kept me part of the Anglo-Welsh literary phenomenon and therefore of the Welsh cultural scene. Of anyone else I would by now be saying: 'It's about time he shut up', but every rule demands its exception, and no exception can be as compelling as that self-made for oneself. Also, I am as pleased as I am privileged by the accolade of your invitation to discourse yet again on a subject so dear to my heart and so important to the cultural life of our country.

One great change from fifty or even thirty years ago is that it is no longer necessary to over-define one's subject, and discourse at length about what it isn't as well as what it is. The term Anglo-Welsh has by now not only an acceptable but an accepted meaning. As adjective or noun it is a descriptive and defining

Reprinted from the *Transactions of the Honourable Society of Cymmrodorion*, 1987.

literary term. Anglo-Welsh literature consists of the poems, novels, short stories, autobiographies and the like, together with the critical and attendant apparatus they engender, written by Anglo-Welsh authors. In turn, Anglo-Welsh authors are those men and women of Welsh blood, valid claim or affinity, the compulsions of history and geography, and the accidents of education and nurture, who either cannot, will not, or in any case do not use the Welsh language for creative purposes. I emphasize that word 'creative', and having done so will illustrate just one of the creative writer's cruces with a statement from our best living Anglo-Welsh poet, R. S. Thomas:

> Because I was thirty years old before I began to learn Welsh seriously, and because I lacked the privilege of being brought up in a Welsh environment, I have neither the instinct nor the confidence which are essential for anyone who wishes to use language in the most skilful way possible, namely in writing poetry. I have therefore refused to commit suicide as a writer . . .

Which is why so ardent a Welshman and so dedicated a poet had by 1977 written 606 poems in English and just one poem in Welsh. His apologia, it is relevant to note, was written in Welsh prose. Conversely, yet supportively, Alun Llywelyn-Williams has testified how his father's passion for the Welsh language and the happy accident of an equally dedicated Welsh teacher in Cardiff ensured his conversion to the art and practice of poetry in Welsh. If books have their destinies even as their owners, poems have their destinies no less than their poets. Few readers, if any, have been heard to complain.

Anglo-Welsh literature then is not only the visible, weighable, purchasable and even readable product of the English-language writers of Wales. It is likewise the rendering articulate of at least two-thirds of our fellow-countrymen—a matter (I choose my adjective) of shattering impact and importance. The term itself arose in a most honourable way out of our high regard for the pre-eminence and temporal priority of Welsh-language literature, and (I speak for many of my friends as well as myself) our anxiety lest our inevitable rivalry might be one more source of damage and diminution of *yr hen iaith*. And if that sounds patronizing, or minatory, or otherwise offensive, heaven knows that was the last thing in our minds. The future of the Welsh language becomes an ever more cruel problem, and it will be a grievous day for Welshmen and Wales if this well-intentioned literary adjective 'Anglo-Welsh' should ever fall into disuse because differentiation is no longer needed.

After those sombre words you will be relieved to hear that I don't propose to rehearse yet again the main critical heresies regarding Anglo-Welsh literature: that it must be written by Welshmen about Wales only; that it can't be Anglo-Welsh because it isn't like Anglo-Irish; and that it is a 'colonial' literature. All three are patently wrong-headed (the third is likewise wrong-hearted), and, blessedly, time and common sense have disposed of them. Nor need I trace the changing relationship, the increased understanding of each other's problems, now characteristic of our writers, whether in Welsh or English. We have come a long way from the bruising years when Saunders Lewis could say of Dylan Thomas that he was a fine young poet but lost to the English, and Dylan could say in reply, 'Land of my Fathers: my fathers can have it.' Saunders would have proved a better prophet if instead of 'lost to the English' he had said, 'given to the world', for in Dylan the Anglo-Welsh have produced the best-known and most widely read Welsh poet of all time. Which is excuse enough for my now disregarding all Anglo-Welsh antecedents and starting with the thirteen lucky years 1934–46, when Anglo-Welsh literature advanced so spectacularly from mid-spring to high summer.

But why A Personal View, with Capital Letters at that? Is this that pride which brought the Angels down? Not so, I assure you. All I seek to do is to talk among friends of how the Anglo-Welsh literary experiment looked to me when it was actually happening, and how I came to be caught up in its joyous compulsions. That there will be some vanity in the narrative is certain—who ever got anywhere wholly without it?—but I offer my story not because it is extraordinary, but because it is so commonplace, so much according to the pattern. And I proffer myself as more of a prototype than an exception: a walking, talking image of the talented Valleys boy born in a typical mining village, in a typical South Wales industrial valley, and raised in a typical South Wales working-class home.

My father, George Henry Jones, a man of good repute and savour, was a miner at Oakdale Colliery in the Sirhowy Valley, and lived in Blackwood. Let me tell you a little about him, and if you have heard it all before—and you have, under many names—that is your good fortune. He had come from Kent to South Wales at the age of 10, and was quickly down the pit. He became a socialist of the old-style gradualist type, worked tirelessly for the cause, and had the trust and respect of all who knew him. He too was a prototype, of the practical, many-skilled, hard-working idealist. A family man devoted to his wife and kids. A thousand, five thousand fathers were saying the same thing: 'No son of mine is going down the pit.' Remember? My brother did go down the pit for a few years. I went to College instead, and with an untroubled conscience rode out the five deepest years of the Great Depression, from 1924 to 1929. It was a tight squeeze even for me by the end. My State Scholarship ran out, and my father got the sack—and I will tell you why. An unloved official was to retire in the late autumn of 1928; there was to be a presentation, and the powers-that-be thought it would be nice if my father, as one of the two longest-serving miners in the pit, would hand over their token of esteem and say something nice as he did so. But Dad declined, firmly, and just as firmly he said why. A month later he was on the dole, and by the mercy of God (in Whom he didn't believe) never got a job down under again. However, my mother was by then the District Nurse and local midwife, and we, Nurse Lily Jones's chicks, got by—*I* in particular got by—surprisingly well, compared with most. If Dad's faith was in social justice and fair-do's-all-round, Mam's lay in love and compassion. With two such parents, it followed that mine was a privileged and assured, if sometimes straitened childhood. True, these were the years when the Valley wits could say of a threepenny-bit: 'The worst thing about a threepenny-bit, see, once you break into it, it's as good as gone.' And it was never a problem, keeping down with the Joneses.

For an impressionable mind, even more arresting than facts

are the mythologies of our personal past and present. Let me then recall my own most influential myth, born of the explosion underground at Senghennydd, Glam., some ten miles seawards from Blackwood. It took place on the morning of October 14, 1913, when I was six-and-a-half years old, and it killed 439 men. Now I must explain that at Blackwood, a stone's throw from our home on Gordon Road, we had an open space called (and rightly so) the Tip, composed of flattened slack and debris and serving as a place of concourse for visiting roundabouts, cheapjacks, politicians, medicine-men, revivalists, and their colourful like. At its lower edge it sheltered our local slaughterhouse. At times of crisis, bafflement, disaster, it was our working-class habit to congregate there, men, women, and children, and I can still smell the actual and imagined expectancy and still hear the quivering silence and mutter of indistinguishable words which charged its darkening air. On the night of the Senghennydd disaster all Blackwood was there. My brother John, a hard-fisted and protective adult of 8, escorted my mother; while I, a timid infant of 6, clung tight to Mam's brother, Uncle Jack, a joyful gladiator about the field for Newport RFC, in whose cause he had sowed his teeth like Indian corn on every gashed and scrum-torn pitch from Rodney Parade to Stradey, and had now grown so careful of his false ones that they never left the safety of his pocket. What a man—what an uncle! Above and around the whispering and fear, the sky, I remember, throbbed with red. I know now that the explosion at Senghennydd Colliery took place twelve hundred feet down, out of sight, out of sound. I learned that long ago, and accepted unwillingly that my childhood vision of God's right hand illuming our mortal tragedy was myth and nothing more. Later again I learned that the red evening sky was almost as regular as supper in the Valleys, when the iron-works north of us at Merthyr and Tredegar were opened to the waiting heavens.

Be that as it may, the disaster at Senghennydd and the red pulse of heaven remain my most powerful other-than-family childhood memory. Inevitably I quickly came to share my father's strong and reasoned political convictions; and not unnaturally I came to press them harder and with a sharper point. After all, if you aren't facing full left at 18 you need your heart tested, just as if you *are* facing full left at 80 you need your head read. Though if you are facing full right at any time of your life you are beyond surgery and past salvation. For there it was: 439 men dead to make money for some damned coal-owner and some equally unspeakable battener on road-rights and royalties.

And Uncle Jack, that man of might and merriment, popular with all—what of him? He died, bedridden in his fifties of dust on the lungs. Speechless, breathless, supine, utterly betrayed by Society and the System. That didn't incline me to eyes-right either.

But let me return from these not uncommon commonplaces to my not impersonal Personal View and the theme of my not unrepresentative status. Born at Blackwood, in the Sirhowy Valley, Gwent, to a miner and his wife; attended Blackwood Infants' and Blackwood Elementary School, and thereafter as a scholarship boy Tredegar County School, and as a scholarship student the University College of South Wales and Monmouthshire, Cardiff, and finally in 1929, the deepest-down year of the Great Depression, off to teach for six years in North of England grammar schools—what could be more representative than that? Meanwhile Me and Mine had weathered the First World War, the coal strikes of 1922 and 1924, the General Strike of 1926, and when I returned to South Wales in 1935 if things were looking up a bit this was because industry was rolling up its sleeves for that Second World War which was coming to look a certainty.

One more glimpse of the obvious and we should be reaching Anglo-Welsh literature head-on. But I still want to stress, and heavily underline, that the Anglo-Welsh writers of my generation grew up in both hard and mind-stirring times. And what lingering inhibition tempts me to omit the further epithet 'soul-searching'? For a good deal of my generation's thinking and feeling took place in the twin realms of Politics and Religion. It could hardly be otherwise. Take a piece of paper and jot down the chapter-headings of the time: The Class Struggle, Socialism in our Time, Unemployment and the Dole, the First Labour

Government and its woeful collapse, Arthur Cook and the South Wales Miners' Federation. And mustering on the horizon the murk of Nazism, Fascism, and Communism. What a post-war world it was turning out to be, fit neither for heroes nor for cravens to live in. Strikes, lock-outs, disarmament, and rearmament: the incipient Anglo-Welsh were conversant with them all.

And Religion? Throughout my lifetime the Nonconformist and Methodist denominations have been in decline, and here too I have followed a trend. But though belief and attendance have gone their way, I cannot take the lessons of Methodism out of my life, nor have I the slightest wish to do so. Rebel as I did, rebel as I do, Nonconformity, Methodism, the Wesleyan legacy, has permeated my whole being with its warmth and immediacy, its untemporizing rule of right and wrong, its missions and witnessings and conversions, its ascetic ideals and carnal fixations, its truth and myth equally impinged upon the mind—religion sadder than elegies, stronger than mead, rich as a coalseam, sustaining as ten tall brothers.

Still, it is often said, and by none more often than myself, that for all its merits and blessings Methodism was in precept and practice at best indifferent, at worst inimical to the arts. Paradoxically, for my generation, class of 1935, nothing could have fallen out better. We had no canons of Anglo-Welsh literature to rebel against; but revolutions need something to rebel against, and we—I had almost said by divine dispensation—we had Nonconformity. So for just one generation, ours, you had this unique and stimulating point of balance, when the heart-deep but romanticized memories of hymn, prayer, and sermon kept charging our emotional and therefore creative batteries, while dogma, shibboleth, and proscription were powerless to run those batteries down.

Another truth not to be forgotten is that for thousands of youngsters in hundreds of Blackwoods the abiding memories would be even more of the rural than the industrial setting. The Horse Pond and the Mucky Wood, the copses near the Old Beech, and the black sparkling river in which we swam naked as newts and noisy as starlings, the linnets and finches

and yellowhammers in the gorse-runs up towards lonely
Pen-y-fan, are no less real, no less poignant than the five o'clock
hooter pushing through the dawn, the crack of naily boots as
the afternoon shift tramped home, the thin all-purpose over-
coats, and the tall tub in which my brother and I vacked our
father's sweat-and-coal-stiffened pit-togs till all lather had
perished. This was the plurality that was still always one, and
always with full measure.

The classic statement on all these matters is Gwyn Thomas's:

Those Rhondda days are, for me, for ever bathed in a brilliant light;
the tumult of political enthusiasms, the white-hot oratory of the
people's paladins, the festivals of folk singing and hymn singing in
the vast chapels, moving groups on the hillsides at night . . . their
echoes can still fill my mind with an intensive creative excitement.
Then the hill-walks across to Llanwonno, or over to the Dimbath,
the Beacons to the north, pulling us towards an even wilder solitude
than we had ever known; and the Vale of Glamorgan to the south,
tempting us to an ordered placidity which it would benefit our souls
to cultivate. And between these two poles of attraction the fermenting
disquiet of the Valley streets, ringing with every note of pain and
laughter contrived since man's beginning. In that small territory of
land and feeling lay the whole world's experience. The years of study
and experiment have driven convenient lines of communication
through it; they have not enlarged its frontiers, nor enriched the
texture of its earth.

But I must move on. Even so, as a codicil to that political
and ecclesiastical statement, and as a reassertion of my all-
pervading representative status, I add that it was my gentle-
hearted mother's dream that when I left College I would become
a preacher and sing a glad song before the Lord, preferably
in Blackwood, and ideally in her very own Wesleyan (later
United) Methodist conventicle just three hundred yards down
the hill from home. Whereas my socialist and agnostic father
hoped that I might enter politics, first locally, then nationally,
and thereby increase justice and mercy among the children
of men.

But that was not to be. Neither role could ever be congenial
to me. It was my altogether better fortune to obtain a teaching-

post at Wigan Grammar School for three years, and thereafter at Manchester Central High for a further three before I returned to what is now (1987) the late lamented and sorely savaged University College, Cardiff, in the summer of 1935 as an Assistant Lecturer on Probation, which was good news for me, and should be even better for my listeners, inasmuch as it brings me within hailing-distance of my subject—the Anglo-Welsh and their books. Indeed, in 1935 I had published two books myself, real books—with hard covers—a volume of translations from the Icelandic and a historical novel entitled *Richard Savage*. But why on earth would I write a novel about that eighteenth-century scallywag and poetaster? Did I see myself as an Anglo-Welsh author? Emphatically not. The word was more or less reserved in those days for rugby teams compiled from Welshmen playing in England for English clubs who made a trip home once or twice a season, received a warm welcome and an even warmer hiding before returning to their chosen or enforced exile. No, I wrote *Richard Savage* because I wanted to, because I had literary leanings, and because I hoped to distinguish myself—or if you like, to show off a bit. These seem to me not merely valid but highly commendable reasons why any would-be author should get down to it and write. I didn't bother my head whether other people would like it. A lot of them did. It was a good seller—almost a best. So what would I write next?

To my publisher's surprise I abandoned the shining pay-lode of the historical novel and wrote *Times Like These*. Instead of a flamboyant narrative about colourful characters and spectacular happenings, I wrote a quiet and honest story about quiet and honest people living their quiet and honest lives in a South Wales mining village in a South Wales mining valley. Why this right-about turn in manner, theme, and purpose? Quite simply, because I was back home in Wales and implicated in things Welsh. Me and Mine were together again. I was at a stroke recognizably not an English author. By virtue of my language I was strictly speaking not a Welsh author. I was, when my novel appeared in 1936 an Anglo-Welsh author, and I was coming to know a couple of others in like case.

The very first I met of this rare and endangered species was Jack Jones. We were practically next-door neighbours in Rhiwbina, where the disparate shades of Kate Roberts and W. J. Gruffydd still haunted the rarefied air. Iorwerth Peate lived there too, for a while, barricaded off from Jack and me by his politics; and had I but known it, in Rhiwbina lived my lifelong-friend-to-be, Glyn Jones. Jack was a revelation. He had published his *Rhondda Roundabout* in 1934, and was by now buckled to his self-appointed task of interpreting the South Welsh to themselves, their fellow-Welshmen, and while he was at it to the whole wide listening world. His energy, readiness of phrase, and abundance of recollection—I had never known anything like it. And his industry! 'Another damned great thick book, eh, Mr Gibbon?' If George the What's-his-number hadn't invented the phrase about Edward Gibbon, I would now be inventing it about Jack Jones. He liked big books the way he liked big barmaids. It was how the Good Lord intended them to be: Big, and full of their bindings. I remember Jack and me waiting for a Rhiwbina bus on Kingsway, alongside the Castle, when Glyn came up and joined us. Said Jack, spry as a blackbird, all zip, zest, and affectionate curiosity. 'Writing any books now, Glyn?' ('Books', mark you, not book!) 'Yes, I'm writing a story.' 'Good. What's it about?' 'It's about three boys.' 'Good,' said Jack. 'How many generations you taking 'em through?'

Jack was very good for me. He enlarged my view of mankind. Most of my friends and colleagues were people very much like myself, who had lived very much the same kind of life. But here was Jack, who had been collier-boy and shoni-hoy, had joined the Army to get away from the pit, and then deserted to get away from the Army. But he was back in khaki in time for the retreat from Mons, and on hand to record Captain Haggard's famous injunction, 'Stick it, the Welsh!' In politics he was to march behind Lloyd George and Ramsay Macdonald, Mosley and Karl Marx, till his bewildered mother at last had to ask him, 'What are you now then, Jack?' He was a navvy, party agent, orator, encyclopaedia salesman, cinema manager, employed, unemployed, and finally self-employed as an author.

He believed that Life, like books and barmaids, should come in large sizes.

I have recorded before, and will no doubt record again, the story of how Jack and I first met the third member of our Rhiwbina triumvirate, Glyn Jones. Like my recollections of the Senghennydd disaster, this too is not untouched by its enveloping mythology—Glyn, I believe, would plump for a different railway station—but we are authors, story-tellers, not theologians debating how many rivers flowed out of Eden, or how many Welsh angels can sit unscathed on the point of a needle. It happened this way. In the late autumn of 1936 Jack and I went up to Mountain Ash to hear a performance of Verdi's Requiem at the Three Valleys' Festival. By the time we got back to Llandaff North the rain was pouring down, and it didn't help that we were both bareheaded. The station approach was deserted, its lamps unavailing, and we had a tidy step ahead of us. It was then that we noticed a third traveller moving our way. Said Jack—and nothing could be more typical of his zest and humanity: 'Let's see who he is.' We halted. 'Good night there!' said Jack, and added with the assurance of a man who knows that his name is a household word: 'I'm Jack Jones.' Said I, more humbly: 'I'm Gwyn Jones.' And 'I'm Glyn Jones,' said the Third Man. We were all bound for Rhiwbina, and we all had a book on the bench—and that was my second encounter with an Anglo-Welsh author.

'Bliss was it in that dawn to be alive, But to be young was very heaven!' And that was the way of it for more than a decade. The Anglo-Welsh literary identity grew from individuals. Next came the first groupings, the most obvious of them in Cardiff (Valley boys to a man) and Swansea, a growing awareness— soon enhanced by the appearance of the two periodicals, *Wales* and *The Welsh Review* in 1937 and 1939 respectively—of the existence, work, and achievement of other practitioners here, there, and wherever. To make a hurried, anxious journey to Ross-on-Wye in response to a distraught-sounding letter from Margiad Evans, or a planned excursion to Corwen to watch John Cowper Powys and Phyllis watch a distinguished Icelander take snuff; to find a young man by the name of Alun Lewis standing expectantly on your doorstep, or to arrange to meet an unknown newcomer named Gwyn Thomas in London and get him to write for *The Welsh Review*—to say nothing of bearding Caradoc Evans in his Chinese-carpeted lion's den outside Aberystwyth—encounters such as these were manna from heaven for each and every one of us.

And not only books and authors were beginning to abound. Roughly coeval with the full flowering of Anglo-Welsh authorship we beheld the entrance on both the Welsh and world stage of an astonishing group of singers and actors: Geraint Evans, Elizabeth Vaughan, Gwyneth Jones, Stuart Burrows, Emlyn Williams, Stanley Baker, Rachel Roberts, Siân Phillips, Hugh Griffith, Richard Burton. And painters: David Jones, Brenda Chamberlain, Ceri Richards, Kyffin Williams as well as Augustus and Gwen John—and shall we not add Josef Herman here too? Those who maintain that the performing arts today have taken over the energies and skills and self-dramatization that used to adorn the pulpit have more than the tail-end of a truth in their hands.

Well, so far I have stayed with my subtitle: A Personal View. The time has now come for a personal judgement—which cannot be other than a professional one. To further this, I propose to set out a brief list of authors and publications during the years 1934 to 1946, designed to show the emergence and sustained presence of Anglo-Welsh writing during that decisive period. It was not compiled on strict bibliographical principles. I had rather describe it, in rugby parlance, as our all-conquering Anglo-Welsh squad of the time. When shall we look upon its like again?

SOME ANGLO-WELSH AUTHORS AND THEIR BOOKS, 1934–46

1934

1. Dylan Thomas, *18 Poems*.
2. Margiad Evans, *Turf and Stone* (her *Country Dance* had been published in 1932).
3. Jack Jones, *Rhondda Roundabout*.
4. W. H. Davies, *Poems*.

1935

1. Rhys Davies, *Honey and Bread* (he would complete his South Wales trilogy with *A Time to Laugh*, 1936, and *Jubilee Blues*, 1938).
2. Emlyn Williams, *Night Must Fall*.

1936

1. Geraint Goodwin, *The Heyday in the Blood*.
2. Gwyn Jones, *Times Like These*.
3. Idwal Jones, *China Boy*.
4. Arthur Machen, *The Cosy Room*. (Machen's best work had been completed by 1925 or so.)

1937 A good year.

1. David Jones, *In Parenthesis*.
2. Glyn Jones, *The Blue Bed*.
3. Jack Jones, *Unfinished Journey*.
4. Lewis Jones, *Cwmardy*.
5. Llewelyn Wyn Griffith, *The Wooden Spoon*.
6. John Cowper Powys, *Maiden Castle*.
7. Keidrych Rhys's periodical *Wales*.

1938–9

1. Dylan Thomas, *The Map of Love*.
2. Richard Hughes, *In Hazard*. (*A High Wind in Jamaica* had appeared in 1929.)
3. Richard Llewellyn, *How Green was my Valley*.
4. *The Welsh Review*.
5. Saunders Lewis, *Is there an Anglo-Welsh Literature?* (Saunders decided there wasn't.)

1941–2

1. John Cowper Powys, *Owen Glendower*.
2. Vernon Watkins, *Ballad of the Mari Lwyd*.
3. Alun Lewis, *Raider's Dawn*.

1943–5

1. Idris Davies, *The Angry Summer*.

2. Glyn Jones, *The Dream of Jake Hopkins*.
3. Alun Lewis, *Ha! Ha! Among the Trumpets*.
4. Leslie Norris, *Poems*.

1946 A very good year. The Year of the Thomases.

1. Emyr Humphreys, *The Little Kingdom*.
2. Dylan Thomas, *Deaths and Entrances*.
3. Gwyn Thomas, *Where Did I Put my Pity?*
4. Gwyn Thomas, *The Dark Philosophers*.
5. R. S. Thomas, *The Stones of the Field*.
6. Lest We Forget. During these years Caradoc Evans published five novels and two volumes of short stories. The offering for 1934 was *This Way to Heaven*. That for 1946 was *The Earth Gives and Takes All*. No irony is intended. He will always have a place in our First Fifteen. He had, of course, delivered his awesome and wondrous hammer-blows much earlier: *My People*, 1915; *Capel Sion*, 1916; *My Neighbours*, 1919; and *Taffy*, 1923.

I ask a second time, with some anxiety, when shall we look upon its like again? But a still more pressing question awaits an answer, and to it I now turn: the pre-emptive question of the achievement and quality of the Anglo-Welsh in my time. For in the arts there is only one thing that lasts and matters, and that is Excellence.

I begin by offering, not for the first time (that was in my inaugural W. D. Thomas Memorial Lecture, 'The First Forty Years', at Swansea University College in 1957), a passage from a most remarkable talk given by David Jones through the Swansea station of the BBC in October 1954, and published under the unvarnished title 'Autobiographical Talk' in *Epoch and Artist*, 1959.

Four years later again [he has been talking about his service with the Royal Welsh Fusiliers on the Western Front and his conversion to Roman Catholicism] in 1925, without any initiative on my part I was again in Wales, this time not in Gwynedd [the North], but in the Deheubarth [the South]. It was in the Black Mountains that I made some drawings which, it so happens, appear, in retrospect, to have marked a new beginning . . . My subsequent work can, I think, be truthfully said to hinge on that period. All my exhibited work dates from after that period, none or virtually none before it. But that I shall not be seriously misunderstood I must immediately remind you that what truly determines the changes or developments in *any* artist's work is some new or more developed perception relating to the formal problems of his art. An appreciation of natural beauty, a feeling for some specially beloved *patria*, this hill, that sea-coast or whatever it may be, will not, in itself, be of avail to the artist quâ artist.

An example from the Welsh past: Hywel the poet-warrior, the son of Owain Gwynedd, was evidently moved by the natural beauty of the terrain through which he moved his fierce war-bands, and he loved the dapple of that landscape, and the beauty of bright foam and bright weapons, and saffron gowns and white limbs and white gulls, but none of this vivid awareness would have given us a single line of his famous poem in praise of North Wales unless he had first loved an art-form, and had mastered that form, or rather had himself been mastered, by the elusive constraints of that very specialised art, Welsh 12th century prosody. But the principle I wish to bring to your attention is the same whatever the art-form.

The artist, no matter of what sort or what his medium, must be *moved by the nature of whatever art he practises.* Otherwise he cannot move us by the images he wishes to call up, discover, show forth and re-present under the appearance of this or that material, through the workings of this or that art. The artist is not, necessarily, a person vastly more aware than his friends and relations of the beauties of nature, but rather he is the person most aware of the nature of an art.

That statement, powerful and perceptive, brings me face to face with that concluding verdict without which everything I have said so far would be of minor and short-lived significance. How good is Anglo-Welsh literature?

To start with a home truth, I don't think there can be any doubt that it has been very good for Wales and us Welsh for the obvious reason that every region of earth likes to see itself displayed to advantage, or even (to quote a very famous Anglo-Welsh authority) warts and all, on the world-map of literature. It is a matter of pride, and a measure of our self-respect, that we wish to see our country's history, inhabitants, heroes, eccen-

trics, achievements, landscape, way of life, culture and civilization, its distinctive and in all ways assimilable being, depicted
through the media of the arts. Clearly, in a context of writing
considered as literature I am not now concerned with that
considerable body of verse and prose, amiable, adequate, even
commendable, which engages our attention *only* because it is
about, or of, or for Wales, and from a fellow-countryman's
pen. It has its place and its uses, and one wishes it well. But
our present business is with authors who command a higher
suffrage, whom we esteem not only for what they say but for
the way they say it, not only for their insight and observation
but for their degree of perfection in the exercise of their art.
Such is the unfairness, the undemocratic nature of the arts,
that these, the elected ones, are inevitably the best conveyors
of the Welsh heritage. R. S. Thomas's Iago Prytherch, Dylan
Thomas's Ann Jones, Caradoc Evans's Nanni, and characters
and types as diverse as those in A. Edward Richards's
'Worthy is the Lamb', Islwyn Williams's 'Will Thomas's Cap',
and Rhys Davies's 'Canute', and therewith and thereafter
Gwyn Thomas's Meadow Prospect, Brenda Chamberlain's
Eryri, Idris Davies's Rhymney, and Jack Jones's Merthyr—
and why not Cwm Rhondda, Cwm Eithin, Cwmdonkin and
Cwmscwt?—all would be welcome for this reason alone, that
each is the eidolon of someone or somewhere known through
our eyes, ears, and felt experience. Beyond all dispute this is
right enough, and we do well to glory in it. But equally beyond
dispute all this is still not enough. We must raise our eyes,
exalt our vision. Has Anglo-Welsh literature, or some assessable
part of it, a significance for the rest of the world? The answer
is Yes.

Let me start—and this is a subject on which I can say nothing
that I have not been saying with increased evidence and growing conviction over half a lifetime—let me start from the
word 'region' and the term 'regional literature'. For reasons
of history, geography, tradition, social mores, bonds imposed
and ties evolved, sometimes by language and always by
affinity—the sense of belonging together—there are many
regions of earth peculiarly identifiable as themselves, and not

as something or somewhere else. South Wales is a region of Wales, instantly recognizable and fully valid. It is likewise a region of Great Britain, and by inevitable progression of Europe, and the World. So the adjective 'regional' and the term 'regional literature', as I use them—and I trust you do too—have no derogatory connotation. They are the full and honourable designations of much of the world's best literature, and have nothing to do with the parochial or provincial. When Thomas Hardy wrote of 'The seasons in their moods, morning and evening, night and noon, winds in their different tempers, trees, waters and mists, shades and silences, and the voices of inanimate things'—and against them portrayed the tragedy of Tess, he dealt not with love in a corner but with the inescapable and universal rhythms of human life and destiny and the changeless yet ever-changing manifestations of the natural world which mould and moulder us from the cradle to the grave. Regionalism is part, and a very considerable part, and a very important part, of the literary tradition and achievement of Great Britain and Ireland. Think in our own lifetime of Hardy, D. H. Lawrence, Arnold Bennett, O'Casey, Joyce, the Powys brothers. In just the same way regionalism is a very important part of the European and American tradition. Think of Malraux, Giono, Silone, Lorca, Faulkner, Tennessee Williams, Welty, and a hundred other authors of the nation within a nation.

One more word about Thomas Hardy. A regional author, unquestionably. Where would he be without Wessex? And Wessex without him? But a 'national' author in respect of England and Great Britain, a European author in respect of Europe, and a world author in respect of the world. And he is the last three because he was the first, a Wessex author. For it was there he found, in Gwyn Thomas's noble phrase, the whole world's experience, and from there he relayed it to the world. And so William Faulkner—he reeks of Yoknapatawpha County: he is its prophet, recorder, and funeral orator—and thereafter an author of the Deep South, an American author, a world author—and once more the whole world's experience. And what of James Joyce, who lived in Paris and wrote of

Dublin? These three are not necessarily 'greater'—I use the word in inverted commas—than Conrad, Hemingway, and Shaw. The thing to remember is that they are not necessarily smaller.

I am by nature's stamp and the world's usage a soft-walking man. I am not, then, for one moment setting the Anglo-Welsh achievement of the 1930s and 1940s against the achievement of the American South, or of the Anglo-Irish over a measured half-century. Or am I? For when I read, or re-read, *In Parenthesis* and *The Sleeping Lord*, *Song at the Year's Turning* and *Poetry for Supper*, *Owen Glendower*, *A High Wind in Jamaica* and *Unfinished Journey*, *My People*, *The Dark Philosophers* and *All Things Betray Thee, Ha! Ha! Among the Trumpets* and *The Water Music*, *Ballad of the Mari Lwyd* and *The Angry Summer*, *Deaths and Entrances* and *Under Milk Wood*, my modesty is not so dumbfounding as to find me wholly dumb.

But I have to finish soon and somewhere—in that order—and clearly I am planning to finish with Dylan Thomas. Which means that if I should ever be called upon to advance just one name to represent modern Anglo-Welsh literature at the Book Fair under Babel, the name is likely to be his. Not for his short stories and descriptive pieces, his comic gift, his incantatory performances as a reader of his own verse; but because by virtue of his power over words and mastery of poetic form— in David Jones's phrase, his awareness of the nature of an art— and by virtue of his nurture in Swansea and in Dyfed, and the Antaean nature of his essential life-giving and poetry-yielding contacts there—and because he chose in his moments of exaltation to attempt not the middle reaches of poetry or the self-protective dry cleverness of minor modes which is the bane of so much poetic literature today—especially in England—but themes timeless and universal—love, birth, death; joy and grief and the heart's affections; our kinship with all living things; the wonder and blessing of life;—and because with all this, for better and often for worse he was prepared to follow his daemon to the cave's end: for these reasons it was granted to him to write—shall we say a dozen—or twenty?—of the best poems of our time in any language known to me.

As an old-fashioned reader who finds his first favourites also his latest and best, among these poems, regional, national, and for the world as they are, let me set the five specifically Welsh pieces, 'After the Funeral', 'Poem in October', and the incomparable 'Fern Hill', to say nothing of the 'Prologue' and 'Poem on his Birthday', alongside that universal proclamation and prayer, 'A Refusal to Mourn the Death, by Fire, of a Child in London'—or Dresden, or Hiroshima, or Swansea, or wherever over the Earth's torn surface death has rained from the sky in mankind's never-ceasing Slaughter of the Innocents.

And so to finish? Fifty-one years on from *Times Like These* I count myself more than fortunate to have shared in the dawn of recognition and the noontide burst of splendour of the Anglo-Welsh. That there may be new dawns, new noons, of like radiance—that is a blessing to work for and a faith on which to rest.

⫸2⫷

The Golden Cockerel *Mabinogion*
1944-1948

Er Cof Annwyl

THOMAS JONES, 1910-1972
DOROTHEA BRABY, 1909-1987
CHRISTOPHER SANDFORD, 1902-1983

I

The great pest of speech is frequency of translation.
If an academy should be established for the cultiva-
tion of our style, which I, who can never wish to
see dependance multiplied, hope the spirit of *English*
liberty will hinder or destroy, let them, instead of
compiling grammars and dictionaries, endeavour,
with all their influence, to stop the licence of trans-
latours, whose idleness and ignorance, if it be suffered to proceed, will reduce us to babble a dialect
of [*Wales*].

Preface to the English Dictionary, 1755.

IT would be a fine, impressive thing to be able to proclaim
that the Golden Cockerel *Mabinogion* leapt from the press clean,
comely, and complete to the last gleaming toe-nail, even as
Athene from the head of Zeus. And after a fashion it would
even be true. For on the Inglorious Twelfth of July nothing
of it was to be seen, and then on the Lucky Thirteenth *mewn cam*

'A much-expanded version of a paper first given to the Honourable Society
at London shortly after the publication of the Golden Cockerel *Mabinogion*
in 1948' (Editor, *Transactions of the Hon. Soc. of Cymmrodorion*). The essay
printed here from the *Transactions* was written and published in 1989.

ceiliog, as at a Cockerel's stride, there it was, in folio and orange cape, t.e.g., and free of all blemish. But no one will be surprised to learn that preceding the Cockerel's final consummatory footprint there lay a hundred or two others, all taken in pursuit of perfection, and that so superb an artefact came into being not by an impulse, however inspired, but by a continuing process of trial and error, hard work and high expertise, by the will to succeed, and a helpful Providence which I am not disposed to paraphrase as a bit of good luck.

It all began this way. In the spring of 1944 I sent to Owen Rutter, Christopher Sandford's partner at the Golden Cockerel Press, a copy of Richard Savage's *An Author to be Let*, which I thought he might be interested in publishing. He wasn't, and he returned it, but in his covering letter of 21 May he asked whether I had a 20,000-word story of my own to send him. It happened that I had a long story fluttering in my head and heart, and I wrote back to say so. There was a two months' silence, I finished *The Green Island* and sent it to Rutter, and a further silence followed. Then in early September I received my first letter from Mr Sandford; Rutter had died of overwork at the Admiralty, his partner had been invalided out of the Army, was coming down to Llechryd for a five-day holiday, and wondered whether we could reach an agreement about *The Green Island* there. He ended his letter thus: 'I shall be seeing Mrs Rutter on the 20th and shall ask her whether the *Mabinogion* reached Rutter safely. Was it a gift to him, or a loan, or for us to consider as a publication?'

Clearly then, sometime early in 1944 I had sent Owen Rutter a copy of the Everyman edition of Lady Charlotte Guest's *Mabinogion*. Unfortunately I have no copies of my earliest correspondence with either Rutter or Christopher Sandford, which is a tribute to my then modesty rather than my common sense. But that I sent Rutter that particular book in no way surprises me. Early in 1938 I had first read the *Math vab Mathonwy* of W. J. Gruffydd, that formidable and by now legendary Professor of Welsh at Cardiff. Of late years the critics have dealt sternly if regretfully with Gruffydd's poetic and creative scholarship, but it appealed greatly to me, and I regard his *Math* as one of the quickening influences of my literary life. In particular it plunged me head over heels into the world of the *Mabinogion*, from which I have never climbed, nor sought to climb, back out. When in my story 'The Dreamers', written in 1942-3, I said of my hero, 'He was a great scholar, and could tell you the colour of Vivien's eyes or what size shoes Rhiannon wore. It is likely that no man since Lancelot was more intimate with Gwenhwyfar, and what he didn't know about Olwen, Culhwch didn't know either'—save for my opening clause, we are not far from autobiography. It is one thing to read and professionally study old stories; it is quite another to be so possessed by them from time to time that they become part of your imagination, and so of your very being. I had, for example, been so seized by the story, the deep vistas, the sheer magic of the 'Matter of Math' that I was drawn to redress Gruffydd's deliberately barbarous but fascinating rendering into a more palatable English with the disparate help of the previous translators and Sir Ifor Williams's *Pedeir Keinc*, and while still at Cardiff attempted versions of *Branwen*, *Pwyll*, and *Manawydan*, in that order. Inevitably I also meditated a retelling of 'The Saga of Pryderi'.

Mr Sandford and I duly met at Cardigan for luncheon. As Sancho Panza constantly maintained, 'Everything is better with food.' I have little recollection of our talk together, but inevitably I must have been more concerned about *The Green Island* than the *Mabinogion*. But I do remember Mr Sandford putting a straight question: 'Which is the one Welsh book which Welshmen would choose to see in a Golden Cockerel Press edition?' I must have talked to some purpose, for in his next letter (2.10.44) Mr Sandford wrote that he had discovered a copy of a letter written by Rutter during his illness (but presumably never dispatched), saying that he thought the *Mabinogion* would make a grand book but one which couldn't be undertaken till production had become easier. Mr Sandford agreed, but added: 'But that consideration should not stop you preparing the text *now*—it will take some time!' Since at Cardigan he had talked feelingly about high costs and the shortage of paper and binding materials, I must have suggested that only the Four Branches be proceeded with. 'You say, do just the Four Branches. Now, except to make it short, is there any reason (or excuse) for that? It may be bad taste on my part, or it may be that I am not a Welshman, that makes me actually prefer some of the other tales, and even particularly those which have some French "overlay" in them! Unless you can show a good reason (or excuse), I think it should be the whole thing—the eleven . . . Next, as to the form the edition should take—I fancy *either* making of it one super-book as magnificent as anything we've ever done, *or* eleven little books. In either case we should have illustrations made, I think. The illustrated book is our "line" . . . Next point, I would like you to use Lady Charlotte's text as far as possible and only emend where it is mistranslated or watered down. If, after you've had a further look at the text, you feel you could not conscientiously adapt it fairly easily, I think we should reconsider the whole question of whether to embark on it at all.'

'Great oaks from tiniest acorns grow.' By mid-October we had our acorn, and it didn't look so tiny after all. I wrote back strongly for one big volume, not eleven little ones, and in his reply Mr Sandford prophesied publication four years hence. By thus sponsoring a new version of the *Mabinogion* (even though it was envisaged as a revised Guest), Mr Sandford emerged as our translation's 'onlie begetter'—for without the guarantee of publication (and the stimulus of such superb publication) I can pronounce categorically that nothing more would have been heard of our venture.

For a time, indeed, nothing *was* heard of it. But if I kept my mouth shut, I kept my ears open. What entered in at their porches was the impression that every other person in Wales had planned, was planning, or intended to consider the possibility of planning, a translation of the *Mabinogion*. I heard of an incomparably distinguished Welsh writer who was engaged to prepare a version for a press as famous as the Golden Cockerel. I also heard why the project had come to nothing. I heard of another distinguished writer who had actually set pen to paper. I also heard why his pen had not travelled very far. I heard more than I care to repeat about matters I fear to adumbrate.

It was like being in a Ministry of Translation: everybody had a plan, and an excuse for doing nothing about it. To an outsider we must have looked remarkably like the Adélie penguins thus reported on by Antarctic explorers: 'Two or more penguins will combine to push a third in front of them against a skua gull, which is one of their enemies, for he eats their eggs or their young if he gets the chance. They will refuse to dive off an ice-floe until they have persuaded one of their companions to take the first jump, for fear of the sea-leopard which may be waiting in the water below, ready to seize them and play with them much as a cat will play with a mouse.'[1] I confess that I pondered the analogy deeply. Was it my role to be pushed into publication, then, *more celtico*, eaten *pour décourager les autres*? Well, I concluded, if so, so. In innocence (or ignorance), with faith (or presumption), I determined to press on, rush in where penguins feared to tread.

It may be asked, Why? when my qualifications for the task were so meagre, and my immediate disabilities so great. Well, first, I have always delighted in the translator's art and craft, and have practised it assiduously throughout my working life. Then as a man who cannot read Tolstoy, Homer, or the Bible in their original tongues, I unashamedly approve of the transmission of masterpieces. Further, we know our capabilities only when we put them to the test. Certain works encountered in one's career invite, even demand, a deep involvement— *Beowulf*, say, the *Mabinogion*, and *Egil's Saga*, so if my post-1938 involvement with the Four Branches surprises anybody, that anybody isn't me. If the *Mabinogion* is a Welsh treasure of treasures, let it be the world's treasure too, and the gateway to that is to make it available, and worthily so, in a world-language, videlicet English. The recent translations into Dutch and Bulgarian from the Golden Cockerel and Everyman text, and not from the Welsh, are not irrelevant here. Then, second, if I may be allowed a word of a more personal kind, I came to think in 1944, with that firm-wrought if impoverished world of

---

[1] Apsley Cherry-Garrard, *The Worst Journey in the World* (London, 1922), Penguin edn. 109.

our youth in danger of moral, spiritual, and physical disintegration, that to help create something lovely was a gesture of faith, or at least of stoicism, or even of departure, and that to set forth in all possible perfection these glorious fragments from our Welsh past was an affirmation of the values that redress the balance of our human brutishness. Within one's own breast such thoughts are valid; spoken aloud they recall the tired mouthings of a thousand word-worn hacks; but I still contemplate the *Mabinogion* venture the more fondly and gratefully for remembering how much of what was best in me, not only as a writer, during those four years was poured into it.

But good intentions of themselves mean little. Indeed, without performance they are nothing. I went hard at work. With the Four Branches already in good (though still not good enough) shape, I had a head start, and by the end of the year, with a goatlike skipping of cruces, I had finished *Lludd and Llefelys* and *Macsen*. I then rode off with Culhwch in search of Olwen, and in the absence of an edited and annotated text suffered over months that felt like years the full rigours of that awesome quest. In *The Dream of Rhonabwy* the men of Llychlyn and Denmark were naturally more friendly. But I had by now found, as it seemed to me, a literary style and mode of narrative adequate to the Great Task itself. And all the while it had been growing clearer that the original idea of revising Lady Charlotte must be discarded. It was a question of texture, not of altering this word, that phrase, or even a sentence or paragraph, but of changing the whole style of the thing. It seemed wiser to admire than to imitate. I sounded Mr Sandford in the matter; soon he was making anxious enquiries after Lady Charlotte's health; but it was as late as August 1945, on a sunny day in a dark little street in Dolgellau, that Thomas Jones and I finally broke to him the news of her demise and interment. But to revert, a new translation of the *Mabinogion* was an impossibility for me. By the end of 1944 it was time to do what I had been thinking to do from the beginning: find an expert in medieval Welsh to collaborate in, and when necessary to dominate the venture.

Thomas Jones, by now like Christopher Sandford invalided

out of the Army, and safely returned to Aberystwyth, was of all men obviously my man. It is significant that I had raised the question of a collaborator with Mr Sandford in early October, a significant date in the University year. During the Michaelmas term I told Tom I was engaged on a new translation of the *Mabinogion*, and since he knew next to nothing of me in those days he looked less alarmed than might be expected. A month or so later I put to him the question of a brand-new and joint translation, and within minutes we were partners.

Obviously the book had been lifted to a different plane. It had the master-maker of the only great private press working in Great Britain to plan its format; and it had the foremost young Welsh medievalist of the day to guarantee its accuracy. True, it still had me; but I was not disposed to regard that as a calamity. I had just had occasion to read for the first (and so far only) time Milton's *Epitaphium Damonis*, and was determined that my reed-pipe should not hang on an aged pine-tree far away, but like the young Milton's should piercingly give forth a British note for our native Muses (ll. 168–78).

I am aware that a degree of naïvety has characterized this part of my narrative. But in a cynical age our best moments are ingenuous. I call Caradoc Evans to witness. 'I do not think there is any guile in Gwyn,' he has written. 'I do not think he would stoop to defraud even the Income Tax. He might be a Samoan.' Alas, I can only conclude that the Income Tax does not read Caradoc, and I have never met a Samoan. I don't suppose Caradoc had either.

II

The greater part of readers, instead of blaming us for passing trifles, will wonder that on mere trifles so much labour is expended, with such importance of debate, and such solemnity of diction. To these I answer with confidence, that they are judging of an art which they do not understand; yet cannot much reproach them with their ignorance, nor promise

that they would become in general, by learning [it],
more useful, happier or wiser.

Preface to Shakespeare, 1765.

To the many who knew Thomas Jones, whether as friend,
colleague, or teacher, and to the many more who know the
quality and quantity of his publications—to all these little need
be said about our *Mabinogion* partnership. Two words will
suffice: We worked.

I find from Mr Sandford's letters that on 15 April 1945 we
sent him a typescript of the Four Branches as a Pisgah sighting
of the Promised Land. To produce this Tom's magisterial hand
had traversed, corrected, and signally improved my prentice
drafts. It was now for me to prepare a new typescript, which
was sent off to Mr Sandford at Eye. His reply, when it came,
expressed both pleasure and approval. This we had assumed
would be the case, and we were already launched on *Lludd*
and *Macsen*, with Culhwch waiting in the wings. On the whole
we made fast progress here, because though my version looked
very different indeed after Thomas Jones's scrutiny, at least
we had a version to work on, and a style of English as our
medium. The important thing, we both felt, was to reach what
might be called a penultimate stage, that before the preparation
of a typescript for the printer. Until then it would be hard for
the illustrator to go confidently ahead, nor could we fully call
in the Helping Companions of our venture. So the minute we
finished our second revision of *Culhwch* we decided to press
ahead with *Breuddwyd Rhonabwy* and the three Romances.
But in the immediate post-war years we soon found ourselves
having to meet ever-increasing demands on our professional
and private time. So for the Romances Tom dictated what
was in large measure a literal translation, with all problems
either solved or signposted, which I took home with me over
a period of many weeks and brought into line with our by now
agreed stylistic principles. Thereafter we went through our joint
version, and were not displeased with it. The success of our
stratagem may be measured by the reader's unawareness of
it. Despite our changed working method for the Romances,

the Golden Cockerel and Everyman's *Mabinogion* came in
its entirety from the same two minds working with a single
purpose, and is all of a piece.

We reached our penultimate stage by October 1946. Well
under two years may appear a short time to those fully cognisant
of the size and nature of our task, but we were two, and we
were engaged on a labour of love. And we had the vacations
to further us, especially those of Easter and the summer. We
were as strong as horses, and as a matter of working habit and
pride drove each other hard. To recall just one day will be
sufficient. It was in mid September. With sun and sea and sky
the world was magically beautiful. We worked together all the
morning, and all the afternoon, took twenty minutes off for
tea, then worked till seven o'clock. I felt pretty fagged, but
had no intention of saying so. But as I walked home up the
Prom my head felt physically enlarged and there was a trembling in my knees. I didn't like it at all. So I thought it best
to swallow my pride, and as we were settling down to work
next morning I told Tom I thought we should cut out the
after-tea session. To my relief he said he had been thinking
the same thing, and that the day before he had only just
managed to reach home under his own steam.

In this fashion then, by the end of 1946 we had been through
Peredur and *Gereint* twice, through *Macsen, Lludd, Rhonabwy*, and
Owein three times, and through the less transigent passages of
Culhwch and the Four Branches so many times that we had
lost count.

Also, like Culhwch, we had our Helping Companions. He
had Cei and Bedwyr, Cynddylig and Gwrhyr, Gwalchmei and
Menw. We had Professor J. Lloyd-Jones from beyond the Irish
Sea and Professor Sir Ifor Williams of Bangor, and ours was
the stronger team. Thomas Jones and I have already recorded
in print[1] that no version of a Welsh classic ever received

---

[1] See the Everyman *Mabinogion*, pp. xxxii–xxxiii. It was Mr Sandford's own
idea that the Golden Cockerel translation should appear in Everyman's Library,
and on his initiative that it forthwith did so in 1949. He had been much impressed
by the declared opinion of reviewers and correspondents that our version should
be made available to the widest possible circle of readers. For the subsequent
history of the Everyman volume, see the newly revised edition of 1989, pp. xl–xli.

warmer or more ample aid than this. It is a simple thing to say that Professor Lloyd-Jones read our versions from *Pwyll* to *Iarlles y Ffynnon*. The heroic nature of his service becomes clearer when I say that he *read them word by word against the Red Book and the White*, and commented minutely on every point where comment might be useful. I can only say that Thomas Jones and I had the grace *not* to be ashamed of ourselves in the face of this superb generosity from a devoted scholar carrying all too many burdens of his own. To Sir Ifor we were already deeply in debt for his editions of some of the tales, and typically we showed our gratitude by sending him lists of posers. Typically, he showed his magnanimity by sending us lists of answers. As for small points of exact and specialized knowledge—no one was safe. Archaeologist, botanist, classicist, ploughman, historian, topographer, all demonstrated how *this* might be right but how *that* was assuredly wrong.

This brings me to a consideration of what we tried to do in our translation. It would be idle to say that we wished to put the Welsh *Mabinogion* before English readers: this had already been done, twice over. Bluntly, the only public justification for a new translation from any language and at any time is that it shall be better than those that precede it. But when I use the word 'better' I am aware how vague and uncritical a term it is. Thus a new translation can be considered 'better' in so far as it meets the needs of a new age; and in language and tension conveys to the contemporary reader what his generation demands from any particular classic. I fancy most great feats of translation have been of this kind: translation for today and not tomorrow. In this genre, at least, posterity may go hang. But when we talk of translation for today, we assume that the medium is the very best language of today; and by 'best' (another singularly uncritical term) I mean the cleanest, richest, most exact and yet most evocative language of today. In other words, translation demands no less pains if much less genius than creative work. Where such pains are taken, and there are no destructive deficiencies in the translators' equipment, a degree of excellence is guaranteed.

But there is another sense in which one translation may be

better than another. After all, an author has a meaning, and it is important to convey it. He has a way of saying things, a style, and it is this style which distinguishes a great writer from his fellows, and makes what he says of such passionate concern to us. Style admittedly is of the very texture of an author's native language, and no one supposes that it can be transposed without loss into any other. But some languages allow a closer approximation than others; and I am sure that every language may be well rendered into English, with its vast and subtle vocabulary, its tremendous range of stylistic effects, its sense of period, and its titanic literary tradition, and perhaps above all its power to re-create every alien element till it seems native as turf and stone. The prose rhythms of most (or for anything I know, all) of the Indo-European tongues can be fairly matched in English; the greatest difficulties of a prose translator arise, I should think, when he is confronted with the lapidary effects of a highly inflected and intensely compressed tongue—the Latin of Tacitus, for instance. But difficulties are a challenge, not an excuse, and when every allowance has been made for them, I expect we shall agree that if Translation 'A' keeps closer to the meaning of the original than does Translation 'B', more nearly reproduces all those devices which constitute its style, and reads as a more expressive piece of English in its own right, then 'A' is better (with or without inverted commas) than 'B'. It is better because it is more accurate and, a different matter, more faithful.

Accuracy can be more easily determined than faithfulness. The one is of the letter, the other of the spirit. Complete accuracy produces the perfect crib. Sometimes the problem is recondite, like the *penngwch pwrquin, penguch pwrqwin,* of *Owein,* which carried us through a score of authorities before we came out with 'bourgoyne coif', and were none too clear what that meant either; or like Thomas Jones's remarkable new readings from the White Book MS. Sometimes it is glaringly obvious, maddeningly on the tip of your tongue (only it never gets past the tip), like the *lau heb lau* of *Branwen* and the *lle drwc yd ym,* 'we are on the spot' so to speak, of *Math.* Sometimes it is to remember that if you heave a great sigh on page 10, you had better not give a loud groan on page 11; that if you start with a 'commotion' you must not end in an 'uproar'; and that a stuffed owl is not the same thing as the Discobolus.[1] To say nothing of whether in a medieval context you keep 'thee' and 'thou' (as we did) or settle for 'you'. But all this will be held self-evident. But a translator can go much further than ask himself: What is the meaning of this word in English? He can ask, for example: Is it a common or rare word? It is crude or maybe precious? Has it any poetical connotations? Was it already obsolete or obsolescent in the author's or the scribe's day? Having asked all this (and Thomas Jones and Professors Lloyd-Jones and Ifor Williams having provided the answers), you will translate *amkawd* as 'quoth'—a deliberate archaism (and the hawk-eyed Christopher Sandford writes to ask why you should affect the antique in parts of *Culhwch and Olwen* only?). In this example, I would say that accuracy becomes faithfulness. Faithfulness is the higher virtue, but without accuracy it cannot be. They are like the Inner and the Outer Rule of the medieval anchoress: the Inner Rule the Lady Rule,

---

[1] 'In the Montreal Museum of Natural History I came upon two plaster casts, one of the Antinous and the other of the Discobolus . . . banished from public view to a room where were all manner of skins, plants, snakes, insects, etc., and, in the middle of these, an old man stuffing an owl.

"Ah," said I, "so you have some antiques here; why don't you put them where people can see them?"

"Well, sir," answered the custodian, "you see they are rather vulgar."

He then talked a great deal and said his brother did all Mr Spurgeon's printing.'

'And I turned to the man of skins and said unto him,
　"O thou man of skins,
Wherefore hast thou done thus to shame the beauty of the
　Discobolus?"
But the Lord had hardened the heart of the man of skins
And he answered, "My brother-in-law is haberdasher to
　Mr Spurgeon,"
　　　　　　　　　　　　　　　　　O God! O Montreal!

"The Discobolus is put here because he is vulgar—
He has neither vest nor pants with which to cover his limbs;
I, Sir, am a person of most respectable connections—
My brother-in-law is haberdasher to Mr Spurgeon."
　　　　　　　　　　　　　　　　　O God! O Montreal!'
　　　　　　　　　　　　Samuel Butler, *A Psalm of Montreal.*

which cannot exist without the Handmaiden. Of the accuracy of the Golden Cockerel translation I can speak without fear of immodesty—since to accuracy of so rare of kind I had nothing to contribute. In scores of places Thomas Jones and the Helping Companions put the exact in place of the approximate. I doubt whether the history of the translator's art can show a more accurate rendering of a classic into English.

As for faithfulness—a question intrudes itself. To what must the translator of a medieval text be true? No one today reads an eleventh-century composition exactly as men did in the eleventh century. Or even as a scribe in the fourteenth century read it. Changes in language and literary convention alone would make this difficult. Worse, we are heirs to a new world; our beliefs are different, our points of reference have been fixed anew; what we have lost and what we have gained are like barriers to a possession of the past; how shall a man be sure he knows either the content or the processes of the medieval mind? In the case of the Four Branches of the Mabinogi can we believe that the author himself knew the full significance of his material? Yet by close study, exact knowledge, and an imaginative transposition, one may find oneself *not too unreasonably distant* from an eleventh-century standpoint. Should we then offer a version which puts our reader in much the same relationship to our translation as we ourselves are to its original? Or should we say, 'Today's *Mabinogion* would probably be thus-and-thus', and that is the effect we should aim at? According to our answer, we shall take a very different view of our responsibility towards our text. The kind of thing that might result from the second theory and practice is a version of the Four Branches comparable, let us say, to Robert Graves's version of *The Golden Ass*—genially conflated, oftentimes paraphrased, almost as much a variation on a theme as a translation.[1]

But for the *Mabinogion* we felt that even the happiest para-

---

[1] The logical sequence of this was reached in the eighteenth century with the theory of Imitation. This would be impossible in respect of the *Mabinogion*. It presumed, first, a marked similarity between the world and thought of Rome's Horace and Juvenal and, shall we say? England's Dryden and Pope; and, second, an intimate knowledge and understanding of what was imitated.

phrase, the most exquisite 'improvement', would not do. We aspired to the ideal, and notoriously the ideal is never to be attained. As though we said, Somehow, by a particular combination of gifts and an especial concatenation of circumstances, by inspiration and hard slog, it should be possible to produce a translation which conveys the original work with a word for word accuracy and yet sounds in English the same kind of great literature as the original sounds in Welsh; which brings to today's general reader the intellectual and emotional stimulus of the *Mabinogion*, and yet meets every demand of the strictest scholarship, linguistic, literary, and historical. It would be wrong for me to say that we succeeded; it is right, however, for me to state that we tried. And proper to add that we were sometimes aware that compromise was inevitable.

Once we were over the Lady Guest hurdle we had a style of translation quite clear in our heads. But I find it hard, or even impossible, to say what it was. It is much easier to say what it wasn't. We were of one mind about not being 'modern' and 'with it' and up to the minute, and we wanted to steer clear not only of Wardour Street but of Malory and pseudo-Malory too. Gawain was not to take a stroll, nor Goewin possess an abdomen (I am quoting from our predecessors); on the other hand a single 'peradventure' would have struck us dumb. The mental image I had was of this nature: Here is a branch so thick with leaves and twigs that neither light nor air can get through (brocaded prose, pseudo-Malory); let us take a bill and strip away all verbiage, till what is left is strong and graceful, fresh and bright. Or to abandon metaphor, we wanted prose with a manner, but clear, vigorous, rich, exact.

With hesitation I proffer the four following versions of a passage in *Math*, to illustrate how different was our aim from our predecessors'. Lady Guest chose to convey the *Mabinogion* in a magnificently sustained antique prose; Messrs T. P. Ellis and John Lloyd sought 'to give a literal translation in a literary form, retaining, as far as possible, Welsh idioms, so long as they can be reproduced without violence to the genius of the English language'; Professor Gruffydd, for the purpose of his exposition of *Math*, set himself (I quote) 'the task of frankly providing a mere "crib", keeping as near as possible to the idiom of the Welsh, though the result should be a particularly atrocious form of Welsh-English'. So I offer this quotation as a touchstone of literal accuracy by which the rest of us may be tested. For the style of all three versions is necessarily bound up with their obligation to reproduce yet another style—that of the original. The Welsh text is that of Sir Ifor Williams.

Hwynteu a doethant at Math uab Mathonwy, a chwynaw yn luttaf yn y byt rac Aranrot a wnaethant, a menegi ual y paryssei yr aruei idaw oll. 'Ie,' heb y Math, 'keisswn ninheu, ui a thi, oc an hut a'n lledrith, hudaw gwreic idaw ynteu o'r blodeu.' Ynteu yna a meint gwr yndaw ac yn delediwhaf guas a welas dyn eiroet.

Ac yna y kymeryssant wy blodeu y deri, a blodeu y banadyl, a blodeu yr erwein, ac o'r rei hynny, asswynaw yr un uorwyn deccaf a thelediwaf a welas dyn eiroet. Ac y bedydyaw o'r bedyd a wneynt yna, a dodi Blodeued arnei.

First, by way of touchstone, W. J. Gruffydd:

And they came to Math son of Mathonwy, and they made complaint the bitterest in the world against Arianrhod, and made known to him all the story how he had procured the arms. 'Yes,' said Math, 'let us, me and thee, by our magic and our enchantment make a wife for him out of the flowers.' And he then was of man's estate, and the most beautiful youth that man had ever seen. And then they took the flowers of the oaktrees, and the flowers of the broom and flowers of the meadow-sweet, and with those made by enchantment the fairest maiden above all and the most beautiful that man had ever seen, and baptized her with the baptism which they practised at that time, and placed 'Blodeuedd' upon her.

And now Lady Guest:

They went thereupon unto Math the son of Mathonwy, and complained unto him most bitterly of Arianrod. Gwydion showed him also how he had procured arms for the youth. 'Well,' said Math, 'we will seek, I and thou, by charms and illusion, to form a wife for him out of flowers. He has now come to man's stature, and he is the comeliest youth that was ever beheld.' So they took the blossoms of the oak, and the blossoms of the broom, and the blossoms of the meadow-sweet, and produced from them a maiden, the fairest and most graceful that man ever saw. And they baptized her, and gave her the name of Blodeuwedd.

Ellis and Lloyd:

They came to Math, the son of Mathonwy, and complained most bitterly about Aranrod; and he (Gwydion) told him how he had procured all arms for him. 'Yes,' said Math, 'we will seek, I and you, by our charms and our illusion, to enchant a wife for him out of flowers.' Now he had come to man's stature, and he was the handsomest youth that man had ever beheld. And they took the flowers of the oak, and the flowers of the broom, and the flowers of the meadow-sweet, and out of them invoked the fairest and most comely maiden that man ever saw. And they baptized her with the baptism which was used there, and gave her the name of Blodeuwedd.

Gwyn Jones and Thomas Jones:

They came to Math son of Mathonwy and made the most sustained complaint in the world against Aranrhod, and made known how he had obtained all the arms for him. 'Aye,' said Math, 'let us seek, thou and I, by our magic and enchantment to conjure a wife for him out of flowers'—and he then a man in stature, and the handsomest youth that mortal ever saw. And then they took the flowers of the oak, and the flowers of the broom, and the flowers of the meadowsweet, and from those they called forth the very fairest and best endowed maiden that mortal ever saw, and baptized her with the baptism they used at that time, and named her Blodeuedd.

With these four quotations I arrive at a point where I would negate my entire account of the translators' purpose and practice in producing the Golden Cockerel text, if I do not press the inevitable comparison to a self-congratulatory verdict. So be it. Everyone will be convinced that I am claiming not merely that our rendering is the most accurate of the three (i.e. not counting Gruffydd's), but that stylistically considered it is the best. And everyone will be right. Further, as Efnisien said in Ireland, 'An enormity the household would not think might be committed is the enormity I shall now commit.' I want to quote another passage in the three versions, and a famous passage it is, the description of Olwen. The Red Book and

White Book texts offer a very pretty problem indeed, both of words and word-order.

WB. Y chennatau a orucpwyd. A'e dyuot hitheu a chamse sidan flamgoch amdanei, a gordtorch rudeur am y mynwgyl y uorwyn, a mererit gwerthuawr yndi a rud gemmeu. Oed melynach y fenn no blodeu y banadyl, oed gwynnach y chnawd no distrych y donn; oed gvynnach y falueu a'e byssed no chanawon godrwyth o blith man grayan fynhawn fynhonus. Na golwc hebawc mut na golwc gwalch trimut nyd oed olwc tegach no'r eidi. No bronn alarch gwynn oed gwynnach y dwy uron, oed kochach y deu rud no'r fion. Y sawl a'e gwelei kyflawn uydei o'e serch. Pedeir meillonen gwynnyon a dyuei yn y hol myn yd elhei; ac am hynny y gelwit hi olwen.

RB. Y chennattau a orucpwyt. Dyuot a oruc hitheu, a chamse sidan flamgoch ymdanei, a gwrddorch rud eur am vynwgyl y uorwyn, a mererit gwerthuawr yndi a rud emeu. Melynach oed y phenn no blodeu y banadyl, gwynnach oed y chnawt no distrych tonn; tegach oed y dwylaw a'e byssed no channawan gotrwyth o blith man gaean ffynnawn ffynhonws. Na golwc hebawc mut, na golwc gwalch trimut nyt oed olwc degach no'r eidi. Gwynnach oed y dwyuron no bronn alarch gwynn, cochach oed y deurud no'r ffuon cochaf. Y sawl a'e gwelei kyflawn vydei o'e serch. Pedeir meillonen gwynnyon a uydei yn y hol pa fford bynnac yd elhei; ac am hynny y gelwit hi olwen.

For Lady Charlotte Guest the problem was much simplified. In common with her contemporaries she knew only the Red Book:

So a message was sent, and she came. The maiden was clothed in a robe of flame-coloured silk, and about her neck was a collar of ruddy gold, on which were precious emeralds and rubies. More yellow was her head than the flower of the broom, and her skin was whiter than the foam of the wave, and fairer were her hands and her fingers than the blossoms of the wood anemone amidst the spray of the meadow fountain. The eye of the trained hawk, the glance of the three-mewed falcon was not brighter than hers. Her bosom was more snowy than the breast of the white swan, her cheek was redder than the reddest roses. Whoso beheld her was filled with her love. Four white trefoils sprung up wherever she trod. And therefore was she called Olwen.

The Ellis and Lloyd rendering is a composite one, based on both texts:

And a message was sent to her. She came. And a tunic of flame-red satin on her, and a massive torque of red gold upon the maiden's neck, and priceless pearls in it and rubies. Yellower was her head than the flowers of the broom; whiter was her skin than the foam of the waves; fairer were her two hands and her fingers than the petals of the campion in the midst of the gravel-bed of a welling spring. Neither the gaze of the moulted hawk, nor the gaze of the thrice-moulted young falcon was a brighter gaze than hers. Whiter were her breasts than the breast of the white swan; redder were her two lips than the reddest foxglove. Such as saw her were filled with her love. Four white clover blossoms would spring up in her footprints what road soever she might come by. And for that reason was she called Olwen.

And so to our own:

She was sent for. And she came, with a robe of flame-red silk about her, and around the maiden's neck a torque of red gold, and precious pearls thereon and rubies. Yellower was her head than the flower of the broom, whiter was her flesh than the foam of the wave; whiter were her palms and her fingers than the shoots of the marsh trefoil from amidst the fine gravel of a welling spring. Neither the eye of the mewed hawk, nor the eye of the thrice-mewed falcon, not an eye was there fairer than hers. Whiter were her breasts than the breast of the white swan, redder were her cheeks than the reddest foxgloves. Whoso beheld her would be filled with love of her. Four white trefoils sprang up behind her wherever she went; and for that reason was she called Olwen.

It will be seen that our rendering too is of a composite text. One might define a composite text as one which a reviewer always deplores, an editor often succumbs to, and a translator invariably delights in. Clearly, some of the details of the White Book are sharper and more beautiful than those of the Red. And the 'Whoso beheld her' of Lady Guest, and the 'welling spring' of Ellis and Lloyd, are so just and perfect that once read they are not to be forgotten. No one needs assuring that we were very much upon our mettle when approaching passages as celebrated as this, and we admit the considerable advantage of being third in line.

Our greatest good fortune as translators, it seems to me, was that our gifts were complementary. Two Toms and certainly two Gwyns would have been a weaker combination. From the beginning we worked as closely together as a pair of hands and assumed joint responsibility for each and every word of our version. Our working sessions (there must have been a hundred of them) took place in my old room at the head of the staircase leading from the Balcony just two along from the Library in Old College. It was an eyrie, and though the old proverb has it that 'Eagles fight beak foremost', it was a peaceful one. Our overriding concern at all times was for our book. And Tom was a lovely man to work with, his immense textual and lexicographical learning matched by his good temper and generous spirit. Our collaboration was a unique experience, and we both knew it could never come our way again.

III

'Will she come hither if she is sent for?' 'God knows I will not slay my soul. I will not betray the one who trusts in me. But if you pledge your word you will do her no harm, I will send for her.' 'We pledge it,' said they. She was sent for. And she came.

Culhwch and Olwen

So much for the aims and progress of the translation. What meantime of its physical habitation, the book *quâ* book?

Christopher Sandford, remember, had early decided on one splendid volume to contain the eleven stories, and from October 1944 onwards was feeling his way towards its exact format. A problem of first importance was the nature of the illustrations. I wish I could quote in full the letters written by Mr Sandford during the next fourteen months, till some of the illustrations were in being. They discuss, and illuminate, questions of this kind. Should the book be (*a*) illustrated, or (*b*) decorated, or (*c*) scrupulously plain? When the decision had gone against (*b*) and (*c*), the real difficulties began. 'Should the artist aim at *period and keep that period a uniform one throughout?* If so, should he or she aim at the true Celtic of the Four Branches or the early French of, for example, *Geraint and Enid*?' In any case, what was the true Celtic? (16.12.44) As part of his pilgrimage Mr Sandford entered Lindisfarne and Kilpeck and (it was a safe guess) came out sadder than he went in. The Franks Casket and the Book of Kells were next investigated. 'Does no early Celtic naturalistic representation exist in illustration, *architectural* sculpture, mosaic, or *any* medium?' What of the Franco-Saxon school? The book must have a Celtic flavour, but not a pseudo-Celtic one (8.1.45). 'The more I think about the illustration of the *Mabinogion*, the more I incline to think that the artist should adopt 2 conventions: (1) based on early Saxon for the Four Branches, (2) based on, say, the Bayeux tapestry for the Frenchified stories. But I await your views.' (19.1.45)

Then a decisive letter, 28 March 1945. 'Have you got any further ideas about illustration? The artist (Dorothea Braby) is going to London shortly and I want her to do some research to decide on some conventions which will provide each story with a suitable historical setting. It seems to me that there should be 4 or 5 periods portrayed. *Do you agree? Let me know*, so that I can instruct her:

1.   Ancient British: The Four Branches.
2.   Roman Britain: *Maxen's Dream* and *Lludd and Llevelys*.
3.   Sixth Century: *Taliesin*. (Are we including this?)
4(a). Pre-Norman: *Kilhwch and Olwen* and *Rhonabwy's Dream*.
4(b). Norman: *Owain and Lunet, Peredur*, and *Geraint*.'

With this mention of Miss Braby's name, had we but known it, all our troubles were at an end. Miss Braby started on her research straightaway, but it would be autumn before she began her drawings and Easter of 1946 before she might be expected to finish them—the roughs, that is. Meantime we discussed, approved, and then rejected the notion of including a reproduction of a leaf of the White Book and the Red among the illustrations, and on the 27th of April I find in Mr Sandford's letters the first mention of Mr (later Professor) Emrys Bowen's maps. But the maps are a separate saga.

We saw the first of Miss Braby's rough drafts on 20 October, and it was apparent that the stars in their courses had changed sides and were now fighting for us. Of all the illustrators in this great wide world Mr Sandford had found the right and the best. This part of the undertaking had called for four qualifications, superb drawing, endless application, intellectual comprehension of the subject, and an intense love of the *Mabinogion*. And I think I should add a fifth: a superhuman tolerance of the translators. Let me illustrate four of these five qualities in Miss Braby by transcribing part of her letters about the drawings for *Culhwch* and *Branwen*.[1]

29.11.45. Thank you for your last letter of the 10th. *Nothing* has been allowed to interfere with the execution of *Kulhwch*. I vowed I wouldn't write a letter or get on with Xmas or even do any mending beyond the immediate requirements of seemliness, till K was away to you and C. S.—and now he's ready and away to C. S. who'll forward to you.

. . . I did so hope that you'd want Mabon the son of Modron and the Oldest Animals in Part I in the space I mentioned—but I wanted it to come all from you. For my part my over-weening sense of order rebelled against his inclusion in Part I which was the Statement—up to the end of Yspaddaden's demands—whilst M son of M indisputably belonged to Part II, the Development and Achievement—which was already like trying to find a flat in London! But if you felt it was in order, then that was all I wanted. I think it justifies itself being at the bottom of the page and therefore more or less in sequence. And I think you'll like the Animals—the stag has his first oak sapling, the ousel his anvil, the owl has to make do with one tree stump—the eagle his stars to peck at, and the salmon his river outside Mabon's prison. (How we all worried over this architecture problem—and of course it doesn't really exist at all—all problems just melt into the convention adopted)—and I've got Kei breaking in.

Again you said what I really felt about Arthur and the Black Witch—or rather T. J. did—but that passage was so obscure that I thought a little quiet hairpulling would make a change. Your explanation of it, together with most vivid diagram (!) just made the difference. That space was so prominent—bang in the middle of the whole design—that it really called for no-one less august than Arthur himself, bless him—and the shape lent itself excellently to the two halves of

---

[1] I am much indebted to Christopher Sandford and Dorothea Braby for letting me quote their letters, and especially those in which they were thinking on to paper, with no notion of such a revealing publication as this.

the hag. I don't say that I didn't sigh, as I'd actually worked out the whole design when I wrote and it was all traced ready for completion! I'll enclose my pencil design for your amusement, so you can see the hairpulling trio too. But the other is really better. I feel we all know what we're aiming at and nothing less will do—and the question of 'trouble' is simply irrelevant.

About the shears—this is beyond me to distinguish in drawing. Would you have a careful look at both shears, both razors, Arthur's knife Karnwennan, and all the swords and spears—*not* up my street, really . . . Will the two-headed briar pass? . . . I don't know whether you'll pass the grave—I really don't know what they might be expected to look like . . .

You'll notice the three poisoned arrows—but I have deliberately omitted Y's 'eye-lid forks' as being altogether too obscure to convey by picture. Instead I've drawn eyes so overhung by lids and brows that the 'eye-lid fork' reference does make sense. I decided he would have 'taken them out for the picture'. As it is, probably you and I and T. J. are the only people who will really appreciate what it's all about anyway!

The decorative motif is the same basically in both, but the requirements in each design caused different variations on the same theme . . .

I remain worried about Olwen's hair . . . I can keep that MS indefinitely for now, can't I? It's hardly fair to leave me only Charlotte and the Lilac Fairy Book.

Memory stirs. I've shelved the map question . . .

At the foot of this letter I find I pencilled: Nazi Eagle; 3 arrows; coffer; Kaledfwlch; clods: swallows; Salmon; Arthur striking; collars; Trefoils; Classical lovemaking; Log. Thomas Jones and I were hereabouts at our most pernickety and trying. Our reply must have crossed Miss Braby's first letter about *Branwen*.

3.12.45. On to *Branwen*:—(Suggested lay-out, *still embryonic*):
A. Ships—one apart, ahead with shield lifted up above side of ship, point upwards.
B. Olwen [*sic*] bestowed on Matholwch.
C. Efnisien disfiguring horses.
D. Branwen as cook, receiving blow.
E. Branwen teaching starling.
F. Bendigeidfran and host covering sea.
G. Gwern being thrown into fire by E.

H. Cauldron—dead man beside it—live warrior emerging from within it.

I'm afraid you'll want some reference to the Entertainment of the Head—possibly other things too? Meanwhile I'll put my case: Bendigeidfran's immense size is going to throw things out if we're to have a lot of him. I think *Branwen* only calls for *one* illustration, yes? So the majestic sight of the 'forest and the mountain' etc. will, as it is, dominate the picture and set the scale (one will have to compromise a little) for the rest. So I have omitted the tremendous scene of the *bridge*, and any other ref. to B.

Can you help me as to 'all that there was of string minstrelsy on his back'? Does this include instrumentalists as well as instruments?

We replied to this letter too, and awaited an answer with anxiety.

11.12.45. *Branwen.* Yes, I thought you'd say this—and I'll completely abandon the rather fetching mould I was casting this in. I'll start afresh and recast the whole thing. You give me just the help I want in your suggestion of Heilyn opening the third door.

No, alas, my nearest approach to Harlech was . . . I suppose a post-card of the rock isn't up your sleeve, it it? But on the other hand—the convention we are adopting doesn't lend itself to anything architectural or topographical, which things we have in fact vigorously eschewed, allowing the pattern to be entirely human. Nonetheless I must clearly make myself aware of this rock just for the feel of the thing—and maybe it *will* draw itself in.

The 'string minstrelsy' is one of those nightmares that I propose to draw while entirely unconscious. Lord!

Culhwch. Greyhounds' collars—guilty. Indefensibly. Thank you.

Ysbaddaden's spears—Charlotte has 'dart'. I hereby give notice that I shall strike if again asked to work without *your* MS. Man cannot draw by Guest alone.

Yea, I agree with you about the clods like swallows, but I thought (*a*) better be adaptable to any interpretation and (*b*) clods qua clods not very decorative and therefore not contributive to the design.

Can't do much about Nazi eagle. I drew it from a pre-Boer war animal book.

Goreu in *stone* coffer. Right.

'Tubs' problem easily solved, I think, by removing knife from A's hand—it can be on the ground—having *been thrown* by him—and when witch's bisection achieved he would have approached and struck his dramatic attitude. Arms if necessary may need modifying. Alright?

I can't take T. J.'s comment re K and O as lovers, as I think you've omitted a phrase; anyway it's ambiguous: 'T. J. feels the K and O love-making in the classical convention—i.e., a kind of cloud-borne effect, as of Cupid and Psyche.' Does he mean it is and should not be, or isn't and should—or is there a phrase missing—'he feels that etc.'?

I take you up over spry, plump Blackbird looking too young. *The smith's anvil is there in its entirety*! If he were to look (what later became) his age—there would only be a bit left the size of a nut.

Miss Braby also took me up over my contribution to the problem of Olwen's hair, severely. I thought we ought to see it, Miss Braby thought not. She won. In any case, while I was picking myself up and dusting the headrails and wimples off my elbows, Thomas Jones with the blessing of the Librarian and the assistance of the Staff of the National Library was assembling a conspectus of the Rock of Harlech throughout the ages, in all media, and from every angle and elevation.

18.1.46. Many thanks for the lovely prints. I feel rather hang-dog about this, letting you go to immense trouble, possibly for no result. But I couldn't say 'Don't bother' until I had seen—*(you never know)* and now I have, whilst I am in awe for the majesty of the rock itself, presented realistically, in perspective, and all that can help make it real to the eye, I still think, as far as art is concerned—especially the *highly stylized* Celtic art, where almost *no* realism, and certainly little natural features are attempted—that a mountain or a mole-hill or a pile of manure for that matter, are little more than ∩ in some variation or another, and I honestly don't think a geographic feature (which isn't even an essential of the plot) is going to be *right*—certainly not in isolation. The whole keynote of Celtic Art seems to be resolving it into the most formal, stylized, conventional and decorative forms possible. Well, my concern is—am I conventionalising my drawings *enough*? My justification is that these are illustrations first and foremost, not decorations solely—therefore they must be functional enough in that respect—but the whole genre we have agreed upon is the conventional treatment—and all architectural and geographical feature (and there's the hub—*all*—because we can't really select Harlech just because it is itself a striking feature) must be left out unless operative in the plot—e.g., the river the salmon swims up to Mabon's prison. If Harlech rock is represented accurately, that river should be, and so on. But we've made the river the minimum convention to express the idea of water, and M's prison no more than the strap-work pattern itself—except that Kei must break in—so the minimum amount of stonework is supplied to give him something to break. I think this whole principle is logical and tenable and Celtic—and I put it to you to consider as a policy for *all* the work.

Going back to my *Branwen* design—I have practically finished this—altho' there is a point at which I could introduce the rock—where B. sets out mountain-like wading with his hosts. But on solemn consideration I am dead against it myself for this reason: B. raises utterly fantastic questions of scale anyway . . .

My final *Branwen* contains: 13 ships; Branwen giving her hand to Matholwch (just the two of them—can't cope with B's scale more than once, and one can't have others without him); E. maiming horses; cauldron, dead man by it, live warrior emerging; butcher giving Branwen a blow; starling; B. wading with his ships at sea (stringed minstrelsy too small to be seen—out of sight anyway at his back. *There is a limit!*); E. squeezing bags of 'flour'; E. throwing Gwern into fire; Branwen's falling broken-hearted; Heilyn opening door towards Cornwall—conscious of grief—the Head and feasting seen behind him.

Would you like to send this argument [the rock] on to C. S. for his view?

The result, as always, was dead right. Oddly enough, the overall pattern of the finished drawing was adapted from a motif found in a mid tenth-century grave-mound at Jelling, Denmark. But odd or not, the Branwen drawing on the verso and the printed page opposite, with its perfect capitals, are to my mind the best double-opening of the completed work. But nothing of this came without thought or pains. And that was the way of it throughout 1946, till a fortnight before Christmas we beheld the design for the title-page, the last drawing of all—except for the maps. But before I touch, however briefly, on that three-year endurance test, let me quote Mr Sandford's account of these illustrations in *Cockalorum*, the third part of his bibliography of the Golden Cockerel Press; not only for its technical information, as yet another indication how our book evolved into the lovely thing it is.

Looking at the illustrations, I am reminded of my excitement when, during a lunch at Prunier's, the artist showed me the first product of her research and experimentation. Never can an illustrator have taken more trouble to achieve a perfect interpretation of the great literature of a nation in the terms of its own art. The first trials were made on scraper-board, and the intention was subsequently to transfer them on to wood. After two of the subjects had been transferred in this way, the great truth dawned upon us that, in certain exceptional circumstances, the medium of the scraper-board may be made to produce better results than those obtainable from engravings on wood. This was a case in point. The engravings, though executed with complete mastery of the medium, were actually not so good as were prints from photographic blocks made from the original scraper-board designs. I therefore used photographic blocks for all the illustrations, except in the case of the frontispiece, for which I used the engraved block. Clients may like to compare this engraving with the scraper-board variant of the same subjects printed on p. 102. I do not wish to be misunderstood in my view—this is an exceptional case, for normally engraving, with its sensuously tapered lines, is by far the better medium. Furthermore, the large photographic blocks were, for a number of reasons, very difficult to print.

I have already said that by the end of April 1945 our colleague Emrys Bowen was enlisted in the *Mabinogion* army. To adapt the old slogan: We wanted the best maps; he had them. But it was to take us a long time to agree on what kind of best maps we wanted. It took us some time to learn what kinds of maps there were.

I cannot hide that the whole business of the maps has for me still the troubled vagueness of a dream. Miss Braby lamented that they hung over her head for a full year with 'Damocletian direness'. Mr Sandford never ceased from wondering how we fell into the barbed wire; while Professor Bowen accepted Voltaire's advice: that to the man who feels these things are tragic, to the man who merely thinks, comic. At least, he managed to keep smiling. We began in Professor Bowen's room, the Aberystwyth squad poring over collections of the most exquisite early maps imaginable. We were in at the dawn of map-making, in more senses than one. And we received the first-fruits of Mr Sandford's thinking, couched as usual in urbane and flattering terms:

9.6.45. About the maps, I entirely agree that we want something decorative and 'period' (if possible—but it may *not* be possible). Of course, what period to adopt is what we are up against all through this edition, as the stories have the overlay of so many centuries on their original form. But we can at least limit ourselves at the later end, by saying 'nothing later than Norman'. For the map it would be well to go earlier than that. I wonder, are there any early Celtic maps, say in the Book of Kells, or elsewhere? (Everything to do with this book requires research.)

If not, we should, I think, model our map on pre-Christian Greek maps *for style*, but without any preoccupation with latitude and longitude. We do not want to be medieval. I am inclined to think that pictures on the map, of, for instance, Gwydion driving his pigs, would give a too-late flavour, creating a sort of perspective (which is renaissance), and anyhow they would have to be incredibly small not to occupy too much space on a small map, wouldn't they? Perhaps we should discuss this when next we meet, and perhaps a preliminary would be, if Mr Bowen would oblige, to have a pencilled *rough*—very rough—of the main outlines—the coastline, rivers, and mountains, as applied to the size we have in mind, and then we can see what it looks like and discuss whether we should add little pictures of hill-forts, mounds, etc. and whether events could also be portrayed. I think that the size I mentioned to you would probably have been a double opening for use as an end-paper, in which case the size would be about . . . [diagram] . . . or in those proportions of 13 to 16, as we could (if in those proportions) reduce or enlarge to our requirements photographically. Dorothea Braby could perhaps put a thin Celtic border round it, and also be consulted as to whether she would put little pictures on it. (We should avoid, I think, having pictures by two people in the same book.)

A gruelling time ensued for all. Emrys Bowen prepared a rough draft of a 'medieval' map of Wales, with a monk and a boar and various other adornments touched in, but *tot homines*—we could not agree whether this was the *kind* of map wanted, though we were all agreed that it was the jewel of its kind. Eighteen months later we were as far from agreement as ever, though a second kind of map 'without any preoccupation with latitude and longitude' had been conjured forth for us. And now, from five separate one-man parties we came to coalesce into two. Mr Sandford and Miss Braby reached a common conclusion, and after a time Thomas Jones crossed the floor of the House to join them. This left Emrys Bowen, who alone possessed the expert knowledge which could make the maps credible and who longed, I am sure, for nothing more devoutly than that happy consummation of his effort, and myself, now re-christened by Thomas Jones, Gwynn Hyfar, Gwyn the Irascible, 'one of the nine men who plotted the battle of Camlan'. My recalcitrance, need I say? was based on a complete misapprehension of what the book's designer and illustrator were after. However, time was rolling by, and something had to be done. So we next begged our map-maker to produce two formal maps of the kind that adorned the Gregynog *St Louis*, and I confess that these seemed to me just what was wanted, with their caers and castles and sailing ships and a glorious stylized compass in the top right-hand corner. But this time I was in a minority of one. It was June 1947, we were all growing very concerned about our demands on Professor Bowen, and the way in which, the more closely he met our wishes, the more certainly we went on to suggest something new. On October 16th there came a *cri de cœur* from Mr Sandford underlined in ink and then with red pencil: WHAT ABOUT THOSE MAPS?! Proofs had been read on the text of the *Mabinogion*, the textual notes had been passed, and I at last had retired bankrupt and confused from the map-making business. Freeing his head of all our contradictory notions, Professor Bowen now put forth all his cunning. By St David's Day 1948 he and Miss Braby had performed a miracle, and the maps for which Mr Sandford had argued all along were drawn. Inevitably, they were the only possible maps for our book, and for the first time we were all five rapturously in agreement.

IV

'What craft shall we take upon us?' asked Pryderi. 'We will make shields,' said Manawydan. 'Do we know anything about that?' asked Pryderi. 'We will try it,' he replied.

Manawydan son of Llŷr

Would it be true to say that we now had everything except the book? We had a translation, illustrations, and maps. And these were to be combined with paper and print and glue and thread and binding materials to make a volume. But what sort of a volume?

For this was the Age of Shortages, and behind the Shortages lay Controls, and behind Controls there were some pretty grim fellows dug in behind their desks and enjoying their self-importance: their motto that of the village tailor of my boyhood, who when pressed for a Whitsun delivery would say, 'Never you worry, lovely boy; whoever shall go without, you'll be sure to!' It was therefore impossible for Christopher Sandford to say that he would use a given paper or binding: here again the book had to evolve. In dimension it was to be a foolscap folio, a most harmonious and pleasant size; and I note in various letters such successive notions as these. A paper of the palest saffron shade, an emerald binding with a gold Celtic design, the edges of the book stained lilac? An antique style hand-made toned paper, the binding a blind-tooled heavy dark calf? A classic vellum? Red and green morocco in combination? By May 1946 Caslon's Old Face in Great Primer (18 point) size is running favourite for type, and white paper and vellum as materials. There are long debates about the use of capital letters. 'I approve your use of capitals and lower case. It must have been a great work producing such uniformity. Since you ask me to arbitrate about those black people in *Owein* and *Peredur*, I am putting them in lower case in every instance except "the Black Oppressor". That was his name—he says so, and should be caps. The other black men *are* just black men and the black maiden just a black maiden. He calls her "black maiden" in speaking to her, in one case, just as you or I or Uncle Sam might say "Hullo, gorgeous" or our fathers "Stay, dear lady".'

About punctuation we were for the most part in agreement. Mr Sandford wished to add only one comma to the first 200 pages of our typescript; but in October 1946 two commas on the title-page assumed the dimensions of tailed comets. We were at the end of a protracted and possibly on my part excited exchange about the length of our paragraphs, and Mr Sandford had concluded: 'I do hope that the drone of your own voice during lectures will act as a sedative.' Well! A month later I was still holding out against those commas, but now Mr Sandford has bigger things to worry about. He has seventeen books on his mind and hands, he reminds me gently; Paper Control is the very devil—and then some; dark green morocco (Mr Sandford was an Irishman) has vanished from the face of the earth; and our printer has just lost his monotype caster. 'If you don't have those commas, it will read as if you and Thomas Jones had written the White Book and the Red Book!' We remembered Ossian, and thought of the editors of AD 2948; shaken, we desisted. There were still rocks ahead: to hyphenate or not to hyphenate words like 'to-day', asterisks or numbers for the footnotes, 'my (i.e., C. S.'s) outburst on galley 100', but with our Best of Pilots at the helm we clawed our way safely around them. He 'presumed to mark a few places where you appear to have fallen below your own high standard of clarity or language'—for to work with the Golden Cockerel Press is to enter a new dimension of publishing. But at last the galley proofs were returned, the paper had been ordered, and its delivery assured.

The type had been set up with signal accuracy, but one short sentence had somehow or other dropped out of *Branwen*. With perfection in our sights, Thomas Jones and I decided not to wait for the corrected page-proofs, but immediately, so that our Golden Cockerel might face the world 'clean, comely, and complete to the last gleaming toe-nail', to check the entire translation one more time against our (which means Tom's) beautifully established Welsh text. That was our headache in the spring of 1947. Mr Sandford's was that when the paper arrived, instead of being white, it was dark cream toned; and the white paper and classic vellum in a heartfelt phrase had 'had it'. One had known it all along, of course. 'Though thou get that, there is that thou wilt not get. Wakefulness without sleep at night shalt thou have in seeking those things.' However, you couldn't run the only surviving private press in Great Britain (which the Golden Cockerel then was) without reserves of strength and resilience. 'I have an idea that I can make the book even more outstanding on the cream paper than it would have been on white. The dark cream seems to cry out for other colours—the pictures perhaps in green, and the binding in purple vellum with green inlay. I've written to Dorothea Braby asking whether or not she favours the printing of her pictures in colour. We'll see. I take it that you will be happy either way?' As it happened, we none of us fancied the specimen picture in green, and with the green pictures went the purple and green binding; the Contents page was giving a lot of trouble, and there was difficulty over the printing of the blocks. There was only one criterion throughout, need I say? for Mr Sandford: what was best for the book. Trouble, setbacks, enforced changes, none of these affected his purpose. And he handled his team like a master: an architect co-ordinating the work of translators, illustrator, map-maker, paper-maker, printer, and binder, encouraging, advising, humouring, coaxing, prodding, consulting, and sometimes even deferring, and always bringing us nearer to his ideal. We saw this ideal in July 1948 when in Poland Street we signed (for my part with trembling hand) the 'special' copies. Our nonpareil wives were there, sharing our triumph as wholeheartedly as they had shared and alleviated our travail. Side by side in happy contention we watched the pages turn by way of the wondrous Frontispieces, the Maps, and our Introduction, to where on page 17 we saw the proud Dedication of the work 'TO ALICE and MAIR.[1] At the same time I saw red—red morocco—though everybody else insisted on calling it orange. It must have been the final revelation to Mr Sandford that I didn't even know what colours he had been talking about.

We began as strangers, we ended as friends. I crave one touch of sentiment in this otherwise dispassionate account of our adventure together. The last lines of Mr Sandford's letter of 29 June 1948 are these:

---

[1] A word of explanation. Thomas Jones (Mair's husband Tom) died in 1972. My wife Alice died in January 1979. Mair and I were married in September of that year.

'I saw copies when in London. It is my best book. I am very happy about it. I hope you will be too.

God bless you.

Christopher.'

We *were* very happy. A blessing is a good thing, and in Culhwch's words to our Welsh Arthur: 'May there be none without his share of it.' And in Arthur's words to Culhwch: 'God's truth, so be it!'

⚕3⚕

Three Poetical Prayer-Makers
of the Island of Britain

IT is a humbling admission for a Welshman to make—and
humbly I make it—that in the course of a life which while not
yet grown long grows longer by the hour, and a career much
given over to trafficking in history and legend, fiction and
myth, I have never once invented a triad. Let me, under your
protective shield and benevolent helm, here and now redress
this injustice to the Threeness of Three, and begin by hanging
three small flower baskets of verbal amplification on the bare
trellis-work of my would-be triadic title. Thus:

Three Poetical Prayer-Makers of the Island of Britain: Cynddelw the
Great Poet, who praised the Princes of Earth and the King of Heaven,
and requested his dues of both; James Kitchener Davies the Deathbed
Poet, who in extremis prayed to God to deny him all those things
he had most worked and prayed for; and Saunders Lewis the Poet
of Arduous Causes, who prayed that the Good Thief who died with
Jesus on the Cross should pray for us, that we too may know Him
in the hour of our extremity.

Which brings me to the second paragraph of my preamble.
Having read my terms of reference I am aware, acutely
aware, that the Warton Lectures of the British Academy are
unambiguously entitled the Warton Lectures on English
Poetry. I am even more acutely aware that my Warton Lecture
is strictly speaking *not* precisely, entirely, exclusively, or even
predominantly on English poetry, and lifetime apostle of the
blurred edge though I am, I would expect no one to believe
me if I said it was. So I need indulgence—and as I hope, with

Warton Lecture on English Poetry, 1981. From the *Proceedings of the British
Academy*, Vol. LXVII (1981).

good reason. For Cynddelw Brydydd Mawr most decidedly
was not an English poet. His praise-poems to his patrons the
Welsh princes made all they could of the mischief, murder,
and mayhem those same princes tirelessly inflicted on the
English foe, who it must be admitted as tirelessly inflicted an
equal uncharity on them.

> In arms against Angles, in Tegeingl's lands,
> Blood spilling in streams, blood pouring forth . . .
> In strife with the Dragon of the East,
> Fair Western Dragon, the best was his.
> Ardent the lord, sword bright above sheath,
> Spear in strife and outpouring from sword,
> Sword-blade in hand and hand hewing heads,
> Hand on sword and sword on Norman troops,
> And constant anguish from the sight of death . . .
> I saw war-stags and stiff red corpses,
> It was left to the wolves, their burial;
> I saw them routed, without their hands,
> Beneath birds' claws, men mighty in war;
> I saw their ruin, three hundred dead,
> I saw, battle done, bowels on thorns;
> I saw strife cause a dreadful uproar,
> Troops contending, a rout collapsing . . .
> I saw lances red with Owain's rush,
> I saw for Saxons sorry corpses . . .

Not an English poet, did I say? He wasn't even pro-English.
Nor was James Kitchener Davies pro-English, though somewhere along the line (he was christened James) he must have
been pro-Kitchener. Nor is Saunders Lewis pro-English either.
He is pro-Welsh. The dearest wish of his political life has
been to preserve the Welsh language, achieve Welsh self-
government and national independence, and arrest and reverse
the twentieth-century process of anglicization and alienation
which seeps and creeps through much, indeed most, of Wales
today. But to drive my own horses and fly my own hawk—it
has been my conviction throughout most of my adult life that
it is not only our Welsh business to know what we can of English
poetry, but the Englishman's business to know what he can

of Welsh poetry. These separate businesses being part and parcel of our common business of being and belonging with and to each other and to the ever-expanding sphere of family, locality, region, country, and as far thereafter as our modest fund of humanity may carry us. This isn't as pious—and certainly not as pi—as it may sound, for I am also a convinced believer in what, within the law and the bounds of regard, is separate and different and individual in us all. Welsh poetry has various characteristics, qualities, ambitions of manner and matter, and above all of metrical and verbal patterns and congruences of sound, not much met with in English poetry. Few among you have more love for English poetry than I—or a warmer admiration—but it is without any constricting modesty, as it is entirely without arrogance, that I am seizing my opportunity to touch lightly, and with the help of two inspired translators,[1] on a subject that the mildly aberrant and erratically enquiring Thomas Warton would, I am sure, approve of.

Which brings me urbanely to the three less than urbane poetical prayer-makers of my lecture this evening. They belong, be it noted, to widely separated centuries. Cynndelw's *floruit* was the second half of the twelfth century, one of the outstanding ages of Welsh poetry. He acquired the cognomen *Brydydd Mawr* during his lifetime, and though at first it may have remarked the width of his shoulders, it served soon to acknowledge the magnitude of his mind. He was thus not only the Large Poet but also the Great Poet, and either way accepted the appellation without demur.

He was a poet of the Gogynfeirdd. The first great age of Welsh poetry was that of the Cynfeirdd, literally the First or First-Come Poets. The Gogynfeirdd were the Next-to-the-First or Next-Come Poets. They are also known as the Court Poets

[1] The translations of Cynddelw (in *The Earliest Welsh Poetry*, Macmillan, 1970) and of J. Kitchener Davies are by Professor Joseph Clancy of New York. Those of Mr Saunders Lewis are by Dr Gwyn Thomas of Bangor. I owe them warm thanks, as I do Mrs Mair K. Davies and Mr Saunders Lewis. [It is with sorrow that I record the death of Saunders Lewis in 1985, and of Mair Davies in April 1990. Mrs Davies died attempting to rescue her grandson from a burning house. G. J., 1991.]

and the Poets of the Princes. The Cynfeirdd or First Poets produced and in part preserved a substantial body of heroic and tragic verse, exemplified by the poems associated with the names of Taliesin and Aneirin on the one hand, and the saga-names of Llywarch the Old, Heledd, and Cynddylan on the other. The emphasis was on the heroic kinds: eulogy, elegy, and commemoration. Gnomic and nature poetry survive too, vaticination and religion; but the age was a Heroic Age, and its verse mirrored and portrayed it.

The circumstance is relevant to Cynddelw and his peers. The Gogynfeirdd were in every good sense of the word professionals, who inherited, practised, and transmitted not so much an art as a highly organized and strictly regulated craft of verse-making. What you did and how you did it—in what words, in what form, and with what techniques—these things were prescribed. One has heard the phrase, 'a painters' painter'. Cynddelw was of all things a poets' poet. He knew all modes, all means, all measures, and knew that he knew them. His patrons knew it, his fellow-poets knew it, his disciples knew it, and after eight hundred years we know it. He was the greatest of the Gogynfeirdd for two chief reasons. The first is that just mentioned: he was so accomplished a performer (and I stress that word) that whatever task he took in hand he performed superlatively. Like his fellows he had taken over from Taliesin and Aneirin the poetic kinds proper to a professional poet. He seems to have begun his career as court poet to Madawg ap Maredudd, lord of Powys, for whom he composed a classical eulogy while he lived, and a classical elegy when he was dead. Ah, that we might all have our Cynddelw!

Madawg dead and dirged, Cynddelw went on to ply his skills before other great ones of the Welsh world, Owain Gwynedd in the north, and the lord Rhys down south, and again and again discharged with resource and authority whatever a patron might properly require and a craft would rightly permit. Which brings us to the second reason why he was the greatest of the Gogynfeirdd. Word-master, song-master, rule-master though he was, the very personification of the bardic ideal, he brought something more to verse-making: he brought himself. He made a little more room within the tradition, a little more elbow-room for the poet to work in. And so we find Cynddelw addressing Madawg's young daughter Efa in an innovatory poem which combines ardent respect with respectful ardour, private devotion with public regard, the innocent friendship due to a child (and your lord's child at that) with the awakening compliment welcome to a young woman. Cynddelw was gallant in his ode to Efa as Dryden in his day would be gallant in his address to the Duchess of Ormond, all things wondrously subdued by a master of his craft and made concordant with the purpose, the pleasure, and the duty of a court poet who is also a Great Poet, Prydydd Mawr. He made use of the *llatai* or love's messenger in a fashion prophetic of Dafydd ap Gwilym; somewhat surprisingly wrote a poem after the death in battle of his own son; and in the grammarians' discussion of the modes of versification there is reference to the 'manner of Cynddelw', with its suggestion that he experimented there too. And on everything he composed he set his own unmistakable stamp and impress.

I came to Cynddelw late—and that not to my regret. There is much to be said for postponing some major delights and enlightenments till one is old enough to appreciate just what it is one has been missing. He instantly looked a poet for me. His confidence appealed to my feeling for authority, his courtly arrogance to my courtly humility. Here was a man who at all times was conscious of what God had given him. 'Be silent, bards—a bard is speaking!' I judged him true brother of my old friend, the tenth-century poet Egill Skallagrímsson of Borg á Mýrum out in Iceland, who stepped before kings, opened his mighty jaws (which were also melodious), and instantly had silence; and to my still older friend the unknown author of *Culhwch and Olwen* in the *Mabinogion*, that exultant master of early Welsh narrative prose. Like Cynddelw, because they were supreme craftsmen they could meet the severest demands of their art; and like him, because they were supreme artists, they left a savour of their unique selves with the products of their craft.

But I resist the temptation I find almost irresistible, and

approach, as Cynddelw had to in the end, that prayer to God which makes him part of my talk this evening. Like Egill a skald, bard, court poet, and friend of princes, and a warrior whose sword knew the colour of red, Cynddelw would have acquitted himself well at Ragnarok, had Christianity boasted such a luxury. Since it didn't, he would write a set piece in classical form, with every rule of language and structure obeyed, stamp it with his bardic authority, and concurrently make it eloquent of his distinctively eloquent personality. This set piece was the verse-composition known as *marwysgafn* (that is, Deathbed Poem), addressed by a bard not to his lord on earth but to his Lord in Heaven. Let me at this point again remind you of the secular inheritance of the court poets of the twelfth and thirteenth centuries, who had taken over the traditional rights and duties of their British or Celtic heroic age predecessors. Theirs was an essential and indispensable function of the society they lived in. For behind the bloody catalogues and brutal exultations of heroic poetry (and believe me, they *are* bloody and brutal, and none more exultantly so than the Welsh), behind these lies a deep, enduring, and imperative grasp on reality. In a heroic society, if the hero-king had need of his people, his people had equal need of him; and it was the bard as celebrant and memorialist who could do most to enhance him in life, sustain him and his house before posterity, and (perhaps most important of all) define and hold up for approval and emulation those standards of personal and public worth and conduct which were a man's best, most precious, and least alienable possessions in life and death. It was these standards and their expression in terms of war, valour, service, reward, loyalty, contempt of death, and love of fame everlasting, which were the bond and buttress, shield and stay, of tribe, confederacy, people, and nation, in a warlike and hierarchical age.

Of all these matters Cynddelw was fully seized and cognizant. Had he not said so, many times, to many princes?

> Britain's regal hawks, I chant your high song,
> Your honour I bear,

> Your bard, your judge I shall be,
> Your assistance is due me.

What more natural, and what more inevitable, than to enunciate these patent truths yet again, this time to the Prince of Princes and King of Kings, with whom in justice and mercy they would count most? Which he did, in a formal composition of an established kind, the *marwysgafn* or Deathbed Poem, a mode of address at once personal and public to Almighty God, and one which he brought more into line with secular eulogy than his contemporaries did.

The Deathbed Poem opens with our author's customary ease, authority, and assurance:

> I salute God, asylum's gift,
> To praise my lord, bounteous, benign,
> Sole son of Mary, source of morn and eve
>   And teeming river-mouths,
> Who made wood, and mead, and true measure,
> And harvests, and God's overflowing gifts,
> Who made grass and grove and mountain heather . . .

The entire introduction is excellent in manner and exemplary in sentiment. So is his second section, which begins with Cynddelw nudging God's elbow—or was it the lesser though still exalted humerus of the Archangel Michael?

> I salute God, I solicit acclaim
> For the piece I perform . . .

And less ambiguously than is usual he speaks of a gift to be given, a reward to be received. In the third section his eloquence heightens, and he lets sound his grand diapason of words, phrases, and poetic counters. This is the very stuff of twelfth-century poetic rhetoric, and from first line to last Cynddelw is in control of it.

> Almighty Ruler, when you were born,
> Came mercy for us, came redemption,
> Came Adam's sons from faithless faction . . .
> Came Christ incarnate, mainstay, master,
> Came in Mary's womb the wished-for Son,

Came the world's five ages from torment . . .
And He is our helm and our haven
Who judges our deeds by our doing,
And He, heaven's Lord, portion of peace,
Brought us forth from perdition when pierced,
And He rose for us, and won His reward,
And the Lord will not deny us His help.
And as a reward He was seated
In full might, the sun's road His domain.
The man whose hand will give his tithe to God,
He is not thwarted of his reward.
I am a bard, flawlessly fashioned:
In my Creator's hold, legion's Lord,
I, Cynddelw the singer, grace I ask;
Michael, who knows me, welcome be mine!

The masculine strength of the diction, the compulsive
appeal of the imagery, the pressure and timing of the emotional
sequence would conceal, if concealment were possible, or even
desirable, the gradual merger of redemption and reward which
grows explicit in the second half of Cynddelw's exposition of
God's justice and mercy. Christ won his reward, the man who
pays his tithe wins his reward: shall not God's bard, flawlessly
fashioned, win his too? Something well past reason if short of
common sense tells me, Why not? If we can approve of the
juggler of Notre Dame who brought the tribute of his one skill
to a private performance before Our Lady, why not a performance, public or private, to the glory of God by that conjuror
with words and magician with metre, Cynddelw Brydydd
Mawr? 'Be silent, bards; a bard is speaking!'

> Almighty Ruler, when of you I sang,
> Not worthless the piece I performed,
> No lack of fine style in the lyric . . .

And so to the poem's ending. Cynddelw's skills, his largeness
of utterance, his power and conviction, do not for one moment
desert him as he moves from claim to appeal, and from appeal
to his plea for salvation. I will read it, then leave it to speak
for itself, for its poet, and for the poetical resources, intellectual,

emotional, linguistic, and metrical, of Welsh twelfth-century
poetic prosody:

> Almighty Ruler, deign to receive,
> Reverent request, harmonious,
> Flawless in formation of language,
> My song in your praise, fair land's candle.
> Since you are master, since you are monarch,
> Since you are prophet, since you are judge,
> Since you are kind, since you are benign,
> Since you are my teacher, banish me not,
> In your wrath, from your fair land.
> Refuse me not your grace, exile's Lord,
> Scorn me not amidst the wretched crew,
> Spill me not from your hand, vile dwelling,
> Throw me not to the black loveless throng.

And so, leaving Cynddelw the Great Poet behind us, to
confront God with his greatness, we approach over the gulf
of eight centuries the second and third close-set spider-legs of
my wide-spanned poetical tripod. By way of a bridge it was
my intention, as it is still my hope, to proffer a few sentences
about religious poets and their poetry in Wales today, in both
our languages; a remark or two about the erosion of Christian
belief which we share with the rest of Great Britain; and the
sparest of spare words about the decline of Nonconformity and
Methodism, which to me, as to so many of my South Wales born
and bred generation *were* Christianity in those kingfisher days
when life's pasture is green and youth's cup runneth over.

I would not, of course, be misunderstood as saying that Welsh
poets are more notoriously or even more numerically back-
sliders from the Lord than their readers or the generality of
their English, Scottish, and Irish peers. On the contrary, mighty
exceptions at once spring to mind. In the English-language
literature of Wales, for example, that so-called Anglo-Welsh
writing whose flowering over the last half-century or so has
been so variously rich, R. S. Thomas and David Jones are
not just religious poets: they are specifically and eminently
Christian poets, the one a priest of the Church in Wales, the
other a convert to Roman Catholicism. A Christian upbringing

and a Christian witness are not in themselves, need I say? enough to make even a religious man a religious poet. Nor can a religious fiction greatly avail. Dylan Thomas, who despite Swansea and 'Where Tawe Flows', belonged at heart with uberous Dyfed and tidal Tywi, fostered a poetical attachment to a deity who was old before Zeus and Yahweh were young—a deity human–animal–divine, part Polar Bear, part Father Christmas, with a spoonful of Merlin to taste.

> Animals thick as thieves
> On God's great tumbling grounds
> Hail to his Beasthood!

And why not? But it is a long way off from the Whitsun Walk of childhood and the Easter Sacraments of age. Any religion deserving of the name, though the dictionaries are beginning to give ground, requires a God, and demands that he be worshipped. Pleasure before a sunset, awe on a mountain's height, wonder at the struts and hinges of a seagull's wing, are not enough. The 'Author's Prologue' to the *Collected Poems* of 1952, whose hundred lines, we are told, it took Dylan a whole year to compose, may well be the most discreetly evasive poetic evasion of the Christian God in twentieth-century literature.

Then there was John Cowper Powys, a giant—nay, Titan— of our age, whose life was a baffling search for Truth between the sulphurous chasms of the First Cause and the sleety highlands of the Fourth Dimension. And what was the Truth he came up, or down, with? 'To be at the death of God is my single quest.' Few of us had thought to go as far as that. We were modest, tolerant men with no taste for Deicide, but rather a disposition to find old beliefs grown empty of meaning, so that we let them go. For better, and partly for worse, men like Gwyn Thomas, Idris Davies, Raymond Williams, Rhys Davies, and myself, took shape in the evening of our teens as religious men without a religion, men of faith without a faith, who had still to learn the saddening lesson that Pelagius was a born loser, and his genial Celtic heresy concerning the goodness of man a non-starter from the start.

Hedge and dyke a little and who will be surprised to hear

that the situation in Welsh-language poetry is not too dissimilar? The last eighty years or so, the years encompassing T. Gwynn Jones, R. Williams Parry, T. H. Parry-Williams, Saunders Lewis, Gwenallt, Waldo Williams, and Alun Llywelyn-Williams (I have drawn a birthday line under the outbreak of the First World War), have been the most splendid age of Welsh poetry since the Age of the Cywydd. Of religious poets three are outstanding: Saunders Lewis, Gwenallt, and Waldo Williams. Of the three the best for my purpose is Saunders Lewis, which implies no criticism of the others; for there is no doubt in my mind that a handful of his religious poems, and especially 'Mary Magdalene' (*Mair Fadlen*), 'To the Good Thief' (*I'r Lleidr Da*), and 'Ascension Thursday' (*Difiau Dyrchafael*), are our supreme modern Welsh artefacts of their self-declared unequivocally Christian kind. Here is a man who in Thomas Merton's phrase is 'writing for God', and bringing to that exalted task every literary skill, every exercise of care, and every quality of unremitting exactitude of which he is capable. You don't have to share Mr Lewis's religious convictions to feel this. Each one of these poems, as a made and finished thing, has a completeness, a 'truth' which is its own, even more than it is the poet's—a statement which may well seem to you in need of explication. But a poem, we should from time to time remind ourselves, is not a poet, though it sometimes coincides with, and is quite often confused with, its maker or his supposed outlines. Rather, it is a poet's artefact, a poet being a man with the will and means to make and perfect a statement in verse entirely adequate in its manner and matter to fulfil the intention of its maker and the expectancy of its hearer, or reader.

That expectancy need not precede acquaintance. A poem can arouse and gratify expectancy simultaneously, at a first hearing or a fiftieth. As we hear it, possess it, and are possessed by it, we acknowledge the highest and most effective mode of communication of which human speech, our highest human communicant, is capable. Something significant and necessary has been stated, made manifest, in the best words and in the best structured form. This is the empyrean function of a craft employed in the service of what we nowadays call an art. This is what Cynddelw believed, though he would certainly have expressed himself differently. There can be found (indeed, there *has* been found) a right way of expressing a theme of general rather than private import (to be merely private, personal, self-exploratory, and self-indulgent—such is the theory—is to diminish, to slough significance), and to achieve that rightness is the first and full business of a poet.

One speculation always leads to another. Were Saunders Lewis to write a Deathbed Poem, after the fashion of the Masters, it would certainly be found one of the most striking and effective of its affecting and formalized kind. Most of our mortal vicissitudes have befallen him, often as though by personal invitation, his longings higher and his disappointments correspondingly deeper than those of his fellows. Like his friend David Jones a convert to Roman Catholicism, unlike his friend an authoritarian by temperament and conviction, he is in all things a man of burning and self-sacrificing beliefs, in religion, national and nationalist politics, and unaccommodatingly devoted to the preservation and enhancement of the Welsh language and his concept of our Welsh destiny. He has been a lifelong fighter, braced by the knowledge that you must not take on only those battles you expect to win. That would be the easy satisfaction of fighting for glory. You must fight for your cause because it *is* your cause, even though it may carry with it the bitter lesson that the majority of your fellow-countrymen neither approve your struggle nor want your sacrifice. For much of his life he has been among the most notable public figures in Wales, and is certainly one of the most distinguished Welsh poets, dramatists, and polemicists of the century.

By his own definition he is a craftsman who has learnt to trust technique, and knows that a good poem is an impersonal thing. It can be so, no question of it; but for me there is equally no question that a good poem may also be found a personal thing. But there is no particular dilemma: the inexactitude of language and the imprecision of thought, personal weightings, and private refinements (of which I recognize a great many in myself), make many literary disagreements more apparent and soluble than real and permanent. But before I go on to look at an 'impersonal' poem of his which impresses me as a poignantly 'personal' one, let us consider a poem, not his, where the critical proposition that a poem has its own truth, which is not necessarily or wholly the truth of its poet, brings comfort and admiration, whereas a belief in its literal, professed personal truth would bring desolation and grief to the reader. This is James Kitchener Davies's *Sŵn y Gwynt Sy'n Chwythu*, 'The Sound of the Wind that is Blowing'. I have no wish to deal in absolutes and bests, but this poem, because of its autobiographical content and social commentary, its cry of pain for the self and despair for the nation, the Old Testament nature of its appeal to God in hope's destruction; and because it shows the selection, shaping, and reshaping of material proper to a work of art; and because of its effect upon every kind of reader, whatever his politics, religious faith, social background, and life's history; for these reasons, along with its command of words and metre, it is among the most remarkable statements made about industrial South Wales and its people during the harsh decades of poverty and strain between the two world wars.

It coheres with my general purpose in that like Cynddelw's Deathbed Poem (and not unlike the effigy of some early seventeenth-century divine portrayed while still alive in his chosen shroud and coffin), it is an address to God postmarked for Earth as well as Heaven. *Sŵn y Gwynt*, as it fell out, was literally a deathbed poem, commissioned by Radio Wales, and composed in hospital between two surgical operations a short time before its author's death in 1952. Most of it he was himself too weak to write down. 'It was from a few notes of his on paper,' wrote his wife, 'and from listening to my husband's spoken words line by line, that I set it down on paper, there by his bedside.' It is a work simple in structure but complex in intention. The poet's life was neither commonplace nor, in South Wales terms, all that remarkable. At the age of 24 he had left the farm and fields of Tregaron in Mid-Wales for the fields and pits of the Rhondda Valley in South Wales, where he became a teacher, married, wrote some interesting plays for a playless land, espoused the Welsh nationalist cause with fervour, 'ventured in elections', and played an active though not dominant part as orator and preacher in what Gwyn Thomas has called the 'fermenting disquiet' of the busy, harassed, can't-be-kept-down life of the strung-out Valley townships.

He was, let us say, dedicated to good causes. Certainly to good intentions. A life so dedicated, so occupied (and pre-occupied), so demanding, so prone to set-backs, and so slow to harvest—who among us, trapped in the murk of disappoint-ment and the opacity of doubt, but might ask himself, 'Why do I do it? Why should I? And, God help me, to what end?'

> Remember,
> There was no need for you, more than the rest of your fellows
> To scream your guts out on a soap-box
> on the street-corners and the town squares;
> no call for you to march in the ranks of the jobless,
> your dragon-rampant hobnobbing with the
>   hammer-and-sickle;
> there was no need for you
> to dare the packed Empire and the Hippodrome on Sunday
>   evening,
> —you a dandy bantam on the dung-heap of the spurred cocks
> of the Federation and the Exchange—
> but you ventured,
> and ventured in elections for the town Council and the County
> and Parliament all in good time
> against Goliath in a day that knows no miracle.

When I say I don't know how much of this is hard fact, and how much is metaphor, that is not indifference. If I add that their precise boundaries require no drawing, that is not heartlessness. Truth in a court of law is one thing: the truth of distilled or rearranged experience is another, especially in a poet's auto-biography, and perhaps above all in his *marwysgafn* or Deathbed Poem.

> For it not only blows where it will, the tempest,
> But blows what it will before it where it will.

And one thing it can blow before it, shedding a little here and heaping a little there, is literal truth, which is a commodity that Ancient Mariners and Cider-drinkers with Rosie have always managed to do very nicely without. May we not assume that Kitchener Davies at a fraught period of his life entered as many men must within the dark night of the soul, and from that unsettling experience of insight and self-deception, anxiety and regret, together with such incidentals as every writer's longing for a subject to write about, our human need to explain our uniqueness, to tell how it was and is with us (reinforced by the Welsh tradition of the poetic set piece and work of public significance), Kitchener's being in hospital and undergoing surgery for abdominal cancer, his wife's sustaining presence— from these things, and others guessable, came incomparably the best poem he ever wrote, and the one by which he will be remembered.

To recall past happiness (he was to say that the tumbledown walls of the farmhouse of Y Llain set a brand as of Cain on him in the Rhondda); to have literary, professional, and political ambitions, and know oneself grown older with no great matter accomplished; to brood on pain and survival—these are the black crows of middle age. To suspect oneself a failure, and fall prey to self-doubt, self-pity, self-accusation—these make the crows look bigger and blacker. 'What shall I cry?' saith the Preacher. 'Birds build' was Gerard Manley Hopkins's cry in Crowland:

> Birds build—but not I build, no, but strain,
> Time's eunuch, and not breed one work that wakes.
> Mine, O thou lord of life, send my roots rain.

The wind that in childhood ruffled the sheltering hedges of Y Llain and spared the shelterers in its protective ditch; that made squirrels of boys in the tossing branches; the wind that blew broken hopes and soiled ambitions with yesterday's tins and newspapers along the gutters of the Rhondda; the wind he had courted and challenged to brace and cleanse his soul—

> May God who is slow to anger forgive my presumption,
> pulpiteering, singing hymns and praying to Him . . .

I asked for the wind that was probing the skeletons
to breathe into my dry bones the breath of life.
I pleaded with the tempest to winnow with the whirlwind
my desert's draff, and drench with its rains
my wasteland's parched ground till it bloomed as a garden.
I appealed with fervour without considering—
without considering (O terror) He could take me at my word,
He could take me at my word and answer my prayer,
And answer my prayer.

Self-accusations, however unjust and unnecessary, are a
destructive burden for a man wasted by a cruel illness, a weight
of foreboding, and a longing for the lost normality of home,
family, peace and quiet. But God is merciful: Can one yet
unpray one's prayers, unhope one's hopes, undream one's
dreams? Can one by God's grace renege? It was of the Father
of Mercies that Kitchener asked this impossible boon.

O Father of Mercies, be merciful,
Leave me my comrades' company, and my acquaintances' trust,
And the strength that is mine in my wife and children . . .
    Atonement who purchased freedom,
Do not tangle me in my prayers like Amlyn in his vow,
do not kill me at the altar by whose horns I have blasphemed,—
but let me, I pray, despite each wound, however hideous,
fail to be a saint.
    O Saviour of the lost,
save me, save me, save me,
from your baptism that washes the Old Man so clean:
keep me, keep me, keep me,
from the inevitable martyrdom of Your elect.
Save and keep me
from the wind that is blowing where it will.
So be it, Amen,
    and Amen.

When I first read this astonishing exercise in self-revelation,
as one born in the crumpled blanket of the coal valleys, bred
to the innocence of book-learning, and raised on the breast of
religion, it seemed to me the almost unbearable expression of
a poet's truth. Nowadays, for all the seas and cities in between,

still Antaeus to my native plot; my judgement sharpened but
my ideals unimpaired; my theology under snow but my sym-
pathies vernal in leaf and flower; I see it rather as the *poem's*
truth, to which the poet's narrower truth has been legitimately
accommodated. It is no compliment to a work of the creative
imagination to catalogue it as a factual record. Our poem is
not fact unadulterate and unadorned, but fact transmuted,
selective, recharged and re-ordered. *Sŵn y Gwynt Sy'n Chwythu*
'The Sound of the Wind that is Blowing', is a deeply moving
poem because it is a beautifully contrived poetic artefact, whose
truth is to human nature and experience.

There can be no doubt that for all its public aspects *Sŵn y
Gwynt* is an intensely personal poem, a poem of Me and Mine
and Here and Now. We left Saunders Lewis after remarking
his opinion that a good poem is an impersonal thing, and after
my promising to read an 'impersonal' poem of his which
impresses me as being not only personal but poignantly so.
It is a poem called *Caer Arianrhod*, which means 'The Fortress
of Arianrhod', *arian* meaning 'silver' and the whole phrase
the apt Welsh name for the Milky Way. It is a poem of just
eight lines, and purports to be the soliloquy of Owain Glyndŵr
(Owen Glendower) before he was encountered on the Berwyn
mountain in North Wales early one morning by the early
rising Abbot of Valle Crucis. 'You have risen early,' said
Owain. 'No,' answered the Abbot; 'It is you who have risen
early—a hundred years before your time.' Whereupon Owain
disappeared. It was Owain Glyndŵr, you remember, who last
led a revolt in arms to restore an independent kingdom of
Wales, was defeated by the English monarchy, disappeared,
and died in 1410–17. Whatever the rights and wrongs of it,
Glyndŵr's rising and its failure remain a somewhat throat-
constricting episode in Welsh history. Here are the thoughts,
the words, one national leader found for a predecessor of 500
years before:

> I saw the night closing its wing over the moor,
> Over a few frail homesteads, fallow land, infrequent furrows,
> And the stars came and the Milky Way, a dense miracle,

To spatter the feathers of the firmament with their myriad
   peacock-eyes.

I spread the wing of my dream over you, my country,
I would have raised for you—had you willed it—a joyful
   stronghold;
But my lot is like a shooting star that's cast out from among
   the stars
To stain the darkness with its hue and to burn out.

Earlier I congratulated Dylan Thomas on a masterpiece of
evasive evasion. Now I congratulate Saunders Lewis on a
triumph of personal impersonalism. The impersonalism is
there, all right, in the distancing of the subject, the appeal to
history and legend, the vast unrolling of landscape and stars,
the loftiness of the diction and control of the emotion, the
balanced structure. Paradoxically, these same things make it
a deeply personal poem. The protective wing of the night, the
wing of my dream; the raising of Caer Arianrhod, and the
joyous stronghold I would have raised for you, my people;
the dense miracle of a myriad stars, and the star which was
not chosen, but was rejected to fall alone; the more public and
impersonal, the more private and personal, with the truth of
the poem and the truth of the poet in classical equipoise. And
a poem of painful ironies, for poet and reader alike.

But our real business with Saunders Lewis is not in respect
of this beautifully designed allegory, parable, metaphor—what
shall we call it?—of a poem. It is rather with him as one of
our Three Poetical Prayer-Makers of the Island of Britain. In
prayer, as in eulogy and elegy, in patriotic diatribe and vaticination, he belongs with the bards, the men of professional skill
and technical exactitude, above all the men of high and noble
utterance. Like Cynddelw's, his voice is the voice of a living
tradition. And like Cynddelw he made a little more room within
the tradition. During my meditations and procrastinations
and changes of direction for this evening's talk, I at one time
thought to choose a poem each from Medieval Welsh, Old
Norse, and Old English, to illustrate—no, just to proclaim—
the fascination they have for me: Cynddelw's *Deathbed Poem*,

the *Sonatorrek* of Egill Skallagrímsson, in which the poet, shattered by the loss of his sons but canny even in his grief, railed at Othin, threatened him with his sword—and then took him back into favour for his poetry's sake—and that most beautiful, tender, and moving of all Old English religious poems, *The Dream of the Rood*. It was not to be, but it would be a present enrichment if the last of these, *The Dream of the Rood*, were in your minds now, as I begin to read, without comment, without explication, without praise—for the poem needs none of these things from me—Saunders Lewis's poem *I'r Lleidr Da*, 'To the Good Thief'.

> You did not see him on the mountain of Transfiguration
>   Nor walking the sea at night;
> You never saw corpses blushing when a bier or sepulchre
>   Was struck by his cry.
>
> It was in the rawness of his flesh and his dirt that you saw Him,
>   Whipped and under thorns,
> And in his nailing like a sack of bones outside the town
>   On a pole, like a scarecrow.
>
> You never heard the making of the parables like a Parthenon of
>   words,
>   Nor his tone when he talked of his Father,
> Neither did you hear the secrets of the room above,
>   Nor the prayer before Cedron and the treachery.
>
> It was in the racket of a crowd of sadists revelling in pain
>   And their screeches, howls, curses and shouts
> That you heard the profound cry of the breaking heart of their
>   prey:
>   'Why hast thou forsaken me?'
>
> You, hanging on his right; on his left, your brother;
>   Writhing like skinned frogs,
> Flea-bitten petty thieves thrown in as a retinue to his shame,
>   Courtiers to a mock king in his pain
>
> O master of courtesy and manners, who enlightened you
>   About your part in this harsh parody?
> 'Lord, when you come into your kingdom, remember me,'—
>   The kingdom that was conquered through death.

Rex Judaeorum; it was you who saw first the vain
  Blasphemy as a living oracle,
You who first believed in the Latin, Hebrew and Greek,
  That the gallows was the throne of God.

O thief who took Paradise from the nails of a gibbet,
  Foremost of the nobilitas of heaven,
Before the hour of death pray that it may be given to us
  To perceive Him and to taste Him.

⊰4⊱
A Mighty Man In Sion
Caradoc Evans, 1878–1945

I

A MAN here and there becomes a legend in his own lifetime, and in their register is Caradoc Evans. I first met him not long after I moved to Aberystwyth in 1940. My introducer was the epigrammatist Sarnicol, a sharp-nibbed man and neat excoriator of our human rind. He took me out to Brynawelon (the Hill of the Breezes, rightly so entitled), where Caradoc, always the man for a gesture, awaited us in the open air, at the head of a flight of stone steps, and gave me a grave Mid-Wales appraisal as I came thrusting up in my spring-heeled South Wales fashion. He was polite, even gracious, but wary. We went into a room whose floor was covered with a dimmed-down, ageing, but entirely sumptuous black Chinese carpet, on whose receptive pile we proceeded to circle each other like a couple of Cardiganshire corgis. Later we adjourned to the field outside, and I had my first sample of his good-humoured, well-paced, and mordantly libellous conversation. Sarnicol, looking very old-world in what used to be called a come-to-Jesus collar and glasses, played the benevolent ringmaster, and I assumed, wrongly, that our encounter would be immortalized in four lines of well-wrought verse, rapiered with satire, commas, and *cynghanedd*. The afternoon ended with Caradoc saying 'Come again', and clinching the invitation by reaching for a toy pencil and adding 'When?'

By the midsummer of 1941 we knew we would be friends, and I was honoured with his warmest term of approbation: 'Old Bloke'. Once or twice we had met by accident on the street, Caradoc and his second wife Marguerite (alias Oliver

Sandys and the Countess Barcynska, the romantic novelist) had come to tea, and we had swopped ideas mightily, though still a bit chary one of the other. I best recall a superb day of sun and breeze at Brynawelon in July 1941, when we lay out in the garden above and behind the house, watching four hares playing near the tree line, while Caradoc discoursed with his impressive voice and enchanting intonation of his days in London, of W. H. Davies, Arthur Machen, T. P. O'Connor, Denis Bradley, and Norman Douglas. Even had they heard him, they would have been too entertained to sue him for libel. He declared himself contemptuous of a merely Welsh reputation; of a vain woman writer he reckoned, 'Aye, no doubt she thinks her blood will be communion wine in heaven'; and he had a rich story of the local woman who because a Gors heathen persisted in walking all the way to Aberystwyth and back on Sundays for his non-nonconformist rites, demanded, 'Why! isn't the God of the Baptists good enough for him?' He recited with zest his own savage and blasphemous rejoinder. Later, we walked to Llanilar for dog biscuits. A couple of farm-women by a gate gave us the white of their eye for greeting. 'How d'you get on with them, Caradoc?' 'Not too bad,' he said; 'only they are afraid I'll put them in a story.' Right down the hill and all along the river he put to me, courteously but inexorably, the five hundred and five leading questions which his wife has gently summarized in one: 'What is your origin?' 'By dam,' he concluded warmly, 'you have done well!'

The art of pleasing (and no man had this more than he) implies a little flattery. Later that summer we took Glyn Jones and B. J. Morse out to Brynawelon, and with my right ear I could hear Caradoc catechizing Glyn. 'By dam,' I heard him conclude, 'you have done well!'

After John Cowper Powys I rate Caradoc the best listener in Wales, and women in particular found this charming after domestic half-attention. However long he might stay silent he was not absent from the conversation. He would sit with his head hung forward, his lids drooped like a bird's, and his short black pipe rising and falling like a little boat on his big lower lip, amused and absorbed and awaiting his moment. During

this same visit Glyn Jones's wife happened to say that she was
not all that impressed with her own Christian name, Doreen.
Suddenly Caradoc surged forward into our hesitant pros and
cons. 'Do-Reen!' he cried, with emphasis, astonishment, and
an almost voluptuous appreciation of the two syllables, 'By
dam, that's a fine name! Do-Reen! That's the *hell* of a fine
name!' There was play-acting in it, of course. He was a play-
actor to his heel-butts. And immensely appreciative of play-
acting in others.

The Welsh are natural actors. They are the playboys of Europe.
Whether he is in a tree scaring the crows, or on his knees libelling
his neighbour to God, or telling off the Devil from the pulpit, the
Welshman is always acting. The best actors are in the pulpit. I have
shuddered at a Welsh preacher's portrayal of a man who was so
hungry that he ripped open his feather-bed and ate the fleas. I have
seen a preacher as the Prodigal Son scuffle with shrieking pigs as he
fought for a morsel of food from their trough. I have seen a preacher
commit a man to the earth as if he were a kindly God receiving him
into his arms on the other side. Indeed we Welsh are actors. The pity
is that we are nothing else.

Unlike so many personalities, who are a grief to the eye,
Caradoc looked the part. Yet he was not a big man; indeed,
his chest was narrow and his shoulders, towards the end of his
life at least, were somewhat folded. But he had a fine head,
and his features were unforgettable—that Evan Walters portrait
is a gem. He had a long bony peasant's face, with a good strong
nose, prominent black nostrils, and thick upstanding grey hair.
His eyelids were crinkled and pink, like a parrot's. His mouth
was loose and wilful, with a long upper lip after the Irish fashion,
and the lower swollen and purple, with a small self-coloured
lump on it; and he often carried it pouted outwards. The sides
of his jaws were pink, and I never saw him when he did not
look newly shaved.

His clothes were never less than colourful, and often bizarre..
By the time I met him he had long crawled from his drab
chrysalis of black coat and striped trousers, to face the world
as a Tiger Moth. In the way of hats nothing was too fantastic.
Most of them were cut-down women's hats. Once he bought

a woman's hat, and in reply to expostulation: 'But that's a woman's hat, Caradoc!' he crushed it down over his ears and said bluntly: 'Well, it's a man's hat now!' Later he consented to have its brim pruned. It was of fine straw, red, green and yellow, and after pruning the very image of a small beehive, but he wore it with Red Indian gravity. Add a green and blue tweed jacket of violent check, a white cricket sweater with red and black club colours round the neck and waist, a navy blue shirt with a sewn-on scarlet collar of Viyella, and a green tie, and you are beginning to get the picture. Add black corduroy trousers, white socks, and sun-smiting polished brown toecaps, and you complete it. I must say, he looked exactly right. Nothing about him but proclaimed with glory: I am Caradoc Evans!

It is strange that with all that has been written about Caradoc's work there has been so little critical appraisal of it. He threw his first thunderbolt in 1915 with *My People*, his last in 1943 with *Morgan Bible*. In between came (the list is neither exhaustive nor chronological) *Capel Sion*, *My Neighbours* (by the Big Man's mercy he never got round to writing *My Friends*), *Wasps* (the first issue of this, withdrawn on a threat of an action for libel, is very much a collector's piece), *Nothing to Pay*, his play *Taffy*, and *Pilgrims in a Foreign Land*. A novel and the uncollected stories have been published since his death. Of the novels I think *Nothing to Pay* by far the best; ten or a dozen of the short stories guarantee him a place among the best short-story writers of his time.

The virulence of his libels on the London Welsh, the savage disproportion of his picture of rural Wales, are matters of literary history. The reactions of Little Bethel, the Sewing Guild, and the Parish Pump are equally chronicled. Macaulay, ruminating on Byron's exile from England, decided that there was nothing so ridiculous as the English people in one of its periodical fits of morality. But he lived fifty years too early, and knew not Wales. Grotesquerie, ferocity, the bitter black of caricature were to earn Caradoc a thousand enemies, and even lilliputians are formidable in a count of heads. His attacks on Welsh religious life, on sport, on the Eisteddfod, on Welsh music and singing were, of course, generally mischievous and sometimes malevolent. He paid back with interest the humiliations, the miseries, the thwarted hopes and the sweated labour of his boyhood and early manhood. Thus while most of his writing has the startling truth of high caricature, it is significant that his caricature was never kindly. His emotions were naked and raw, and he loved to hate. If he felt (and he felt more deeply than most) for a creature broken and destroyed, he expressed his sympathy by a castigation of hypocrisy, greed, or lust, which at times is itself shocking. To read the most passionate of his stories is to live again those long-healed-over moments when we felt on our shrinking flesh and sickened brain the primal revelations of the horrors that stalk the world. He needs no battles, earthquakes, plagues, to strike and numb us; a handful of peasants in a handful of houses take us to the limits of endurance. Much of his best writing has the cruel simplicity of folk-tale; he was less an inventor or recorder than a translator or (in the old poetic sense) a re-maker of once-was or yet-could-be fact. In other words, an artist not a chronicler, an author not a reporter. Even when he exploited recorded or observed fact, he rarely deserted his private world of fantasy. In the earlier volumes he was always ready to visit Heaven and eavesdrop on the Apostles; in *Pilgrims in a Foreign Land* and the posthumous *The Earth Gives All and Takes All* he invented a whole farmyard of animals and birds with human characteristics, who lived on terms of full communion and communication with their attendant Cardis. Criticism could hardly go farther astray than it did with those who trounced these essays in the grotesque as 'realistic' misrepresentations of the Welsh peasant-farmer and his labourers.

'The best-hated man in Wales'—so said only too many Welsh journals when it was known that Caradoc had laid aside his iron-shod boots for ever. And once it had been true. In his own evocative sentence: 'The repute of the man who defrauds servant girls with coloured bibles was fairer in Wales than mine.' Many local authorities banned him from their libraries; and to one of them fell the distinction of burning his books in the public incinerator. University societies passed resolutions against him, threatened to duck him in various sacred rivers; and the London Welsh shouted down Miss Edith Evans in his savagely entertaining comedy of Welsh village life, *Taffy*. For in English writing we had grown used to a Wales of the sweet singers and the great congregations, to a gallant little Wales, all tenors and wing-threequarters, and to the homely humours of the bucket-and-backyard. To be presented with a new picture, of rural troglodytes and urban milk-waterers, was more than we could stand. As book after book left his gall-dipped pen, we found the same Big White Shirts and Little Red Pennies, the same flowers of lust, greed, and hypocrisy, burgeoning in the familiar tub of dung. A vexing man he grew to the upright, a grief to the righteous—to say nothing of the self-righteous. Yet good intentions were not lacking towards him; the impulse to 'save' him (in the Welsh theological sense) filled a thousand bosoms. He was implored with loving-kindness, sweet reason, ingrown resentment and at last black fury, to mend his ways and write to please his critics not himself. Alas, he was deaf to pleading, hardened to abuse, and mischievous enough to promote new trouble and then revel in it.

His public announcements which forced our eyes upon ourselves, were yet more maddening than his stories, which exposed us to the derision of the English. 'People say hard things about our preachers. But Welsh preachers are not nearly so bad as their sermons.' 'The Eisteddfod is our national circus of clowns, and a rattling symptom of Welsh intellectual famine.' 'Every bardic robe is the flaunted shroud of a third-rate artist.' 'Nonconformity has made us an unhappy, embittered people. All that is beautiful it has taken from us. Forgotten are the Welsh dances and Welsh customs, and forgotten is Welsh folklore, and in their stead we have these morose entertainments of screeching sermons and doleful hymns.' And so for almost thirty years his relations with Wales (though not with individual Welshmen) were, according to taste, comical or tragi-comical. He was like an actor who falls victim to his own best role, and plays it so sustainedly that he can play no other. He must be the one and only Caradoc, the Scorpion of Nonconformity,

and One of the Three Sour Scourges of the Cymry. For this
he shares the blame with his expectant audience. His role was
to decry his people, to flout honoured convictions, and demolish
sacred prejudices. And all the time he was fostering his image
with sardonic care, so that he became a folk hero, or monster,
in his own lifetime.

II

When Caradoc set up as author he had an adviser, his fellow-
Cardi, Duncan Davies of Lampeter, an argumentative young
orator at street corners on behalf of the Shop Assistants' Union,
and to him we owe almost all the facts we have concerning
Caradoc's years of poverty and early authorship in London.
'We were always talking together about the Welsh peasantry.
Like Caradoc, I had been born in a remote country place,
and I had stored in my memory a large bundle of stories
and incidents which I had gleaned from round my home.'
Caradoc thought such things worthy of literary record, and
according to the tradition the first to be written down was 'Be
This Her Memorial'. It is the ninth story in *My People*, and
proceeds thus:

Mice and rats, it is said, frequent neither churches nor poor men's
homes. The story I have to tell you about Nanni . . . contradicts that
theory.

Nanni was religious; and she was old. No one knew how old she
was, for she said that she remembered the birth of each person that
gathered in Capel Sion; she was so old that her age had ceased to
concern.

She lived in the mud-walled, straw-thatched cottage on the steep
road which goes up from the Garden of Eden, and ends at the tramping
way that takes you into Cardigan town; if you happen to be travelling
that way you may still see the roofless walls which were silent witnesses
to Nanni's great sacrifice—a sacrifice surely counted unto her for
righteousness, though in her search for God she fell down and worshipped at the feet of a god.

This god, with a small g, was the minister of Capel Sion, the
Respected Josiah Bryn-Bevan. Upon this nauseating young

hypocrite Nanni poured out all her love, and to him she gave
all her devotion. But alas, the Respected Josiah received a call
from a wealthier sister church in Aberystwyth, and because
it *was* wealthier the Respected Josiah hearkened and obeyed.
This was heart-breaking news for Nanni; she bent her stiffened
limbs before God, with a capital G, and prayed that she might
live long enough to hear the Respected's farewell sermon and
be enabled to give him a parting present. This would be a big
coloured Bible, and in order to purchase it this peasant woman
first starved herself, then ate of strange diet.

Two Sabbaths before the farewell sermon was to be preached Nanni
came to Capel Sion with an ugly sore at the side of her mouth; repulsive
matter oozed slowly from it, forming into a head, and then coursing
thickly down her chin to the shoulder of the black cape, where it
glistened among the beads. On occasions her lips tightened, and she
swished a hand angrily across her face.

Nanni did not attend the Respected Josiah's farewell sermon
after all. She now lived with a piece of calico drawn over her
face, and knew herself to be too horrible. So she asked her
neighbour Sadrach Danyrefail, another nauseating hypocrite,
to present the Bible for her, which he did. The Respected Josiah
graciously accepted it: it was a book to be treasured, he said,
and he could think of no one more fit to treasure it than Sadrach
Danyrefail, to whom he forthwith handed it over.

In the morning the Respected Josiah Bryn-Bevan, making a tour of
his congregation, bethought himself of Nanni. The thought came to
him on leaving Danyrefail, the distance betwixt which and Nanni's
cottage is two fields. He opened the door and called out:
'Nanni.'
None answered.
He entered the room. Nanni was on the floor.
'Nanni, Nanni!' he said. 'Why do you not reply to me? An I not
your shepherd?'
There was no movement from Nanni. Mishtir Bryn-Bevan went on
his knees and peered at her. Her hands were clasped tightly together,
as though guarding some great treasure. The minister raised himself
and prised them apart with the ferrule of his walking-stick. A roasted
rat revealed itself. Mishtir Bryn-Bevan stood for several moments

spellbound and silent; and in the stillness the rats crept boldly out of their hiding places and resumed their attack on Nanni's face. The minister, startled and horrified, fled from the house of sacrifice.

This appalling but wonderful story heralded a phase of Anglo-Welsh fiction which by its very nature would not last long. Mainly, I believe, because Caradoc was *sui generis*, and had neither stable-mates nor disciples. In modern jargon, it was a one-off thing, and five years and three books, *My People*, 1915, *Capel Sion*, 1916. and *My Neighbours*, 1919, saw the best of it. It is difficult to find any other Welsh author to set in brackets with him, and I am alarmed by my own temerity in thinking what a Heroic Age poet he would have made, what a panegyrist after Catraeth or Argoed Llwyfain—completely disciplined, utterly unflinching, the master of his craft and enhancer of its moral and technical conventions. But I let wisdom, or caution, prevail, and say no more than that in *My People* 'A Father in Sion', 'The Woman Who Sowed Iniquity', and 'A Just Man in Sodom' strike me (and the choice of verb is deliberate) as stories of comparable quality and impact.

Any writer must be judged by what he says and the way he says it. Caradoc's style and subject-matter were each highly distinctive. He came to English as to a foreign language, and shouldering the risk made of it what he wanted. By his own witness the two main influences on his story-telling were Genesis for style and Marie Lloyd for narrative.

I joined a grammar class at Toynbee Hall, but I gave it up, for grammar is the study of a lifetime . . . Somehow I came to read Genesis again and when I was about the middle of it, 'Jiw-Jiw, this is English writing' I said to me. On a Saturday night I went to the Hammersmith Palace and there I saw Marie Lloyd, and 'Jiw-Jiw,' I said to me, 'she tells not by what she says but by what she does not.' I kept up Genesis and Marie Lloyd.

For Genesis read the whole Authorized Version. Here are some paragraphs from 'Lamentations':

The night of the Hiring Fair Evan drank in the inn, and the ale made him drunk, and he cried a ribald song; the men with whom he drank mocked him, and they carried him into the stable and laid him in a manger, and covered him with hay; and in the stall they put a horse, thinking the animal would eat Evan's hair and beard. But the Big Man watched over Evan, and the horse did not eat his beard.

'What shall we do,' said the light men, 'to humble him before the congregation?'

One said: 'Let us strip the skin from the horse that perished, which is buried in the narrow field, and we will throw it over his head.'

Thus they did, and Evan went home with the skin of the horse covering the back of him like a mantle.

This is a fair example of his hard, clean, pungent biblical prose. Also, the Lot-like incident is no idle flourish: Evan's return home thus outlandishly attired finally addles the wits of the daughter whose flesh he has already polluted in his drunkenness. She runs naked into the fields, is taken with a snare, and Evan puts reins on her, and 'In this wise he drove her before him, in the manner in which a colt is driven, to the mad house of the three shires, which is in the town of Carmarthen, and the distance from Manteg to Carmarthen is twenty-four miles.' It is only fair to Caradoc to add that he had made Evan clothe his daughter before driving off to the mad-house. And it is only fair to Evan to add that 'After this he did not sin any more; his belongings increased . . . and his house remained religious as long as he lived.'

III

And now, out of a dozen topics inviting discussion I must of necessity confine myself to three. The first, of piquant interest to all word-bibbers, idiom-hunters, and practitioners of the tricky art of translating one tongue, one language, into another, is Caradoc's typically mischievous but consistently clever manner of rendering Welsh words and phrases in re-creative English. He offers us idioms which are strange but pleasing, like 'forehead of the house' and 'kill the hay', and others easily swallowed, like 'large money' and 'hundred and a half'. But other of his 'literal translations' gave deep offence, because they are in effect, and often in fact, grotesqueries designed to degrade his characters and make them stupid, ridiculous, or even hateful in our eyes. Especially our religious eyes. Of this kind are 'the Big Man' for God (i.e. *y Bod Mawr*, the Great Being), or 'Little Big Man', or yet more affectionately 'Dear Little Big Man'; the undear departed's choice of 'the White Palace or the Fiery Pool'; and such variations in the announcement of a death as 'Old mam has gone to wear a White Shirt' or 'Twm bach is in the Jordan'. The normal verbs of saying or not saying are eked out with 'Mouth you to the wench fach', 'What iobish do you spout?', 'Shut your chins' or 'Shut your throat', 'Speech him to the Great Harvester'. What, one wonders, did Caradoc really make of Yahweh? And, even more, what did Yahweh make of Caradoc?

Second, at the risk of repetition, I emphasize that he was one of the most painstaking authors imaginable. I cannot speak of his unsigned day-by-day journalism (I remember his calm description of a paper he had worked for, that only fools bought it and luckily their number was increasing day by day); nor of his ghost-writing (he claimed to have set several reputations higher than his own); but over everything he signed he was meticulous. At the head of the 'Men and Women' articles he wrote for my *Welsh Review* he would inscribe the menacing rubric: 'To the Printer. Do not alter anything in this article.' 'Printer' was a tactful way of spelling 'Editor'. His manuscript showed his never-ending fight for perfection, and after one experiment I never again sent him a page-proof. He was indefatigable at winnowing, and could say as much in a sentence or two as any man since Swift. Thus, from 'According to the Pattern':

Even if Abel had land, money, and honour, his vessel was not filled until his wife went into her deathbed and gave him a son.

And from the same story:

Though his daughters murmured—'We wake at the caw of the crows,' they said, 'and weary in the young of the day'—Abel obeyed his son, who thereupon departed and came to Thornton East to the house of Catherine Jenkins, a widow woman, with whom he took the appearance of a burning lover.

And this, the opening paragraph of 'Unanswered Prayers':

When Winnie Davies was let out of prison, shame pressed heavily on her feelings; and though her mother Martha and her father Tim prayed almost without ceasing, she did not come home. It was so that one night Martha watched for her at a window and Tim prayed for her at the door of the Tabernacle, and a bomb fell upon the ground that was between them, and they were both destroyed.

Some thirty years later the eye was undimmed, and the tongue edge unblunted.

Some time ago I bought a pint of beer at a public house round here. As I was preparing to depart, the bright-eyed, skinnyish, yellow-faced woman of the place said to me: 'Come to the cellar and I'll show you where my dog died. Oh, he was a fighter, he was!' She lit a candle and I followed her. In the grey-hued cellar she said: 'We found the old dog here on the morning of my husband's funeral. Dead. There was one wreath too many for my husband's coffin and so I laid it on the body of my dog.' 'And,' I asked, 'whose wreath was that you cast away so lightly?' She answered: 'Mine.'

This kind of matter, this kind of manner, are the flesh and bone of his writing. It is the agreed convention of the civilized world to judge authors by their best, and Caradoc's style at its best is remarkable for its purity, strength, and precision. He never wrote a flabby or a formless sentence in his life; and it is therefore instructive to consider why many consider him not a great writer, and why he falls short of Maupassant, say, even in the eyes of his admirers. His writing, with all its fine qualities, was irremediably stylized; it was designed for one set of effects, and with those he was content. It lacked suppleness and adaptability. But a worse handicap was his narrowness of vision. What he saw and chose to write about he saw with extraordinary, and at times demoniacal, intensity; but he was blinkered. Greed, hypocrisy, and gross and brutal appetite—he wrote of these with power and fidelity and, it must be confessed, with tiresome iteration: but generosity, self-sacrifice, love, and the kindlier humours of men—of these he has nothing to say. Or almost nothing. His books are filled with hints of a greater writer lost. But he chose to be *Malleus Brittonum*, and a hammer must be always striking.

Ever since the publication of *My People: Stories of the Peasantry of West Wales* in the year 1915, a chorus of clamant voices had been asking, Why? Or even, Why Us, *yng ngwlad yr Efengyl*, in the Land of the Gospel, the Prophets, and the Preachers? Were the most outrageous stories a revenge for his foiled hopes of becoming a schoolteacher or preacher? He was born in Welsh-speaking Wales, and apprenticed not to the arts, pedagogy, or the pulpit, but to the Rag Trade, whose hirelings, he tells us, were required to dress like Cabinet Ministers on the wages of a dustman. For long he had an incomplete command of literary English, and his early writing was done after a full day's work of twelve hours or more, on the wrapping paper and discarded box-lids he found behind the counter. His friend Duncan Davies has preserved the record of those pinched years of struggle into journalism and full authorship, and the record is a brave one, a page out of Grub Street: poverty, loneliness, belittlement, and frustration. 'Cruel is the world to a boy with nothing.' He could not be brought to talk about it: it had no place in his anecdotes. Just an occasional sick and savage sentence. 'I wrote the truth as it was at that time, and it was the stinking truth. The stink of it will be in my soul for ever.'

Others found a simpler explanation. Mishtir Caradoc Evans was no enigma to them. He just happened to be the most arrogant, ungrateful renegade of the century— and hadn't he said as much himself: 'Mam, Mam, was the milk in you sour that I am Me?' The debate continues.

Much must be left unsaid, and a little be said briefly. Until the flowering of the mid-1930s (and in his own opinion till the day of his death in the mid-1940s) he must be accounted, if only because the most notorious and hardest to come to terms with, the most important figure of the Anglo-Welsh literary movement. After all, he was not merely a legendary being himself: he had created a legendary Wales to the wonderment and annoyance of his contemporaries. Nor should he be grudged the satisfaction this gave him. For he had a twofold significance: the first the high excellence of his best work, and the second what I may call his work of liberation. That his battling was disinterested I very much doubt, for he was as ready to libel as to satirize, but before most of us set pen to paper he had fought savagely and successfully against philistinism, Welsh provincialism, and the hopelessly inhibited standards of what little Anglo-Welsh literature there was. For good (or if you prefer, for bad) he destroyed the dynasty of Allen Raine and the Maid of Cefn Ydfa, and sank it in the sea. The great waves dashed against him and shook him more than he cared to admit, but none whelmed his head, and the Rock of his Salvation was unshakeably founded on his vanity and ignorance. There is no evidence that he ever read a line of any Anglo-Welsh author of the mid-1930s renaissance, his published strictures were as silly as they were sour, and if in the grand debate for the artist's freedom he was on the right side, it was as often as not for wrong reasons.

Which brings us to our third, and last, and therefore mortuary note on Caradoc. Here again much must be left unsaid, and a little be said too briefly. He had lived much, even most, of his life in London, and left to himself would pretty certainly have opted to remain there for good. His recent foray with Marguerite into West Wales (1933–7) had produced no small harvest of stress and strain. The wreckage of his first marriage, to Rose, had continued to fall all too publicly about his ears. (Indeed, on one occasion, her handbag fell all too publicly about his ears, when at a chance confrontation outside the Aberystwyth railway station she felled him to the ground before an audience of taxi-drivers well-versed in strict metres and local charges.) Nothing so forthright was to be feared at the hands of Marguerite, but of his second marriage too he could say without fear of contradiction, 'I am too much for her', with the equally indisputable rider: 'I am too much for myself too.' And now for the second time, in the nervous pre-war summer of 1939, to Marguerite, West-Wales looked a very good place to be. Not only for its own sake. Every bit as important, residence there, she thought, would distance Caradoc from various temptations inimical to their marriage. He might demur, but was he not a kept man, not earning enough in a year to keep himself in tobacco for a fortnight? While Marguerite with her two best-sellers a year, and her self-induced vision of a Happiness Stone awaiting her under the splendour of the Setting Sun—Marguerite held the purse-strings and the casting-vote.

This time they crossed the mountains not to the comforts and known amenities of their earlier home in Aberystwyth, but to the village of New Cross, a few miles inland, where as I have already recorded I first met Caradoc in late 1940. His fires were fast dying down, but for all his switched-on charm, his gift for gnomic utterance, and his epicure's relish of a good phrase in others, he remained a creature closely in touch with malice and pride. It was the natural corollary of his hard eye for his fellow-men that he had a soft spot for dogs. At this time he and Marguerite had no fewer than three, a quiet old lump called Jock, the handsome Taffy whom I cannot remember, and a lynx-hued, sly-eyed, neurosis-ridden lip-lifter named Timber, whom on a closer acquaintance I grew to mistrust and pity in equal measure. In many ways he and Caradoc were in like case. Kennelled richly though they were, they lived very much under starter's orders, took exercise on a lead, and were beleaguered by a possessive, even proprietorial love. Each bit the hand that fed him, and for good measure Timber bit Caradoc, though it is not reported that Caradoc ever bit Timber. Each suffered his own kind of ruin, and was not the sole proponent of his woe.

Nor did Brynawelon prove the benign refuge Marguerite had been hoping for. It stood open to the winds and weather, and in winter was cold and draughty. Worse, Caradoc's health was now calamitously in decline, and in October 1943 they removed to the shelter of Aberystwyth, and it was there that he died on 11 January 1945. His funeral service was at Horeb, New Cross. Of his resting-place he had given this account in his Journal: 'The garden of graves is two fields higher than this house (*scil*, Brynawelon). A man is cutting with a scythe the grass for hay. I do not know who the man is because I cannot see his face. But he must be a Methodist and a tee-totaller otherwise the grass would not be given to him. This grass is religious.' The grave's modest headstone bears this inscription:

CARADOC EVANS
Died

11th January 1945

'Bury me lightly so that
The small rain may reach
My face and the fluttering
Of the butterfly shall not
Escape my ear.'

Caradoc Evans

Caradoc had been a chapel-goer and sermon-tester all the Sundays of his life, and was curious of the life to come, though he had no wish to share in it. 'If survival is possible, I have told Marguerite that I will prove it to her in three's, should I die before her. But I do not imagine there is anything after death except peace and quiet and a hole in the ground.' The epitaph at Horeb is probably Marguerite's carefully chosen version of a much earlier rumination. By a curious quirk of truly Caradocian circumstance it now serves for Marguerite too. She had stayed on in West Wales after Caradoc's death, removing first to the nearby village of Penrhyn-coch where, without Caradoc to guide her, she sorely mistreated the beautiful Welsh name of her cottage. From there she moved to Aberdovey, where she had an actual Happiness Stone standing as a kind of tourist attraction in her front garden. Then, finally, she broke away to the Border, to Church Stretton, where she died in the wintry March of 1964. After a funeral service at Llanfihangel-y-Creuddwyn, she was laid to rest on 13 March with her husband at Horeb, New Cross. There had been a heavy fall of snow, the mourners were few, and the officiating Minister assisted in carrying the coffin up the steep slope to the grave above Brynawelon. Man goeth to his long home, and Woman likewise in her season. But, alas, there proved to be no room on the headstone for Marguerite's name or style, no word of esteem or affection. And though this wrong be one day righted, other echoes and ironies are biding their time, wry, grotesque, and gruesome, in that order.

Be that as it may. Not long after his death (incidentally, his given name was David, not Caradoc), and not long after I had said my second goodbye to this gifted, perverse, and in all ways fascinating man in the March 1945 number of the *Welsh Review*, I was, by invitation, looking through his books and encountered a typical Caradoc *coup-de-main* on the inside cover of one of them, interred there in the sure and certain hope of a glorious resurrection. In that minuscule, unmistakable, and almost illegible hand of his he had written: 'I'll be around somewhere.' In respect of Wales, his personal legend, and his place in Anglo-Welsh literature, I judge he always will be. After all, Old Bloke, it takes two to say Goodbye, and as yet Caradoc hasn't said it. And Dame Wales hasn't said it either.

⚞5⚟

Welsh Dylan, 1914–1953

An Obituary

ON this afternoon of shell-blue sunshine, in the Little Summer of Mihangel (Saint, Swordbearer, First Angel under God), spun on a shining spider's line to the thirteenth day of December, how sit upon this Sabbath ground and tell sad stories of the death of bards? For the world is a prodigy around us, and Dylan's Wales a singing miracle: red campion in the bud-bright woods, fists of honeysuckle on sunken hedgerows, and in the garden raspberries pipped and juicy. Ahead, over the hill, a rook and his wife are driving a buzzard in jubilant sweeps to the next sea-dingle—just for the rooky hell of it, it seems; while gulls, love's messengers, swing their white breasts from plough-land to sea. Behind us, over a forest of round and roseate hills, rapscallion kites and kestrels thrive by talion-law; and covert foxes smile as the first-light lambs of Christmas skip in white riding-hoods from dam to red damnation. Water springs are up there too, flowing to redds of Teifi and Tywi, whose lank and emptied kelts point their hook-jaws for river-mouth and salted estuary. (And somewhere there, under the mumbled walls of Ystrad Fflur, the last dry grains of Dafydd ap Gwilym are stirring, poet of wine-sweet women and greenwood, girls' boon but bane to husbands, gull-and-salmon-sender, words' waggish prince, and servant of our Lord.) To the kite's eye and fox's nostril, to the miltless glands of the fish, by air and earth and water, float sight, scent, and savour of the sun-fronting arcs of south-western Wales, from Swansea in Glamorgan to New Quay in Cardiganshire, Dylan country,

Written December 1953, and published with illustrative passages of the poet's verse (omitted here) in *The Adelphi*, vol. xxx (1954).

where Tawe flows, the Jarvis and Surgeon hills rear, land under Milk Wood, and between unnamed river and unknown hill the wrong-foot-forward, cart-before-horse, fly-buttons-behind parish of Llareggub—the right-sided heart of it all.

Dylan Marlais Thomas: there was prescience in this poet's naming. Dylan, which in Swansea rhymes with villain, for the rest of Wales chimes with his art and sullen craft—but he had a royal indifference to the vowel. 'Call me what you like, except Dilys.' The name itself (and in Wales, to the Joneses, Thomases, Evanses and Davieses, the Christian name is all) he owed to the magician-king Math son of Mathonwy, of whom his scholiast father must have read in the Fourth Branch of the Mabinogi:

She was fetched to him; the maiden entered. 'Maiden,' said he, 'art thou a maiden?' 'I know not but that I am.' Then he took the magic wand and bent it. 'Step over this,' said he, 'and if thou art a maiden, I shall know.' Then she stepped over the magic wand, and with that step she dropped a fine boy-child with rich yellow hair. The boy uttered a loud cry . . . 'Why,' said Math son of Mathonwy, 'I will have this one baptized'—of the rich yellow-haired boy. 'The name I will give him is Dylan.' The boy was baptized, and the moment he was baptized he made for the sea. And there and then, as soon as he came to the sea he received the sea's nature, and swam as well as the best fish in the sea. And for that reason he was called Dylan Eil Ton, Sea son of Wave. No wave ever broke beneath him. And the blow whereby his death came, his uncle Gofannon aimed. And that was one of the Three Unhappy Blows.

Another was the early death of Keats—but that was a long time ago and in another country. 'He received the sea's nature.' The coastal waters to the five-fathom line, Swansea Bay and its miles of yellow sands, Mumbles Head and the corpse-wrack skerries of Gower, Pwll-du, the Worm, and Rhosili, with their hard white bone of rock and the green grass growing to the crabbed and jellied tideline, and later the castle-splashed estuary from Carmarthen to Laugharne, and the cliff-waterfalls and golden beaches of south Cardiganshire. He is our first poet of the sea's side—not the swilling wastes of ocean, black water and torn horizons, but the meeting and mingling of sea, river, and land.

This ribbed and sanded waterland with its low inlying hills is the setting of most of the best poems and all the best stories. Uncle Jim lived here, of the 'long, red, drunken fox's face, with its bristling sidebushes and wet, sensitive nose', and extraordinary little Cough, Katie Sebastopol Street who sang for all comers in the Lord Jersey, and the drunk who lost his bottom down (or up?) in Dowlais. This is the country of Ann Jones and Fern Hill, of the birthdays thirty years and thirty-five to heaven; here flashed the needles of the famed stitch-droppers and the legs of the long-legged Bait. And here from the windy West came two-gunned Gabriel. Lickerish life in London and the four American tours, a trip to Persia and a summer near Florence, oozed late un-nourishing pap compared with this milk-rivered, rock-boned uberous land, this bass-and-cockle water, whose four corners are Swansea docks, Carmarthen bridge, Worms Head, and the quicksands of Pendine.

The natal Swansea first. If a poet must be born at all, this is as good a place to choose as any, with its palmy welcome and humerus friendship, its wetlip kiss and bosomy embrace. It isn't Llanelli, true, scarlet-flannelled and sospan-crazy; nor is it Cardiff, elegant as a gold watch on the griped and griping belly of the coalfield. But it will serve. Swansea during the formative years of Dylan's childhood and young dogdom (I have said this before and escaped with my scalp) was a most engaging South Wales village of 150,000 inhabitants, with its notables and naturals, its musicians and poets and loose forwards packed tight and lordly on the ground. On the Landore flank it rivalled the desolation of shell-shocked Stalingrad: here Jeremiah lamented and Micah cursed, and a Lord knee-deep in brimstone hearkened unto them both. But out at the Mumbles, where the town becomes Gower, it turns Paradise without the serpent. Between these disparities, these bounds seraphic and vile, sprawls as jolly a collocation of docks and seaside, streets and bombsites, pubs and chapels, shops and flicks, as any poet could reasonably expect for his first Christmas stocking—with St Helens and the Mumbles Light Railway thrown in for a

blessing. What all this meant to the youthful Dylan, the excitement with which it full-filled him, and the uproarious glory
he wrote into it, may be tracked in black and white through
the trumpeting chapters of *Portrait of the Artist as a Young Dog*,
or heard through whorled ear-conches in the memorial radio
scripts, *Memories of Christmas* and *Return Journey*. Nor has
Swansea ever let him go. It *made* his riper prose, with its bars
and grogram boys and bumbast ladies, so that 'Four Lost Souls'
in 1953 shows the same full malty head as 'One Warm Saturday'
of 1940 brew. Swansea early, and Soho late; repeating and
repeating on the other. These women with the shabby faces
and the comedians' tongues, squatting and squabbling over
their mother's ruin, might have lurched in from Llanelli on
a football night, on the arms of short men with leeks. So Soho:
we change our skies but not our heartscapes—as they lurched
in last night, after Swansea had held the All Blacks to a somewhat blackened draw, dark and dumply women, well coopered
as to stern, and their short, dark husbands, compact as corgis,
guardroom-trained and glasshouse-broken, scarred, merry and
scabrous, wearing tiny silver saucepans on their lapels, as if
to say: 'Touch that one, boyo, and guess what hit you!' And
in the throbbing streets the Valley dandies; flat-capped fish-
wives with their frails of empties, and chip-shop sirens with
their ear-rings rattling; lascars who slide on felted feet, nose-
trimmers, razor-men; Brazell and the rough Skully, and
Matthews Hellfire crying Whoa! to sin and Woe! to sinners
on the burning sands. 'Never was there such a town as ours,
I thought . . . I'll put you all in a story by and by.'

There was, one knows, in Dylan's childhood another side to
the gaudy-bawdy, night-on-the-tiles Tawe which flows through
'Old Garbo' and 'One Warm Saturday'. But how much he
owed to chapel-Swansea I cannot say. My guess is that he
owed more than he thought or admitted, both because of
and despite the revolt and brisk irreverence he shared with so
many South Wales writers of his shaken generation. For one
thing Nonconformity made drink and pleasure so devilishly
attractive. Baal and Mahmoud winked from every glass's lip,
and Aholibah from every pilfered eyebrow. No artist could

possibly feel himself more of a young dog than he littered in
the debris of Zion. So little Gil Morris wasn't the only one who
etched dissipation under his eyes with a blacklead-pencil every
Saturday night; nor was young Mr Thomas alone in leaning
against a bar 'wishing that my father could see me now and
glad, at the same time, that he was visiting Uncle A. in
Aberavon'.

Besides, the family had its traditions, liberal, pedagogic,
unitarian. There was the father who taught English literature
at the Grammar School, and a great-uncle who, like every
other Welsh preacher, wrote a volume of poems in Welsh,
homely pieces about robins and children and religion, utterly
un-Dylanesque, an essay on 'Books' and a few short stories.
From him, one imagines, the poet got his second name, Marlais,
as he himself by a perilous orthography (or my more perilous
assumption) took his bardic title from that same Marlais stream
which squeezes from the thin-soiled sheep and fox country
under Pencarreg, jinks fast and tinkling to the gold-and-trout-
laden Cothi, and so mingles its waters with the flooding Tywi
in the meadowlands east of Carmarthen. These clean con-
fluences have the beauty of a young embrace, the soft swirls
and glossy currents lost yet distinct in each other, the slipping
trout feeling new lures and compulsions, making their way
divinely among bubbles and pebbles, transparent shallows and
channels of tendrilly ooze. Dylan, poet of pools and tidal swills,
was deep-versed in all such alchemies of bell-throated streams
and hailing rivers, and loved that last floating alembic of waters
where fresh becomes salt and the moss-wombed spring leaps
anew and laughs and lives in the billow. Such confluence was
in his soul too. In the first light, along with the flotsam of Tawe,
the jetsam of the holiday bay, a river went out of Eden to water
the garden: and the gold of that land is good.

Laugharne: I was down there for the funeral. It looked a
pleasant little town where time had time to stand and loiter.
The china dogs in the windows barked of childhood and home,
but it was cockles for coal, and in the river tins for coal-tar.
No hawk hung on Sir John's hill, but a song-thrush puffed
his breast with a weak song at the lych-gate, and a spaniel,

young and ruddy, lolloped through our legs at the church-door. (At Montgomery, I remember, at Geraint Goodwin's funeral, that writer of good prose and lover of poached salmon, it was a brisk little white terrier snuffling ecstatically the new-turned earth and the leaf-mould odours of autumn.) The sun was shining, as through all this magic fall of the year, on the uncovered sands and bottom-up boats, on Pelican House and Brown's Hotel, on the ivy draped ruin of a castle (not bad, even to a Monmouthshire man), and the sage-green cliffs under Wharley Point. Shining too on the cream-stone church, the bushy purlieus of the ancient burial ground and the bright green grass of God's new acre over the bridge, on the press photographers baffled by headstones, and on us, the gravely assembled. There they were, my fellow-countrymen, Morganwg and Sir Gâr well to the fore, two well-marked types among Dylan's friends and contemporaries: men built like bulls, like Welsh Blacks, heavy-shouldered, chesty men, with a commitment of paunch, beef-faced and starfish-veined, their cheeks a-loll from the gallows of their cheekbones, bull's wool over their brows, thick and upcurling; and the lean, dark ones, with a handbreadth of long face, black-eyed, bleak-skinned, five-foot-fivers, bards to a man, meditating elegies in their respites from grief.

How soft and easy a country this estuarine Carmarthenshire looks to dwellers under Plynlymon. No sour stricken upland of brown brooks and bristled reeds, no squelching causeways through the encroaching bog, no bald summits and white-grass pastures, with their squat black farms whistling in the wind. Long sands down here, and a caul of water, small bosky hills of birch and beech and oak, villages by Welsh standards pretty and cared-for. Why did he come here? Strangers were asking: Why did he stay? As though there were room for surprise! Because he wanted to. Because he must. Because this corner of Wales raised him to his full Merlin-height of poetry. In the earlier books of poems he was a terrifying adolescent in a terrified world, juicy as a peeled plum with sexual and vaticinatory conceits, an unashamed explorer of the hero, saint, scoundrel, and fool every man carries under his skin. More was needed.

For the problem of autumn fieldfares and firecrests is that of vernal poets too. 'Where do we go from here?' He had genius, and had deployed it as strongly as narrowly; but one cannot for ever remain an *enfant terrible*. There was a Dylan legend, but it was of the Marvellous Boy. And he was now older than Keats. Who has not lain with his nose in seabank grass, a forest of sword-blades and corkscrews stabbing about him, and watched an ant with his burden of egg climb rapidly to nowhere? Dylan was like that ant, troll-sized, merry, and roc-egg burdened, but for what cerulean void was he bound, and on what breakneck spiral? Had we known it, the answer was no void, no spiral, but the road to Wales, and Laugharne, and the flood-tide of his poetry.

Marriage had come at about the same time, in 1937. Fatherhood followed, and he was made part, as never before, of the elemental, miracle-working cycle: birth, love, and death.

These were the gold-browed years when, sown in seasand, he grew from dragon's tooth to druid, in his own land, among his own people, a land of notable publicans and sinners, and a people among whom the practice of poetry is as natural as adding water to whisky or milk. Where else should a Welsh poet live and have his being? For Dylan was Welsh as a leek or a Teifi coracle. Welsh, let us say, as a *cywydd* or *englyn*. Welsh in the cunning complexity of his metres, not only in the loose *cynghanedd*, the chime of consonants and volleying of vowels, but in the relentless discipline of his verse, the hierarchic devotion to the poet's craft, the intellectual exactitude and emotional compression of word and phrase and stave and poem, the excision of everything soft, blurred, and wavering—and Welsh not least in his ignorance of a Celtic twilight. Indeed, he insisted that his later verse was formal and fugue-like beyond the comprehension of his most percipient admirers. Thus the 'Author's Prologue' to the *Collected Poems* of 1952 is a poem of 102 lines, of which lines 52–102 unwind the end-sounds of lines 1–51, line 52 rhyming with line 51, line 53 with line 50, and so on. Finally, the words with which lines 1, 2, and 3 end will be found unchanged at the ends of lines 102, 101, and 100. (I add, against myself, that when the poet opened my eyes to this unsuspected structural harmony at our last meeting, he gave me figures for a poem of 100 lines, and so fulfilled his warning at our first meeting, twelve years earlier, that it was part of the poet's function to lay trip-wires for critics. Always supposing he could count so high: a thing to my mind far from certain. In any case, the honours rested easy: that same evening I persuaded him to retain his heavy red-and-white woollen coat throughout an incendiary reading of poems, merely that I might advise his audience, if they were ever again asked the rhetorical question, 'And did you once see Shelley plain?' to retort—the poet wet with sweat from knees to nape, and gurgling for a drink—'No, but I did see Dylan coloured.').

As surely his last evangelism, the poems to 'great and fabulous dear God' (Hail to His beasthood!), belonged to Wales. Ask any of his generation of Welsh writers what their mothers hoped for them, and they will confess: the Pulpit. Dylan's pulpit was the Carmarthenshire countryside, God's rough tumbling ground, the rooks' black bethel over the surpliced hill; his sermons those best poems of this century written 'for the love of Man and in praise of God'. How he reached such religious, philosophical, and moral notions as he possessed, I don't pretend to know. His knowledge and insight were prodigious, but he lived unchained by fact and indifferent to circumstance. Finance, politics, theology, commerce—I wonder what these meant to him, with all their paraphernalia of dues and contracts, debts and duties? Very little, very little indeed. Hugh Griffith, who alone of living men has played King Lear both in Welsh and in English, records that he once asked Dylan to play the Fool. 'Boy,' said the poet, 'that's casting close to nature!' For he was the Fool, the Great Fool of legend, Peredur-Percival of Arthur's court and eternal Gipsy Jack, Pied Sandpiper of seashores, and Boy from over the Mountain. And he had the Great Fool's wisdom, the wisdom of poet and prophet, growing like hair and teeth and toe-nails, divinely natural and strong, the princely largess of the last poems. There is a glory of the sun, says the Prayer Book, and another glory of the moon, and there is a glory of the stars in heaven. And for Dylan there was a glory of God, and another glory of Man, and a glory of the 'kingdom of neighbours, finned, felled and quilled', and in the last poems these are a trinity, one and indivisible. And he himself a trinity, god, man, and brother brute: Gwynn with the owl on his shoulder; fag-ended tosspot, cherub, and troll; and affable, hickory shorthorn in every heifered pasture.

And now the sun has gone and Dylan's Wales grown dark. The hawks have done polishing their nails for one holy holly-day more, and the magpies' polls are black under thorn. Owl-light and moontime are on us (the moon has been riding since three). Night in the white giant's thigh, and night in country sleep. Not a fox's bark, not a furred small friar squealing. But the owls are out, their wide wings silent as snowfall down the sloe-eyed dingle. Lords of the half-light, their singer lost, we must leave the night to them. And may there, for that singer's sake, be foxes and owls in heaven.

∗6∗

Son of the Late Earl Rivers
Richard Savage, 1697–1743

I

IT was in July 1739, at an innyard in London, that Richard Savage, son of the late Earl Rivers (to give him the title he never denied himself), parted with tears in his eyes and fifteen guineas in his pocket from his friend, admirer, and future biographer, Samuel Johnson. His journey was to Wales.

Johnson (such is the happiness of poets) had framed sentiments proper to the occasion more than a year before, in his poem 'London':

> Tho' grief and fondness in my breast rebel,
> When injur'd THALES bids the town farewell,
> Yet still my calmer thoughts his choice commend,
> I praise the hermit, but regret the friend,
> Who now resolves, from vice and LONDON far,
> To breathe in distant fields a purer air,
> And, fix'd on Cambria's solitary shore,
> Give to St David one true Briton more.

If he now repeated these lines with the subdued relish of a poet who is friend and prophet too, we must imagine them received by Savage with at best a rueful nod. He was bound, he knew it, for exile. He was bound, but this he did not know, for a death four years hence as dramatic, and as enigmatic, as anything in his mysterious and troubled career. If indeed that career may properly be called Richard Savage's at all.

But if there was never a Richard Savage there was certainly a Richard Smith. Richard Smith's mother was as certainly that

Anne Mason who in 1683 had married the Earl of Macclesfield's heir. Her husband, while still plain Mr Gerrard, had shown his mettle by breaking the neck of a footboy just for the fun of it, while in company with Lord Cornwallis. They had begun, modestly enough, by being offensive to the sentinels in the Park. At the trial of Cornwallis for murder, 2 July 1676, in Westminster Hall: 'The summe of evidence, in briefe, was y^t both ye Ld Cornwallis and Mr Gerrard threatened to kill ye sentinell, and y^t one of them, but wch could not be proved, bid ye sentinell kill ye boy, and said: "We will kill somebody"; and y^t presently after Mr Gerrard killed ye boy.' But those were the days when a lord was still a lord, Cornwallis was acquitted, and Gerrard who had fled to France was later reprieved by His Majesty. His curiosity and high spirits were to put him in need of a second reprieve in 1685—he had taken part in the Rye House plot—but he survived to become an earl in 1693 and a cuckold in 1695. His wife's lover was Richard Savage, fourth Earl Rivers, known too as 'Tyburn Dick'. It was Lady Vane's boast later in the century that she had deceived her husband only with her fellow-countrymen—and if it is virtue to lie only with Scotsmen, it is less than sin to pile earl upon earl: the Countess of Macclesfield kept to her rank and bore Rivers a daughter, christened Anne Savage, in 1695, and a son, christened Richard Smith, on 18 January 1697. Anne Savage died soon after birth, and Richard Smith disappeared at the age of six months and has never been traced since. The Earl of Macclesfield divorced his Countess by act of parliament early in 1698, 'by the first bill of that nature that hath passed, where there was not a divorce first obtained in the Spiritual Court'; and soon afterwards she married Colonel Brett, of Sandywell in Gloucestershire—'a particularly handsome man', according to Dr Young. 'The Countess of Rivers [*sic*], looking out of her window on a great disturbance in the streets, saw him assaulted by some bailiffs. She paid his debt, and soon after married him' . . . and presumably went on paying his debts. Colley Cibber in his *Apology* suggests that the Colonel owed his success to the loan of one of his (Cibber's) shirts, and it seems a pity so potent a garment has not survived for the encouragement of other needy but hesitant suitors. The Earl of Macclesfield died in 1702, and the circumstance that Richard Smith was not his son, but the Earl Rivers', was to lead indirectly to the most famous duel of the century, when the Duke of Hamilton and the bully Lord Mohun, in a squabble over the Macclesfield estates, ran each other through in Hyde Park on 15 November 1712. Rivers had already shogged off on 8 August of this year and in his will 'left legacies to about twenty paltry old whores by name, and not a farthing to any friend, dependant, or relation'. He can hardly be blamed for leaving nothing to the illegitimate Richard Smith, for he had received emphatic assurance of his death.

It was probably in 1712 the Town heard that Richard Smith might not be dead after all. Though the claimant made no bones about taking the name Richard Savage, after Tyburn Dick. Twenty-seven years later he was to write to the blue-stocking Mrs Elizabeth Carter that he had passed under another name till he was 17 years old, but a letter still preserved of the actress Anne Oldfield's to 'Dear Mr Savage', forwarding him £10 as a 'small token' of her sympathy and calling his mother an 'unnatural fiend', confirms what hardly needed confirmation: that Savage was at best a careless reminiscer. His story was that he discovered some letters written by his grandmother to his mother (now Mrs Brett), 'And by those means the whole contrivance that had been carried on to conceal his birth'. He referred many times in all to these 'convincing' documents, but apparently only one man besides himself was privileged to see them. This was Aaron Hill, whose benevolence, self-importance, and gullibility made him not the most reliable witness we could choose. 'The proofs he sent me', wrote Hill, 'are too strong to be easily mistaken.' It is surprising and suspicious that Savage, fortified with this public expression of support, was as secretive of evidence as he was noisy in assertion for the rest of his life. His account of their contents can sometimes be flatly contradicted and at other times contradicts itself. Presumably he approached his mother at once, but with no success. He was later to tell Johnson how he would walk to and fro of an evening through the street his mother lived in, 'only for the melancholy pleasure of looking up at her windows, in hopes to catch a moment's sight of her, as she might cross the room by candle light'. Meantime, if we are to believe Savage's story, Mrs Brett had been at pains to forbid him a legacy of £6,000 which Rivers had planned for him on his death-bed; she had planned to have him carried off to the American plantations; and finally, disappointed in this, she had arranged for him to become a shoemaker's apprentice. It was indeed generally believed that Savage had been 'employed at the awl longer than he was willing to confess'.

It was thought for more than two hundred years that Savage's first written work was his poem 'The Convocation', a contribution to the Bangorian controversy. He published it in 1717, soon grew ashamed of it, and destroyed whatever copies he could collect. It had cost sixpence and was dear at the price. Recently light has been thrown on this earliest part of Savage's career by the discovery of his so-called Jacobite poems, written during 1715-16.[1] They are to be examined in the State Papers 35/7/38 ii. 110-13, not in Savage's handwriting but in that of Robert Girling, a government spy. Girling claims to have transcribed them from copies made by an unknown Robert Tooke of the 'Origanal Maniscript's of Mr Richard Savage's own Wrighting'. We hear further that 'the said Savage was about a Year & half or two Year's ago Pardon'd for Publishing, & being the Author of Several Treasonable & Seditious Pamphlets'. The poems sometimes rise to mediocrity but for the most part are bog-bound, yet Savage (if he ever thought about it) could console himself that Dryden too made a bad start. *And* 'Cousin Swift'. It wasn't every man who, like his patron Pope, could write an epic at the age of 6—and have the good sense to destroy it.

Savage next turned to the stage, as safer and more profitable than pamphleteering. His comedies *Woman's a Riddle* and *Love*

---

[1] They were first brought to light by Professor James Sutherland. I owe my knowledge of the poems themselves to an annotated typescript copy sent me by Mr C. R. Tracy, of Edmonton, Canada, who is now editing Savage's works. [Professor Tracy has since written a biography of Savage, *The Artificial Bastard*, 1953, and edited *The Poetical Works*, 1962, and Johnson's *Life*, 1971.]

in a Veil have some external interest. *Woman's a Riddle* according to Savage was written by Savage, according to Christopher Bullock it was written by Christopher Bullock, according to *Biographica Dramatica* it was translated from the Spanish by a Mrs Price. The contest was clearly for the third night profits rather than the honour of authorship. In the Dedication of *Love in a Veil*, to Lord Lansdowne, Savage strikes a familiar note. 'It is my misfortune to stand in such relationship to the late Earl Rivers by the Countess of——as neither of us can be proud of owning. I am one of those sons of sorrow to whom he left nothing to alleviate the sin of my birth.' On the title-page we read: 'Written by Richard Savage, Gent. Son of the late Earl Rivers.' Savage had begun to hawk his misfortunes, and he went on hawking them on the title-page of his next and last play, *Sir Thomas Overbury*, in 1724. This was a tragedy, and Johnson professes to see rays of genius glimmering in it, but Johnson saw most things as Savage wanted him to see them, and was himself the fond parent of *Irene*. Savage's blank verse is amongst the worst of the century: need more be said? Only perhaps that the unhappy author had to submit to the emending hands of Colley Cibber and Aaron Hill, that Savage acted the name-part of Overbury with much applause and more vexation, and that he stooped in his Preface to a 'liberal encomium of the blooming excellences' of young Theophilus Cibber at which he ever afterwards writhed in shame.

To cast the account: by 1724–5 he had written five bad Jacobite poems, one bad pamphlet, and three bad plays. Meantime what was happening to his claim?

In all save one particular it had prospered reasonably. Most people, including Pope, Sir Richard Steele, Hill, Wilkes, Mrs Oldfield, and an assortment of the nobility, had accepted him as Earl Rivers's son. Most of these helped him with friendship and money. There is abundant evidence that Savage had great charm of manner, that his conversation was elegant and informed; he could adapt himself to every circumstance and please in any company. His knowledge of the world enchanted the shallow, his retentive memory made him no fool among the erudite. Johnson has left the following account of his person:

'He was of a middle stature, of a thin habit of body, a long visage, coarse features, and melancholy aspect; of a grave and manly deportment, a solemn dignity of mien, but which, upon a nearer acquaintance, softened into an engaging easiness of manners.' He was also (it may as well be said now as later) a liar and a hypocrite, treacherous and dishonest; he was vain and he was mean. Above all he was ungrateful. Steele was kindness itself to him, and was rewarded with mimicry and insult; Hill though much of an old woman was a kindly old woman, but he lived to repent his championship of this sharp-fanged poetaster; those he praised today he blackened tomorrow, and sometimes he did not wait the twenty-four hours. Thus while in private he declaimed against the government, in print he praised Sir Robert Walpole; while he lived on easy terms under the one roof with the critic Dennis he published a gross lampoon upon him. These instances might be many times multiplied. He soon grew convinced that it was beneath him to work for a living; he accepted charity as by right, bridled and lickspittled on no other principle than may be discerned in the undoubted lack of balance in his character. He saw no reason to return kindness with kindness; to lend him money was eventually to win his hate. He made many friends, among them some of the most famous people of the day, but few were his friends for long. Johnson can have known him for little more than a year before he left London for Wales. What kind of a *Life* he would have written had he known him five times as long we can only speculate. Nor should it be forgotten that Johnson's much-admired indulgence to the memory of Savage entailed a wicked misrepresentation of Mrs Brett, whose general character was for kindness not cruelty. This was so universally admitted that even her self-styled son once gave her 'a character for humanity with regard to the rest of the world'.

> Yet has this sweet neglecter of my woes
> The softest, tend'rest breast that pity knows.
> Her eyes shed mercy wheresoe'er they shine
> And her soul melts at every woe—but mine.

But mine! So it was, and so it would remain to the end.

What Colonel Brett thought of it all we have no means of knowing. Probably he was too busy among his actors and actresses and his wife's maids to care. Their daughter Anna Margaretta was by 1724 within sight of a unique distinction, for 'it was not till the last year or two of his reign that their foreign sovereign [George I] paid the nation the compliment of taking openly an English mistress. That personage was Anne Brett, eldest daughter by her second husband of the repudiated wife of the Earl of Macclesfield, the unnatural mother of Savage the poet. Miss Brett was very handsome.' Walpole's gossip is interesting, if only because Mrs Brett herself was not very handsome. But the daughter's day was short, for the reigning monarch died in 1727 and she got her marching orders, and not even the promised coronet to march in. From a king's darling she declined to a Lady Leman. Brett himself died in 1724, though Jacob in his account of Savage in the *Poetical Register* for 1719 so early called Mrs Brett his widow. In either case he had not to contemplate the sad fate of our claimant, a left-hand brother-in-law of royalty though much in need of money when he published his *Miscellany* by subscription in 1726. The success of this venture and some miscellaneous cadging made him reasonably easy by the end of the year.

II

In 1727 Savage wrote a poem on the death of King George, best summarized in one of its own lines:

O Exclamation! lend thy sad relief!

Never in the history of literature were more exclamation marks used with less rousing effect. He should have kept them in reserve for his own affairs in the November of this year.

It was on the night of 20 November 1727 that Savage came to London from his rooms in Richmond and fell in company with two acquaintances, James Gregory and William Merchant. They sat in a coffee-house drinking till it was late, and then rambled the streets before seeing a light in Robinson's coffee-house, near Charing Cross. They entered and pushed their way into a room still occupied by late-staying company. Merchant seems to have been the trouble-seeker, he kicked over the table, swords were drawn, and in the scuffle one James Sinclair was fatally hurt. Savage and Merchant at once fled the house, one of them wounding a maid who tried to detain him, but they were caught in a back-court by one of the other party and some soldiers who came to his aid. They were straightway committed by the justices to the Gatehouse, and upon the death of Sinclair that same day were removed to Newgate. They stood trial for murder on 7 December, before Mr Justice Page, of whom Foss tells this story: 'When old and decrepit he was coming out of Court one day, shuffling along, an acquaintance inquired after his health. "My dear Sir," he answered, "you see I keep *hanging on; hanging on.*"' The evidence, while not without its minor contradictions and confusions, bore heavily against Savage. Merchant gave the provocation but he had no sword that night; Savage was the first to draw, and stabbed Sinclair while he was engaged by Gregory's blade; it was Savage who cut the maid over the head. Many times before his death Sinclair declared that he received his hurt from Savage—'from the shortest in black; the tallest commanded my sword, and the other stabbed me'. Savage conducted his own defence, and did so brilliantly. He urged the suddenness of the whole action, that there could be no premeditation, that he sought only to defend himself, that his flight thereafter was to avoid the inclemencies of a gaol and not to evade trial. Robinson's was a house of ill-fame, though he had not known this at the time, the witnesses against him were of infamous life and he on the other hand good-natured and meek-tempered 'even to a fault'. However, Sir Francis Page thought otherwise and according to Savage in later years endeavoured to exasperate the jury with an 'eloquent harangue'. He certainly encouraged them to bring in a verdict that Savage and Gregory were guilty of murder and the unarmed Merchant of manslaughter.

On 12 December Merchant was burnt with a hot iron in the brawn of the left thumb, and having given surety for his good behaviour was discharged. The day before, his two companions

had been taken into court to receive sentence of death, where
Savage pleaded well and manfully though without effect for
an extension of the mercy shown to Merchant. They went
back to close confinement in irons, their one hope that royal
prerogative which had twice been exercised in favour of the
Earl of Macclesfield. Nor did it fail them. The Countess of
Hertford and Viscount Tyrconnel solicited His Majesty, and
Mrs Oldfield Sir Robert Walpole; they were reprieved within
ten days, and pleaded the King's pardon in March 1729.
Johnson reports at length how Mrs Brett exerted herself to
prevent the reprieve by spreading a story that Savage had forced
his way into her house and endeavoured to murder her. This
'atrocious calumny' led him to pen his strongest paragraph
against Savage's mother. 'This mother is still alive, and may
even perhaps yet, though her malice was so often defeated, enjoy
the pleasure of reflecting that the life, which she so often
endeavoured to destroy, was at least shortened by her maternal
offices; that though she could not transport her son to the plantations, bury him in the shop of a mechanick, or hasten the hand
of the publick executioner, she has yet had the satisfaction of
imbittering all his hours, and forcing him into exigencies that
hurried on his death.' Johnson seems not to have enjoyed the
pleasure of reflecting that all the calumny in the relation cannot
be ascribed to Mrs Brett.

Savage had walked from the shadow of a gallows in March.
In April he published his best-known poem, 'The Bastard',
'Inscribed, with all due reverence, to Mrs Brett, once Countess
of Macclesfield'. Hitherto he had alternated between sickly
cant and bitter railing when he wrote of the lady he claimed
as mother. Now he was to combine them. 'I hope the world
will do me the justice to believe that no part of this flows from
any real anger against the Lady to whom it is inscribed.
Whatever undeserved severities I may have received at her
hands . . . I have ever behaved myself towards her like one
who thought it his duty to support with patience all afflictions
from that quarter.' This said, he offers an uneasily jocose
panegyric on bastards and thanks Mrs Brett for making him
one; inevitably he proceeds from the general to the particular,

'Few are my joys; alas! how soon forgot!'; he laments those 'ripening virtues' which might have been Sinclair's had he lived, recalls with satisfaction the Royal Pity, and warmly recommends himself to both Pity and Bounty for the rest of his natural life. But he need not have looked so high, for soon after the publication of his poem Mrs Brett's nephew, Viscount Tyrconnel, offered Savage a place in his household; whether to spite his aunt, protect the family good name, or hire himself a poet for compliments to the Great, we cannot determine. He was to be treated as an equal and allowed two hundred pounds a year. 'The Bastard' had brought its author but a trivial sum from his ungenerous bookseller, but Savage's new turn of fortune made it far and away the best-paying poem he had written or was again to write.

Now came indeed the kingfisher years with Joy and Plenty brooding o'er the calméd wave. For the first and last time in his life Savage was of the 'Gentlemen and Friends' whom even so genial a philosopher as Shaftesbury thought the only part of mankind to deserve more than acorns and a bed of straw. His meat was delicate and his wine was choice, his dress was spangled and he slept on down. And he went on writing. There was 'The Wanderer', a long didactic poem dedicated to Tyrconnel (not even the unique dedication copy in the writer's possession, coronets, strawberry leaves and all, has given him much taste for it); there was the cruel, mean, brilliant 'Author to be Let' in which Savage, now too good for Grub Street, flailed Grub Street's bloody back; there were the toadying 'Epistle to Sir Robert Walpole' and the fatuous verses on the Viscountess Tyrconnel's recovery from a Languishing Illness; there was the affair of the Volunteer Laureate. When Eusden, poor hack, foundered in 1730 there were two contenders for the Laureate stakes, Savage and Cibber. Considered as Pegasus, Cibber was wall-eyed, wind-broken, hollow-backed, and barrel-bellied, but he was too quick for Savage even so. The wits made much of his success:

> In merry old England it once was a Rule,
> The King had his Poet, and also his Fool:

> But now we're so frugal, I'd have you to know it,
> That C——r can serve both for Fool and for Poet.

Savage never forgot what he regarded as his humiliation, though what greater disgrace there could be for a poet in the eighteenth century than to become the Birthday Fibber is a rude speculation. But his impudence was equal to the occasion, and from 1732 onwards he styled himself *Volunteer Laureate* and wrote volunteer odes which assure him a place (though unofficial) on that section of the Golden Roll which starts with Shadwell and terminates in Pye.

III

It would be well for the historian as for Savage if here we might leave him, oiled and brocaded, to bask away the years at Brownlow House. But no—

> My Muse to grief resigns the varying tone,
> The raptures languish, and the numbers groan.

For the man who in 1729 could speak with ecstasy of Tyrconnel's compassion and humanity, his 'most unassuming, sweet, and winning candour', the honour of his conversation, his public spirit and private virtues, was five years later addressing him as 'Right Honourable BRUTE, and BOOBY'. From Savage came charges that Tyrconnel sought dishonourably to retrench his expenses and read him lectures; from Tyrconnel accusations of ingratitude and riot. 'Lord Tyrconnel affirmed that it was the constant practice of Mr Savage to enter a tavern with any company that proposed it, drink the most expensive wines with great profusion, and when the reckoning was demanded to be without money. If, as often happened, his company were willing to defray his part, the affair ended, without any ill consequences; but, if they were refractory, and expected that the wine should be paid for by him that drank it, his method of composition was to take them with him to his own apartment, assume the government of the house, and order the butler in an imperious manner to set the best wine in the cellar before the company, who often drank till they

forgot the respect due to the house in which they were entertained, indulged themselves in the utmost extravagance of
merriment, practised the most licentious frolics, and committed
all the outrages of drunkenness. . . . Whoever was acquainted
with Mr Savage easily credited both these accusations.'

The precise occasion of Savage's dismissal need not be
sought. By 1734 he was tumbled out of his dream of luxury
and in worse case than he had ever been, for he was now used
to standards of comfort and attention he would never again
command, and he had forfeited most of his goodwill. There
are few details for the years that follow, but from being merely
unpleasant his case moved rapidly towards desperation. Friends
dropped off, acquaintances discouraged him. In the days of
his prosperity, sidling along in jackal-style with Pope, he had
rejoiced to make enemies of a hundred poor devils in Grub
Street, and these did *not* drop off. His benefactress Anne
Oldfield was dead behind marble in Westminster Abbey, he
lost his volunteer pension on the death of Her Majesty in 1738;
with poverty came importunity, and the shabbier his shifts the
more arrogant his manner. His best poem, 'The Progress of
a Divine', brought him to trial for obscenity; the charge failed,
but it harmed him. One by one the doors of London shut in
his face, one by one the fobs were fastened against him. He
grew down-at-heel, haunted, hungry; he ate in Porridge Row
and slept with outcasts amidst the ashes of a glass factory. Those
who did offer him hospitality found there was no civil way of
getting rid of him; his complaints and ingratitude wearied the
most tolerant, till at last his indignation against the world was
equalled only by the world's impatience with him. Yet with it
all something of charm remained, his reputation as a man-of-
letters, the air of fine society, the curious observations and
extensive experience that were so to impress Samuel Johnson
when he and Savage walked the squares of London from dusk
till dawn because they had not money enough to purchase
even the 'sordid comforts of a night cellar'. Had he known it,
it was his acquaintance with the uncouth provincial which was
to insure him the immortality he vainly hoped for from his
writings. Even his life-story would be weed-grown in the *Newgate*

Calendar but for Johnson. And when at last, in 1739, certain of his friends, among whom Pope was the most active, contracted to pay him a pension on condition he removed himself to Wales it was Johnson, as we have seen, who stood in an innyard in London and sorrowfully waved him adieu.

But if those friends thought that by putting him on a coach with fifteen guineas in his pocket they had sent him packing they were soon to be disillusioned. Within a fortnight there were demands for money, and they were alarmed to hear that he had not yet reached Bristol, much less Wales. The money was sent, but an embargo on shipping at Bristol was his excuse for remaining in the port on a graceful round of visits and entertainments to which it would be cruel to give its proper name. For by now, we may understand, he was not only the man Savage but the type of those egotistical, vain, ill-disciplined hangers-on of literature and life who win our pity even while they seek our condemnation. He is henceforth never a man with alternatives: he must go the one way. And so while still in Bristol he wrote complaints to his supporters in London till many of them ceased their contributions, and when at last he reached Swansea the promised fifty pounds a year had shrunk to little more than twenty. From Swansea he went on to Llanelli, where he met a young widow lady whose name (incredibly) was Jones. He preferred to call her Chloe, and wrote warmly of her 'swelling charms'. The opening of 'Valentine's Day', with its address to Chloe and its description of the Sospan shore, will bear quotation:

> Adieu ye rocks that witness'd once my flame,
> Return'd my sighs and echo'd Chloe's name!
> Cambria farewell!—my Chloe's charms no more
> Invite my steps along Llanelly's shore;
> There no wild dens conceal voracious foes,
> The beach no fierce, amphibious monster knows;
> No crocodile there flesh'd with prey appears,
> And o'er that bleeding prey weeps cruel tears;
> No false hyaena, feigning human grief,
> There murders him, whose goodness means relief:
> Yet tides, conspiring with unfaithful ground,

Tho' distant seen, with treach'rous arms, surround.
There quicksands, thick as beauty's snares, annoy,
Look fair to tempt, and whom they tempt, destroy.
I watch'd the seas, I pac'd the sands with care,
Escap'd, but wildly rush'd on beauty's snare.
Ah!—better far, than by that snare o'erpower'd,
Had sands engulf'd me, or had seas devour'd.

He seems now to have needed a strong fillip to bring him to original composition. Apart from undressing Mrs Jones in print, his plans were to issue his works by subscription and to revise his unrevisable tragedy *Sir Thomas Overbury*. Next he determined to return to London and bring it upon the stage. But though his revises have now reached Chicago, Savage himself got no further than Bristol. Here he was once more treated with deference and charity and given a present of thirty pounds. But he was past help or self-help. These moneys and others he squandered on his private pleasures, the round of visits and entertainments slowly contracted, the importunities began again, the shifts and subterfuges and dishonesties. In 'The Author to be Let', chin-deep in luxury himself, he had railed at the brethren for their poverty, their prostitute Muse, their pretentions to birth: the oil of his own damnation drips from an eulogistic poem 'On Richard Savage, Esq., Son of the late Earl Rivers, By a Clergyman of the Church of England', and dated Bristol, 15 October 1742:

> Pleasing associate! still with winning ease
> He studies every method how to please;
> Complies with each proposal—*this* or *that;*
> With time-beguiling cards, or harmless chat;
> Or moralizes—o'er the sprightly bowl—
> *The feast of reason and the flow of soul.*

Little wonder that Savage reacted with a snarl to this well-intentioned portrait of a Mr Smoothly. The Reverend Gentleman was a liar, he said—and he said so in the *Gentleman's Magazine.*

But an empty belly needs bread and tired limbs a pallet. Deviously for a while Savage won on these necessities, and then he must avoid daylight because the bailiffs were after him, and in the garret of an obscure inn he faced starvation. A last chance came his way to end these troubles and return to London. He received from the faithful Pope a remittance of five pounds and went out to buy an overcoat to cover his shabby clothes. Fatally he was drawn to his favourite taverns and when he went furtively home he was penniless. A short time afterwards he was arrested for debt and confined in Newgate Goal.

This was in January 1743. For the next seven months he bore imprisonment with mingled fortitude and petulance. His gaoler, Mr Dagge, was a disciple of Whitefield's and unusually humane for one of his calling; on him Savage exercised for the last time, but triumphantly, all the charm and attraction of his nature; he allowed the poet a room of his own and the privilege of standing at the door of the prison, and sometimes took him into the country for walks. 'I found the smell of the new-mown hay very sweet, and every breeze was reviving to my spirits,' writes Savage after one of these jaunts. He was busy about his last poem, 'London and Bristol Delineated', whereby with small gratitude and much imprudence he was to raise the resentment of the whole city. His correspondents were now reduced to one, and then Pope too grew silent after some 'charge of very atrocious ingratitude'. Savage's expressions of grief and astonishment need not surprise us; he was genuinely incapacitated from seeing himself for what he was. In him ingratitude was manly resentment, impudence but candour; upon ordinary financial dishonesty he seems never to have wasted a thought. And selfishness—well, that was the blood in his veins.

Pope's last letter survives, with its message of outrage and rejection. It was the only hurt that could pierce his heart, this dire contempt of the greatest poet of the age. There may well be truth in the story that it helped to kill him. For Pope he had toadied, sneaked, run dirty errands, but in his company he was a fingerbreadth from Parnassus. If Pope finished with him—surely, the black ox had not stamped on his foot till now!

Some days after receiving this letter he fell into a state of pain, languor, and dejection. His decline was rapid. 'The last time that the keeper saw him was on July the 31st, 1743, when Savage, seeing him at his bedside, said, with uncommon earnestness, "I have something to say to you, Sir"; but, after a pause, moved his head in a melancholy manner, and, finding himself unable to recollect what he was going to communicate, said, " 'Tis gone!" The keeper soon after left him; and the next morning he died. He was buried in the churchyard of St Peter at the expense of the keeper.' The exact site of the grave was soon forgotten: the plaque long afterwards erected to his memory has now been destroyed by enemy action. However, he still keeps his place in *The Complete Newgate Calendar*, where he rests between the hapless Catherine Hayes who was burned to death with unusual concomitants of legal horror for murdering her husband, and the happy Margaret Dixon, 'Who was married a few days after she was hanged for murder in 1728'. (She sat up in her coffin as her carrying-party were drowning their sorrows, was promptly bled, and survived in defiance of the law, having stood trial and suffered her sentence.)

There are three choices for the reader. He may believe that Richard Savage was indeed the son of Earl Rivers, but since Moy Thomas published the results of his researches in 1858 I believe Makower to be the only knowledgeable student to urge this; he may believe that Savage honestly but mistakenly thought himself Rivers' son; or he may believe that Savage was a fraud.

In this third belief he would concur with Mrs Brett. She had kept silence during Savage's lifetime: no sneer, no reproach, no calumny provoked her to defend herself after his death. Two husbands, her lover, children on both sides of the blanket, all were in their graves before she was borne to hers, an ancient, enigmatic lady whose life had spanned seven reigns. When she was born Milton was settling the contract of *Paradise Lost*: Gibbon had lost one religion and was in Lausanne losing another before she died.

She was *grande dame* to the end. Rivers, yes. And little Richard Smith, the one who died—she remembered him, with pity.

But Richard Savage? The too-full lips, the little eyes, the powdered pock-marked cheeks—we are not permitted to see her towards the end. She takes refuge in silence as behind a fan. And at 85 it was all so very far behind her. Even to the friendly enquirer, Milady has nothing to say.

7

On First Planting a Library

'GOD Almighty', said Francis Bacon, 'first planted a Garden.'
Bacon wasn't a Welshman, but he did become Lord Chancellor
of England and land himself in prison—the Tower, no less—so
there is no particular reason for doubting his veracity. After all,
Genesis One and Two confirm him; as does the first book ever
published in Welsh, *Yny lhyvyr hwnn*, 1546, containing not only
the Welsh Alphabet, Calendar, Creed, Lord's Prayer, Ten
Commandments, the Sacraments, the Virtues to be espoused
and the Vices to be eschewed, but also month by month directions to the truest of all those sons of Adam, the farmers of
Wales.

On that other purest of human pleasures, the Library, he was
less forthcoming. So are Genesis One and Two. So, surprisingly, is *Yny lhyvyr hwnn*. Who first planted a library we do not
know, nor do we know its Adam, or its Eve, though we can guess
at the taste of its apples. It is a safe assumption that the first
purposeful records of human rumination and practice—let
us call them the first documents—would reflect the needs of
government and religion—probably in the reverse order. Gods
are clamant for religions, religions require texts, texts call for
scribes, scribes call for scriptoria. Kings rule by force and fictions, fictions are the gift of poets and historians, poetry and
history invite transmission, transmission comes to depend on
scribes. Law as it is advanced from custom to proscription
attracts codifiers, codifiers engender codes, codes call for
scribes—and so on throughout the entire sacerdotal, dynastic,
political, and generally regulative aspects of our existence.

Soon—whatever 'soon' means in this time-hazed context—as

An Address delivered at the 75th Anniversary Celebrations of the National
Library of Wales, 25 March 1982.

civilization advances and sophistication grows, Three R'd Man, reader, writer, arithmetician, moves on from these bare necessities. Priesthoods, dynasties, tax-collectors find themselves with more on their hands than alphabets, calendars, genealogies, creeds, and commandments (see our first Welsh book, *passim*). It is the nature and need of officialdom to amass baked tablets, rock carvings, papyri, cylinders, white papers, and the like. History of all things can't be left to chance, and confessions of ignorance are never in order. As Mark Twain said, more or less: 'Many great historical events didn't take place as reported. Most great historical events didn't take place at all. It is the business of the serious historian to repair these omissions.' Serious historians were prompt to do so: Herodotus, Saxo Grammaticus and Geoffrey of Monmouth among them. The process of authorship, once in train, proved irreversible. Scribble, scribble, scribble—I speak as a writer—that's bad enough. But worse—I speak as a reader—the stuff has to be stored. Only the Germanic North, the Vikings, had the presence of mind and lack of imagination to incise their memorabilia in deep runic lettering on huge standing stones bare to the winds of heaven, and thereafter abandon them to the will or whimsy of their hirsute pantheon.

Less pious folk stored them in temples as at Heliopolis, or in palaces as at Nineveh; in custom-built thesauri as at Alexandria and Ephesus; in receptacles private or public. Soon—still a comparative term—the countering forces of decay and destruction, accident and design, natural catastrophe and human orneriness, would providentially lift their heads, lest one good custom should o'erfill the world.

And still we don't know who first planted a library. Or when. Was Assurbanipal the first monarch to open his royal collections for the use of his subjects? Was Aristotle the first man to put together what we now call a private library? Where stand the Ptolemies? What of Athens, Constantinople, Rome? And still in the dark backward and abyss of Time, what of the monastic libraries of England, France, and Ireland?

These are rhetorical questions—and rhetorical questions, as you know, are designed to mask the ignorance of the speaker by hinting at the omniscience of his hearers. But while they invite no answer, they allow a conclusion: that to read a history of the world's libraries is to walk the high road of human civilization, and behold with wonder the part that libraries old and new, functional and cultural, great and small, private and civic, regional and national, have played in the lives of men and nations.

Which brings me at last—at long last you may be thinking—to our National Library of Wales, *Llyfrgell Genedlaethol Cymru*, the beloved and revered Nat. Lib. of students, scholars, researchers, etc., etc., etc., and the prop and stay of my own teaching life in Aberystwyth. We are met today to celebrate the 75th Anniversary of the granting of its Charter. Since I received our President's invitation some months ago I have often bethought me, and during the last fifteen minutes I have many times looked around me, and reminded myself how many of my fellow-countrymen are more worthy of my role by virtue of their service to the Library, their knowledge of its history and organization, or their more extensive and profitable use of its resources as expressed in their contributions to literature, learning, the arts and sciences, and all modes of our national life. But I remain tenacious of my privilege—and since the day I first heard it my favourite theological truth has been the tolerant Welsh maxim: 'When God gave the nightingale a voice, he didn't tell the crow he shouldn't sing.'

For what good it can do me in your eyes, Mr President, and for what virtue it can lay up for me in the bookstacks of Heaven, let me confess here, now, and in public, that I have never stolen a book from the National Library. I have, however—and I confess this with equal self-congratulation—I *have* stolen a librarian, my wife Mair.

I like to think that if I have not spent my life in the pursuit of happiness, happiness has spent a fair bit of time in pursuit of me. Much of my happiness has come from my life's work, by which I mean not only my forty-one years' teaching in the University of Wales, seventeen of them at the proudly-entitled University College of South Wales and Monmouthshire, Cardiff, and twenty-four at the still more proudly-entitled

University College of Wales, Aberystwyth. Not only my teaching—and no one ever liked teaching more than I—but the immersion in language and literature which teaching not only allows but enjoins. Language, the greatest of all human inventions, compared with which a landing on the moon is a tuppenny ha'penny ride on the Saturday-afternoon dodgems; and literature, in all humane branches the repository *par excellence* of human thought, memory, self-knowledge, and creation. All this has meant an involvement with books and a devotion to libraries—libraries as humbly benevolent as the lending room at the Blackwood Workmen's Institute, and the War Memorial Room, all books and pictures, at Tredegar County School—to say nothing of my collier-father's long low shelves of Rationalist Press publications, *The Ragged-Trousered Philanthropists*, Mark Twain and the Fabians, and the assorted glories of English poetry from Shakespeare's *Hamlet* to Southey's 'Blenheim' and Tom Hood's 'Song of the Shirt', from these instructive and deeply-moving glimpses of the immortal past and the all-too-mortal present to the challenging book-laden panorama of the aloofly friendly BM (now, should I shed a tear? the BL), the Cardiff Free Library, linked to this one by that redoubtable son neither of Cardiff nor of Ceredigiawn, but of Gwent, Sir John Ballinger; Rylands and Chetham's, Folger and Fiske, the Royal Bibliotheks of Denmark and Sweden, and finally and most fully, my two College libraries and the National Library of Wales.

When in 1957 Professor A. H. Dodd delivered the Address in English that marked along with Professor Henry Lewis's *Anerchiad* in Welsh the celebration of the Fiftieth Anniversary of the National Library's Charter of Incorporation, he offered a masterly account of the Library's dawn-song and pre-history; the dreamers and the dream they made come true; the patriots and planners and benefactors; the architects of success and artificers of victory: among them the Cymmrodorion Society in its birth and rebirths, the Welsh School in Grays Inn Road, the National Eisteddfodau of Llangollen and Mold, the College at Aberystwyth, its Welsh Library and its Assembly Rooms, which for a while housed the incipient collections, and where I, the College's Rendel Professor of English, have according to my students been many times observed drinking tea out of my chaucer.

But factually, unlike Professor Dodd and the admirable 'Brief Summary' of 1974–75, I have little to tell you. For I have only now, faced with this honourable and honouring occasion, realized the extent to which I have for the last forty years been taking the National Library for granted. Because for me and my generation it was not only there, but always had been. The physical presence—and what a presence it is!—was in every sense there before us. From time to time there are new wings, stacks, blocks. There are new neighbours on the Acropolis. The holdings increase mightily. Books recognizable, with hard covers and a friendly type-face, and books unrecognizable that require machines for their consultation; manuscripts ancient and modern, native and foreign; prints, drawings and maps; records, and archives, national, regional, local, family, and personal; papers cultural, scientific, and industrial; micro-this and visio-that; the whole thing a complex metaphor, oasis and power-house, temple, fountain, and factory, where we may seek information, achieve knowledge, and hope for wisdom.

I wish my sentences could grow to paragraphs, and my paragraphs to chapters. Fortunately our friend David Jenkins has the history of the National Library in hand, and for us all it will prove compulsory and compelling reading. But I must still find time to speak of our National Library as a Welsh National Institution. Every nation, country, people needs symbols of its being, representative images, institutions expressive of its inward and outward ideals and realities. Until a hundred years ago these were few and far between in Wales. Now to our comfort we have four: the National Eisteddfod, while not as old as Iolo Morganwg made out, the oldest of them; the University next; and those twin luminaries, the Museum in Deheubarth and the Library on its hill by the Welsh sea. The separation of the Library and the Museum should perturb no one. It conforms to the immemorial pattern of Welsh life; arose inevitably out of the original part-association, part-identification of the College and the 'foundation collections' of the National Library to-be; and, believe it or not, it takes no longer to drive from Cardiff to Penglais than it does from Aberystwyth to Cardiff Arms Park.

There have always been strong centrifugal forces, influences, tendencies at work in Wales. It has not, of course, weakened our consensus for humanity. Interestingly enough, a Library situated in Aberystwyth is strongly centripetal. So vast and vastly used and vastly influential an institution is at once preservative of the past, invigorating in the present, and inspirational for the future. As an emblem of nationhood it helps us cohere, our sects and segments to keep in touch and sight of each other. As a main custodian of our social, religious, literary, political, and industrial history it gives our sense of national identity a base, multifarious and unpartisan—and this is good. The nation with no depth to its past has only shallows for its future.

Of our National Library we say: 'Here are great riches and a great witness.' Because here is Wales from the Three Hundred who rode to Catraeth to the armies of our brothers who marched to two World Wars; Wales from the petals and thorns of the Celtic Saints to the plumes and prickles of Nonconformity; Wales from Prince Madoc and the Welsh-speaking Indians to Max Boyce and the Welsh-speaking Japanese; Wales from King Arthur to the South Wales Miners' Federation. And as one who warmly welcomes the Library's steady compilation of an Anglo-Welsh literary archive, let me add: Wales from our common heritage of Cynfeirdd and *Mabinogion* to our dual legacy of R. Williams Parry and Dylan Thomas.

And now with so much left unsaid I must make an end. We have in our National Library the first and foremost Welsh library in the world, and one which while never forgetting the primal commitment to Wales, its people and its language, yet every year expands its activities and increases its cover. Today then is a day for celebration and praise. And no less for remembrance. And remember we do, those wise and worthy men whose concerted action here in Wales, and in the corridors of power elsewhere, began a lasting sequence of development, expansion, and librarial enrichment; the resourceful administrators and learned librarians—many of them happily in this room today—who brought it to maturity; the skilled and knowledgeable and courteous and friendly staff who make its material available to all comers; these and all others who throughout the years since its opening have sustained the Library as a challenge to our minds and a comfort to our hearts. To them all, remembrance; to them all, praise; and to them all, our gratitude for ever.

⊰8⊱

The Novel and Society

IN the belief that a South Welshman in foreign parts should always declare his credentials I wish to inform you that I first lectured on the novel to an Honours Class of the then entitled University College of South Wales and Monmouthshire in the enchanted autumn of 1935. Perhaps because I had just written a novel myself. Common Room opinion was divided as to which was the more searing emotion: the Principal's delight when he learned that his new recruit had written a best-seller (*Richard Savage*, 1935), or his horror when he came to read it. In that Golden Age of higher education the English Department was offering a course called 'The Novel'—just that—no strings, no limits, no centuries, no countries, no continents. Eminently mad, outstandingly impossible, and entirely splendid. I carried that course for five years, from Heliodorus to Dos Passos, from the lady Murasaki to the lady Chatterley, from Sindbad the Sailor to Salar the Salmon. I don't know what it did for my listeners, but it taught me two lessons: the immediate one how to keep one jump ahead of the class, the lasting one that there's an awful lot of novel.

Clearly there are several legitimate ways of approaching this great rainforest of a subject. To my way of thinking two of these are particularly rewarding. It immensely enlarges our knowledge to chart its history as a kind of writing developed over a long period of time, yet curiously re-developed in France in the seventeenth and in England in the eighteenth century. In this way we can know a great deal about novels and novelists without necessarily knowing what a novel is, or in the abstract what

The Ben Bowen Thomas Memorial Lecture, North Wales Arts Association, 1980. Published by the Association, with a translation into Welsh (*Y Nofel a Chymderithas*), 1980.

The Novel is. Certainly we have to decide when making what I may call the historical approach what it is we are looking for. And we would probably all agree that we are looking for a fictional narrative of adequate length, written in prose (and not to be confused with historical chronicle or factual narrative), concerned with men and women of recognizable humanity, who are to be observed acting in recognizably human ways in recognizably human situations. If you now ask me where Salar the Salmon comes into this, be comforted: all such finned, furred, or feathered heroes are anthropomorphic and qualify. If we accept this as a rough working definition, we recognize *La Princesse de Clèves* (1678) as what we were looking for in France, and *Robinson Crusoe* (1719) in England. I'm not saying this is *all* these two books are. On the contrary, it is the *least* they are. The definition is their lowest common denominator.

There are, of course, critics who don't accept such a definition. I recall Critic A, who doesn't think prose a necessity of the novel and argues for Chaucer's superb long poem *Troilus and Criseyde* as the first true novel in English—which strikes me as completely daft. I would, of course, agree that the novel can be lyrical, poetical, even rhapsodical, but with all due deference to Goronwy Owen's view that in the absence of *cynghanedd* Milton's *Paradise Lost* must be considered not a masterpiece of English poetry but of English prose, I regard it as categorical that the novel has never been, is not, and never can be a verse form.

Then there's Critic B, a worthy man with sound views of prose and narrative, but believing that the novel—or shall I say the novelist—must show psychological insight into human character; and so the revelation of character, not only through action, practical observation, common sense, and experience, though these are permissible, but also by knowledgeable analysis, becomes an essential, indeed a requisite, part of the novel's nature. To Critic B therefore Defoe never wrote a novel in his life. *Robinson Crusoe*, *Moll Flanders*, and *A Journal of the Plague Year*, to say nothing of *Roxana*, are prose narratives, nothing more; and for the novel proper we must wait upon Marivaux's *La Vie de Marianne* (1731-41) in France, and Richardson's *Pamela* (1740) in England.

Or consider Critic C, in strong revolt against the notion that the novel can ever be merely the imaginary biography of an imaginary person or persons, known to and explicable by their maker, the novelist. This old theory more or less supposed that a man is one, that he has one character, one personality, and that even in his inconsistencies, his growth and change, he will be found consistent. Not in the pseudo-philosophical, maybe pseudo-theological sense of a series of propensities which dominate his life and being, but in the sense that for the overwhelming majority of men there is a recognizable, and to oneself more or less explicable 'I'. But Critic C (a very clever man, invariably) will tell you that this critical immaturity was excusable enough till we read Proust, but Proust has shown us that a man is not one, but many, and a multiple of personalities. The true novelist, says C, indeed the true artist, must show in his work an awareness that man is not *l'homme absolu*, but in Laforgue's phrase (in its turn echoing a phrase of Baudelaire's) an innumerable sequence of human keyboards, perpetually changing and perpetually unique. Pushed hard, this doctrine would lead to the conclusion that to anyone who disbelieves in the continuous and recognizable identity of human beings, most of the classical novelists of England, France, and Russia in the eighteenth and nineteenth centuries, and the overwhelming majority of novelists today, didn't know their business, and that the only true novelists of the Enlightenment are Proust and Robert Musil, with poor old Henry James crippling along like a wooden-legged mendicant, now at their side, now in the rear.

Here I can quote either the philosopher Hume, whom every schoolboy knows, or our fellow-countryman Goronwy Rees, whom every Welshman knows. Goronwy has himself written several novels, one of them *Where No Wounds Were*, very good indeed; but even more to our purpose he has written some very good chapters of autobiography. Here are three paragraphs from *A Bundle of Sensations*:

For as long as I can remember it has always surprised and slightly bewildered me that other people should take it so much for granted that they each possess what is usually called a *character*: that is to say, a personality with its own continuous history which can be described as objectively as the life cycle of a plant or animal. I have never been able to find anything of that sort in myself, and in the course of my life this has been the source of many misunderstandings, since other people persist in expecting of one a kind of consistency which, in the last resort, they really have no right to demand. It has also given me, in the practical affairs of life, a certain sense of inferiority to my fellows, who have always seemed to me to possess something which I lacked, as if I were short of an arm or a leg or were otherwise deficient in what is usually regarded as constituting a normal human being. How much I admire those writers who are actually able to record the growth of what they call their personality, describe the conditions which determined its birth, lovingly trace the curve of its development, and accurately assign to nature and nurture their exact part in this performance; and how satisfactory it must be to be able to say at the end of the story (and no autobiographer is quite without a certain pride in saying it): 'Here I am; this is what made me and what I made of myself, and now you can see exactly why I am as I am, and could not conceivably be any other.'

For myself it would be quite impossible to tell such a story, because at no time in my life have I had that enviable sensation of constituting a continuous personality, of being something which, in the astonishing words of T. H. Green, 'is eternal, is self-determined, and which thinks'. As a child this did not worry me, and indeed if I had known at that time of *Der Mann ohne Eigenschaften*, the man without qualities, I would have greeted him as my blood brother and rejoiced because I was not alone in the world; as it was, I was content with a private fantasy of my own in which I figured as Mr Nobody. For I was quite certain that I had no character of my own, good or bad, that I existed only in the particular circumstances of the moment, and since circumstances were always changing, so fast, so bewilderingly, so absorbingly, how could it not follow that I must change with them? I was quite content, even blissfully happy, that this should be so; the notion of a self, a character, a personal identity, even if it had ever occurred to me, would have seemed strictly one of those things which only adults possess, like bowler hats, or umbrellas, or long trousers.

But of course this kind of thing could not go on. The entire structure of our society depends upon the fiction of an individual and responsible 'I' which shall be the object of rewards and punishments, and into such a society even a child like myself had one day to be inducted.

Not, he tell us, that the induction served any purpose. Unlike most of us he still failed to recognize in himself, or for that matter in anyone else, the 'continuous, identical, responsible self' of which most men, I am sure, have a continuing awareness. Which is surprising in a man whose personality was unusually clear-stamped. But that needn't concern us. What need is, first, everyone's right to treat such a self or other such selves in any form of writing, and especially in a form as genial and embracing as the novel; and, second, the fact that no art exists without conventions, no art can survive without changing its conventions, and the value of every artistic convention rests not in itself but in the work of art which it enables, or helps enable, to exist.

Which brings us to our second approach to the novel. Not the question of kind, but the question of degree. For obviously we need a standard of excellence. Or rather a pattern or complex of standards which will allow us to know the good from the bad, which is easy, and the superlative from the good, which can be hard. We need, for example, standards of narrative and substance, the very stuff of which novels are made. We need standards of character-creation and character-portrayal, which make that narrative and substance worthwhile. And we need standards of writing in the formal sense—prose style, let us say—and construction, which give artistic significance to whatever it was the author had in his head to begin with. In brief, we are no longer concerned merely to recognize the novel as such, but to consider it as literature, as a form of art, or if you prefer, as an art form.

Now if we try not to be literary critics for a moment, but just general readers, two things strike us quickly and forcibly in the world of the novel: the numbers that are written, and their variety. The two are closely bound together. The novel has long been and still remains one of the mass media of information and entertainment. A considerable number of people are in constant need of reading matter, and this the novel, with its protean qualities, is admirably fitted to supply. 'Tell me a story' is one of the oldest and newest cries in the world, and each year's output of new novels in Great Britain alone runs into thousands. For in the novel you have a reputable literary form upon which any variation is both possible and permissible. You can just go ahead with a good yarn; you can use a plot or manage without one. You can have few characters or many; you can choose any setting in time or place. You can preach a sermon through the novel, ventilate a grievance, praise a friend, attack an enemy. You can seek to reform society, redress injustice, tickle the world's ribs or coax forth the world's tears. You can display your muscles and your sores. You can be grim, flippant, admonitory, puritanical, or pornographic. You can experience vicariously, you can show the world what a wise, fine, generous, waggish, wide-awake but warm-hearted fellow you really are. You can even write a good one—the possibilities are illimitable. Not least, you *can make money out of it*. According to H. G. Wells, the novel can be anything save boring—and I don't have to tell you it can be that too. The novel—to recoin a phrase—is all things to all men. How then shall we even begin to evaluate so protean and fast-spawning a monster?

We can begin by taking the author at his own evaluation. Not the one he announces sight-unseen at the customs barrier; but the one his literary luggage reveals. For serious writing will always be a serious business. Let's hear Émile Zola on the subject, shall we? In part of an interview he gave to Robert Sherrard of *The Weekly Times and Echo*, in which the English translation of *La Débâcle*, his novel about the Franco-Prussian war, was first issued. It may appear to you over-long and notably humourless, and to contain everything except the kitchen-stove and the heart of the matter. Humour me, and bear with me. Bear with him, and honour him.

My novels (he says) have always been written with a higher aim than to amuse. I have so high an opinion of the novel as a means of expression—I consider it parallel with lyrical poetry, as the highest form of literary expression, just as in the last century the drama was the highest form of expression—that it is on this account that I have chosen it as the form in which to present to the world what I wish to say on the social, scientific, and psychological problems that occupy the minds of thinking men. But for this I might have said what I wanted to say to the world in another form. But the novel has today risen from the place it held in the last century at the table of the banquet of letters. Today it contains or may be made to contain everything; and it is because that is my creed that I am a novelist.

I have, to my thinking, certain contributions to make to the thought of the world on certain subjects, and I have chosen the novel as the best form of communicating these contributions to the world. Thus *La Débâcle*, in the form of a very precise and accurate relation of a series of historical facts—in other words, in the form of a realistic historical novel—is a document on the psychology of France in 1870. This will explain the enormous number of characters which figure in the book. Each character represents one *état d'âme psychologique* of the France of the day. If my work be well done, the reader will be able to understand what was in men's minds and what was the bent of men's minds—what they thought, and how they thought, at that period.

And a little more if I may. He goes on to discuss his subject:

The subject was to be War. I had to consider. War in its relation to various classes of society—War vis-à-vis the bourgeoisie, the peasant, the workman. How the War was brought about—that is to say, the state of mind of men in France at that time—was a consideration which also supplied me with a number of characters. I had to show, in a series of types, France who had lost the use of liberty, France drunk with pleasure, France fated irrevocably to disaster. I had to have types to show France so prompt to enthusiasm, so prompt to despair. And then there were to be shown the immense faults committed, and to show by character how the commission of such faults was possible, a natural sequence of a certain psychological state of mind of a certain preponderating class, which existed in the last days of the Empire.

Then each phase of action had to be typefied. The question of the Emperor and his surroundings—I had to have characters to explain 'the sick man' and his state at the time. I had to show how it was with the peasants of the period, and hence to equip a character or two for that purpose. The Franc-tireurs played an important part in the epoch; it therefore became necessary for me to incarnate these, to create a typical Franc-tireur. The spies and spying had their influence on the whole; I had to have a spy . . . Then having thus, with a stroke of the rake, dragged all together that I could find as likely to illustrate my period, both historically and psychologically considered, I wrote out rapidly—the work of one feverish morning—a maquette, or rough draft of all I wanted to do, some fifteen or twenty pages.

It then became necessary to see the places, to study the geography of my book . . . So, with my rough draft in my pocket and my head teeming with the shadows of my marionettes and of the things they were to do and to explain, I set off for Rheims and went carefully over the whole ground, driving from Rheims to Sedan, and following foot by foot the road by which the Seventh Corps marched to their disaster. During that drive I picked up an immense quantity of material, halting in farmhouses and peasants' cottages, and taking copious notes. Then came Sedan, and after a careful study of the place and the people, I saw that my novel must deal largely, for the full comprehension of my story, not only with the locality, but with the people of the town. This gave me the bourgeois of Sedan, who play an important part in my tale . . .

We may feel that parts of this are a shade determined, over-serious, portentous even. But that's something you can expect when a literary theory seeks to become scientific, as when French Realism in the nineteenth century developed into French Naturalism. But Zola's view of the novel, so serious in its nature, so demanding of its practitioners, so instructive and beneficent to humanity at large—naturalist or anti-naturalist who will not respect and honour it?

Then take at a far remove the opening chapters of Richard Hughes's *In Hazard*. This is the story of a ship and a hurricane. How does Hughes set about his little masterpiece—for that's what it is? He assumes, for most of us correctly, that we don't really know how a single-screw turbine steamer of 9,000 tons is constructed and how she works. He further assumes, just as correctly, that we don't really know how a hurricane is constructed and how it works. So he devotes two chapters, the first two, to telling us. For this ship, a marvel of construction and performance, and this hurricane, likewise a marvel of construction and performance, are going to meet, and what happens throughout their meeting, a kind of mathematics, some of it human, some of it cosmic, that's the novel.

With these two authors, these two novels, *La Débâcle*, 1892, and *In Hazard*, 1938, we will readily agree on the importance of a man knowing what he's writing about. The novelist has knowledge, and his novel transmits it. It need not be knowledge of a severely factual kind. Remember *Tess of the D'Urbervilles*: 'The seasons in their moods, morning and evening, night and noon, winds in their different tempers, trees, waters and mists, shades and silences, and the voices of inanimate things'—these are the background of Tess's tragedy, and lend it their own majesty and inevitability. But we don't read *Tess* to learn how to milk cows or dock mangolds. It offers us an altogether higher knowledge, knowledge about ourselves. We don't read *Moby Dick* because we propose to harpoon whales, or *The Bear* because we are gunning for Brer Bruin. As we don't read—well, *I* don't read— *Sons and Lovers* as a case-history of the Oedipus Complex, but as a poignant and illuminating story of human relationships— mother and son, husband and wife, and lover and mistress, brothers—in short, the human situation, the human predicament, the nature and destiny of man. Of *me*. Of *you*. Of all of us.

This is a great power of the novel as a literary kind. It offers knowledge and truth about ourselves (the most important knowledge and truth there is), not segmented, insulatory, or abstractive, but in terms of an entire situation and human synthesis. This is Conrad's 'revealed moment', and Lawrence's 'interrelatedness'. Flaubert spoke of the need to study the human soul with the impartiality one applies to the physical sciences, and made good his word with *Madame Bovary*; and the brothers Goncourt saw the novel as 'une clinique médico-littéraire', which sounds, and proved to be, rather dreary; and every week we are invited to read new novels which 'lift the lid off' something or other—usually the poverty of an author's mind. For more than lid-lifting is needed. And more than this is provided. Like poetry, like the drama, the novel offers imaginative truth. Truth, in Wordsworth's phrase, carried into the heart by passion.

With that superb but unfashionable (and not undebatable) utterance belling in our ears, let me pause and ask myself where I am, and what I'm doing. As a moral being I have begun by being moralistic, and now I think that is all I shall be, and that I hereby discard from my talk the in any case rather brief and superficial things I meant to say about style, construction, technique, the new approaches to character, time-sequence, communication and non-communication, the anti-novel and anti-hero, the non-novel. I ask your permission to stay with the single question of values. Because without getting into too esoteric or too naïve a state of mind we must look for more in the novel than the simple requirements of narrative method, human characters, prose, and length. Every great novelist has a set of values—and to pretend that great novels, or great any-things, can be produced without a set of values, or merely with anti-values, is self-deception or plain dishonesty.

'To produce a mighty book'—I am quoting, and not for the first time, a sentence of Melville's, from the 103rd chapter of *Moby Dick*—'To produce a mighty book you must choose a mighty theme. No great and enduring volume can ever be written on the flea, though many there be who have tried it.'

It may be presumed that the values held dear by a novelist will be found in his books. And this, I think, is where Hemingway falls from the highest company. Brilliant performer though he is, there is more than a hint of immaturity in his novels, illus-trated at its worst in the perverted sentimentality of the self-announcing tough guy. He *was* a tough guy. Drop him in any jungle, and he'll always come marching out with the heroine on one arm and his rifle clean and oily-bright under the other. He did a lot to clean up the novel of action and high adventure; his writing at its best was clean and hard as a Gurkha's *kukri*; but he was short on ideas and muddled in his notions; and I'd say therefore that while his stylistic and other technical qualities did important service to the novel and short story—and he has written entirely superb short stories and long-shorts which soar above criticism—he has had little influence on people's think-ing, and that little has been bad. His political thinking is hardly to be called thinking at all. Whereas D. H. Lawrence, like him or lump him, is one of the architects of our age, and has helped shape the thinking, the moral concepts, and the general behav-iour not only of you and me, but of millions who've never read a line of him, and millions more who've read only the worst of him, and still more millions who've never even heard of him. Lawrence in the time-honoured sense of the word is a poet, *vates*: a maker of the present and a prophet of the future.

Perhaps we should all write one novel in our lifetime. No doubt we all do—and happy and wise is he that stops at one. But write one novel—do that—and doing so become a syllable in the long, sustained, magnificent tribute to man which the novel is. For while the novel may be, as many of its critics assert (and I agree with them), deficient in 'pure' artists, it has never lacked for teachers, prophets, and celebrants of mankind. Who doubts that Fielding and Dickens and George Eliot and Henry James were on the side of the angels, which means man's side? And Hardy and Conrad, and Mark Twain and Melville and Dreiser. And Tolstoy and Dostoevsky. And Balzac and Zola. *Their novels are ideas in action.* I don't mean that they are primarily concerned to plead or preach, for slaves and the poor, for exploited women and children, peoples and races, the victims of bigotry and power. These are issues with which as human beings they are concerned, but not necessarily more than you and I. It is their ability to use words and control an art form which makes the expression of their views so much more important than yours and mine. If we believe in human progress and human rights, we can well be thankful for the novel as a literary kind, and grateful to novelists for their contribution to both. The novel has been not only the vessel into which creative genius has flowed so copiously for two hundred years, but the chosen medium of men of high soul and a passion to serve their fellow men. It is significant that it developed so swiftly in the eighteenth century, proceeded to such strength in the nineteenth, and for most of the twentieth remained the poetry and drama as well as the narrative of the masses. Anatole France in an oration after the death of Zola said that he was 'a moment in the conscience of humanity'. I am not myself sold on the notion of art for art's sake, and the tribute seems to me a wonderful one.

But when we talk of values in the novel we can mean something different from this, notable and honourable as it is. Every novel worthy of critical consideration—maybe every work of art, but it's the novel we are talking about now—is written because its author has asked a question about life. I don't have to say that I'm not now talking about the literature of entertainment—the detective story and thriller and sci-fi and other such horror comics of the literate—much of which is admittedly very well done. But that is a genre which calls for cleverness, and cleverness, like contrivance, is a main enemy of high artistic creation. Cleverness is the begetter of artefacts not art. Though when I say that cleverness is the enemy of artistic creation, I don't mean that stupidity is its friend. No. The friend is wisdom.

Every worthwhile novel, I think I said (or meant to say), is written because its author has asked himself a question about life. Comedians can do this, of course, as well as the authors of tragedies. It is also possible to propound a question about life without formulating it in so many words. Determinism, religious faith, human freedom and dependence, historical necessity, the nature of truth, the impulses to thought and action—these were some of the questions in Tolstoy's mind when in his own words he 'spent five years of uninterrupted and exceptionally strenuous labour' on the writing of *War and Peace*. And these are only aspects, partial phrasings of the biggest and most inclusive question of all—the meaning of existence. 'What is it all about?' We cannot bear to think that life—the whole world's living, through all eternity, or just our own—is meaningless. 'What does it mean?' we ask—and have to ask if we aren't just clods or stones. 'Why are we here? What can we hope for?'

To find an answer to this is the life's quest of Pierre Bezukhov; and this is the question that never ceases to rack Prince Andrew Bolkonski. Tolstoy is such a titan of the novel, filled with so godlike and yet so immensely human a gift of creation, that he can reach for his answers on two levels. He presents the general issue, philosophic, religious, and cosmic—and here, like most philosophers, divines, and seekers of First Causes, he sometimes grows confused, baffled, arbitrary. And he can present it through persons, individuals. He can put his question a hundred ways. This was the question Prince Andrew found on the face of his wife in childbirth, in 'her glittering eyes, filled with childlike fear and excitement', the wife who wanted only one thing in the world, the warm love her husband could not and would not give her. 'I love you all. What have you done to me?' And this was the question on her dead face too. 'I loved you so much. What have you done to me? And why?'

And three years later these are the questions—What and Why?—he hears Natasha ask by the window in the moonlight at the Rostovs' house in Ostradnoe. Purposeless, depressed, and irritable, unable to sleep, he opens his shutters on the pale, starless, moonless spring sky. Suddenly he hears voices, girls' voices, from the room above. Suddenly, too, everything is charged with a sense that behind the façade of our existence lies something inexpressibly beautiful that we are not seized of and may never possess.

The questions of the dead little princess and Natasha lead to an answer. Prince Andrew tries again to give his life a meaning by entering the public service. But a new disillusion overtakes him. None of the reforms he is so painfully drafting for the legal code can ever be realized in Russia. 'Why am I here? What can a man hope for?' Then one evening he visits the Rostovs.

After dinner Natasha, at Prince Andrew's request, went to the clavichord and began singing. Prince Andrew stood by a window talking to the ladies and listened to her. In the midst of a phrase he ceased speaking, and suddenly felt tears choking him, a thing he had thought impossible for him. He looked at Natasha as she sang, and something new and joyful stirred in his soul. He felt happy, and at the same time sad. He had absolutely nothing to weep about, yet he was ready to weep. What about? His former love? The little princess? His disillusionments? . . . His hopes for the future? . . . Yes and No. The chief reason was a sudden, vivid sense of the terrible contrast between something infinitely great and illimitable within him, and that limited and material something that he, and even she, was. This contrast weighed on and yet cheered him while she sang.

Prince Andrew left the Rostovs' late in the evening. He went to bed from habit, but soon realized that he could not sleep. Having lit his candle he sat up in bed, then got up, then lay down again, not at all troubled by his sleeplessness; his soul was fresh and joyful . . . It did not enter his head that he was in love with Natasha; he was not thinking about her, but only picturing her to himself, and in consequence all life appeared in a new light.

Why do I strive, why do I toil in this narrow, confined frame, when life, all life with all its joys, is open to me?' said he to himself. And for the first time for a very long while he began making happy plans for the future. He decided that he must attend to his son's education by finding a tutor and putting the boy in his charge; that he ought to retire from the service and go abroad, and see England, Switzerland, and Italy. 'I must use my freedom while I feel so much strength and youth in me,' he said to himself. 'Pierre was right when he said one must believe in the possibility of happiness in order to be happy, and now I do believe in it. Let the dead bury their dead, but while one has life one must live and be happy.'

Not that this renewed acceptance of life is the final answer. In Prince Andrew we come to know a man not born for happiness. He must plumb new depths of sorrow and despair, and be the perpetual fountain of his own disillusion before he learns that love, compassion, understanding, and forgiveness are the values that give to life any meaning it can hope to have.·

To put it another way: the world's foremost artists teach us to care about life, and to care about people. In what I regard as the world's great novels we are implicated, concerned, engaged with what we read about. Sterne's My Uncle Toby, Conrad's Mr Jones in *Victory*, Tolstoy's Prince Andrew and the little princess—great novels are readings in the art of life, and teach us engagement and responsibility. When there is a danger that Natasha (in *War and Peace*) will run away with the worthless Anatole, like Pierre we are loaded with apprehension for her. We are forced to take sides, and Tolstoy leaves you in no doubt as to what they are. They are good and evil. That vile and graceful cheat and libertine Prince Anatole is unforgivable, and utterly so. How one detests him! Nothing can be too bad for him. Till in Tolstoy's unique Olympian way we meet him long after in the dressing station after the battle of Borodino, a forgotten man—gone from our memory—now horribly wounded, the surgeon's assistants pinning him to the table, without drug, opiate, or spirits, conscious and screaming with pain, while the surgeon, without bothering to remove the boot, cuts off his leg. Is this he whom it ennobled us to hate, and gratified us to scorn? For we have reached the moment of truth, and it is time to love our enemy, as Prince Andrew, who detested him, and through whose eyes we now behold him, loves him, and Tolstoy in his tremendous impartiality. I don't say that Book Ten, chapter 37, of *War and Peace* is Tolstoy's supreme chapter—I'm sure it isn't—but only the world's supreme novelist could have written it.

The unhappiest consequence of the New Brutalism, apart from the numbing boredom which it dispenses in increasing doses, is that it denies us this kind of concern. It makes Man meaner. And God knows he's mean enough already.

When I read *War and Peace* and grow into its world—for Tolstoy has the same all-embracing power of creation as Shakespeare—I am convinced it is the greatest novel ever written. A conviction I share with just about everyone except Tolstoy, who wouldn't have it that it's a novel at all. The *best* novel I've ever read—so it seems to me here and now: one can always change one's mind—is *Anna Karenina*. So it follows that I would place Tolstoy first among the world's novelists. Which is singularly unoriginal of me. I have used the word 'greatest' about *War and Peace*, and 'best' about *Anna Karenina* deliberately, because there is this marked difference between them, that *Anna* is, if I can with propriety use the phrase in the light of my own pragmatic approach to the art and craft of prose fiction, more purely a novel than its fellow, and approaches more nearly an ideal concept of this kind of literature. For example, you could argue that *War and Peace* is an epic rather than a novel, with its immense and sustained action, its national, indeed European, theme, its world-figures and protagonists, its relation to history, its abundance of private and public episode, and its range and plenitude of interest from the Emperor Napoleon to Platon Karataev's dog. But by no stretch of the term could you call *Anna Karenina* an epic. It is a love story, *un roman sentimental*, a profound study of sexual attraction, desire, passion, love: their destructive force for Anna and Vronsky, whose lives are lived upon a lie; their power for eventual happiness, both domestic and mystical, for Kitty and Levin. There is no foreseeable time when it will not be read as a profound statement of spiritual and physical love, seen in the whole human context, and when it will not help the reader to wisdom, some further understanding of himself and his fellows, and to the tolerance and compassion that follow upon understanding.

And just one other thing. Earlier in this talk I said that novelists were not necessarily more concerned with values or good causes than you and I, but that it was their ability to use words and master an art form which made the expression of their views more important than yours or mine. For that's what literature is: something to say and the best way of saying it. Both elements, severally and in conjunction, allow every degree of excellence or lack of it. But granted a subject that concerns men and women—it can be tragic, comic, satiric, adventure, intrigue, allegory, what you will—granted this, literature is a matter of using words. The novelist must be able to communicate, and it seems to me that he must communicate in a particularly compelling manner. The poet can rely on a quick strike: he can touch your heart or blow your brains out with twelve lines or twenty, or even one or two. But the novelist requires anywhere from seventy thousand to half a million words. So he needs to be careful. They say—I don't vouch for it—that there's as much general wisdom in Tupper's *Proverbial Philosophy* as in the complete works of William Shakespeare—only Shakespeare is judged to have said it rather better. Without good words an author is nothing.

Many, perhaps all great novelists possess not only great virtues but great faults also. It is sometimes a measure of their greatness how well they carry these last. What they must have is the gift of incessant creation and a semi-divine energy. And this indefinable novel form accommodates them all, and will have no difficulty in accommodating them in the future. Good novels, I've said, propound a question about man and his existence; and not to find the answer is paradoxically to find an answer of a kind. Like drama, like poetry, the novel tells us about ourselves; it communicates knowledge; it offers wisdom. Creators are the best teachers: they teach at levels unplumbed by more formal instruction. *They reach right into us.* 'Truth carried into the heart by passion.' At the same time, happily, they please and entertain us. In the novel, as in no other literary kind since the ancient epic, we are conscious of space and distance, and the wearing power of time. We live many lives and compass many ages. We share dimensions of thought and aspects of experience with rare and chosen spirits. Have we not reason to be grateful to the men and women, English and French, American and Russian, who over two centuries and a half have shaped and furnished this refuge of genius? And are prepared to share it with us, their fit and willing guests.

⚛9⚛

Here Be Dragons

A View of the Nature and Function of Heroic Poetry

I

MY subject of discourse is so huge and so ramified that I propose to be no less resolute in dealing with it than the poet Southey with the History of Brazil. 'Southey'—I am quoting the Reverend Alexander Dyce—'Southey was a somewhat impatient listener to Coleridge's metaphysical and long-winded talk. When Southey was engaged on his *History of Brazil*, Coleridge said to him: 'My dear Southey, I wish to know how you intend to treat of man in that important work. Do you mean, like Herodotus, to treat of man in general? Or do you mean, like Thucydides, to treat of man as man political? Or do you mean, like Polybius, to treat of man as man military? Or do you mean——' 'Coleridge,' cried Southey, '*I mean to write the History of Brazil!*'

In the same narrow spirit, in the first three-quarters of my talk I shall seek to divest the heroic mode of poetical composition of all such divagations and diminutions as the heroic-epical, the heroic-supernatural or mythical, the heroic-sentimental, and the heroic-pseudical. My business will be with the heroic *per se*, the heroic-heroical—pure gold, true grit, mead without waste or water. That done, I propose to offer an ameliorative postscript from our own all too stained and disrupted century, whose chief concern will be the last five weeks in the life of the poet Wilfred Owen, killed in action at the Ors Canal one week before Armistice Day, 1918.

From the Gregynog Lectures of the University College of Wales, Aberystwyth, 1980.

I begin by proffering a number of what my heart assures me are aphorisms but my head knows to be platitudes. Thus: a heroic poet is the acknowledged spokesman of a Heroic Age. A heroic poem is what he speaks, or if you prefer, makes on its behalf. I say 'acknowledged spokesman' with an emphasis on both adjective and noun, because the early poets who speak to us of Urien of Rheged, Eirik Bloodaxe of York, and Hrolf Kraki of Leire were official persons in that they discharged an office of a great man's household. By constant utterance they confirmed his status and origin, celebrated his virtues and triumphs, glossed his crimes and blurred his errors, sometimes extolled his wife and always lamented his death, and most important of all transmitted his memory to posterity. Fame, even immortality, could reside in a rune-locked stone or a verse-locked panegyric. You could, of course, have both, stone and verse, and neither survive. But when a heroic poem survives it survives as a best product of its age, because it expresses the conventions, aspirations, and practice of that Age in the heightened and selective fashion characteristic of an artist.

Artists exist within a society for celebration and display, and of their artefacts a gratifying number manage to survive the ravages of Father Time and Brother Man. In our present context, on which time imposes manacles of iron, one such artist fashioned the Migration Age dragon ship-head from the river Scheldt, a second the Sutton Hoo standard, a third the Romano-British cavalry helmet recently unearthed at York, a fourth and fifth the 'Men went to Catraeth with the dawn' stanzas of the *Gododdin* and the exhortations of heroes in the *Bjarkamál*. Like ship-head and standard and helmet, a heroic poem is neither more nor less than the esteemed and essential artefact of a heroic society, and exists only because such a society, as a deliberate endorsement of its own view of itself, provided the conditions that allowed it to exist. Which is why heroic poetry has been not so much a dying as a dead, and one suspects unresuscitable genre, amongst civilized peoples for almost a thousand years. Heroic poetry belongs to the past. It is not to be confused with such apparently related kinds as war-poetry, imperial or patriotic poetry, political and state poetry, to say nothing of the poetry of brave men and the poetry of brave deeds. It isn't 'The Charge of the Light Brigade'—which is neither heroic nor poetry—or 'A Private of the Buffs' or 'Toll for the Brave'; it isn't Kipling, not even the best of him; and it is light-years away from Siegfried Sassoon, Ivor Gurney, and Wilfred Owen. Heroic poetry is a loud clear voice from an age which saw war between men as the richest flower of human experience; a voice clamant, magnificent, and unashamed, but today unthinkable.

And so to a second even more summary generalization: What is a Heroic Age? With my hand on my heart, I admit that I am not entirely sure; but like a great many others before me I carry in my head a learned lumber of facts and fictions from which to assemble a long and at the edges evasive answer. Still, with your permission I shall instead venture on a very short one—and that not my own—and now I come to think of it, not so short either.

Each branch of the Indo-European family of peoples to which most of us here present belong appears to have experienced a Heroic Age, seems indeed to have experienced it for much, even most, of its traceable existence. About that existence we know both surprisingly much and astonishingly little, by virtue of its literary records, which tend to be late, and what in a broad sense we will call its archaeological remains: weapons, harness, personal adornments, drinking vessels, tools, ships, coinage, hill forts, dwellings, images, evidence of war, funerary practice, sacrifice, worship, and the like—which can carry us back farther in time, and from which new or confirmatory evidence can always be hoped. I suffer under no compulsion to be precise: I accept the generalized verdict of the historian and the archaeologist that the conditions characteristic of and requisite for a Heroic Age existed for some millennia before the establishment of that Feudal Society which inherited and needed so many of its principal tenets. In respect of its literature the Heroic Age, or better, a Heroic Age is where you find it. You find it, or can hopefully prospect for it, in Germanic and Norse heroic lays, in part of Gothic or Ostrogothic ancestry, somewhere after the fourth and fifth centuries AD; you find it in Welsh poetry of the Cynfeirdd (the First or Earliest Poets, down to *c*.1100) and the Gogynfeirdd (the Next to the Earliest Poets, who succeeded them). To attempt a date or two, the Old High German *Hildebrandslied* comes from the mid-eighth century; the Old Norse *Second Lay of Helgi Hundingsbane* from the mid-ninth; the Old English *Beowulf* is of or near to the eighth century, and the *Battle of Maldon* was written no long time after the battle it celebrates was fought in 991. The core of Aneirin's *Gododdin* may have been composed near to the year 600, though few if any scholars would ascribe so early a date to the poem in its present form; most would set it some centuries later. The Norse *Bjarkamál* (if we can trust to Snorri Sturluson) was still being chanted to rouse and cheer a worried host before a battle of the year 1030. Our all too exultant and bloodthirsty Welsh poems on the battle of Tal-y-Moelfre are necessarily later than 1157—a powerful confirmation of the strong root and self-renewing leafage of the Welsh tradition of heroic verse.

From the literary and archaeological remains—let us call it the historical evidence—we can observe at close quarters a society with three broadly defined classes: a ruling warrior-élite, the free-born user of land or comparable free-born person, and the slave. You may well ask, how did an arrangement so gratifying to the warrior-élite come about? Or more useful to our present purpose, how did the poets and priests and law-makers of Germanic and Celtic heroic society assume it came about? Well, even as Genesis One and Two offer the least arguable contemporary account of the Creation of Mankind, and Genesis Three and Four the simplest explanation of Mankind's crushing heritage of violence and guilt, so a tenth-century poem composed in Scandinavia but with marked Celtic undertones propounds the most authoritative contemporary theory of the origin of these divinely ordained classes. It is called *Rígsthula*, the Song of Rig (*Rígr*, a cognate of Latin *rēx*, *rēgis*, the Irish *rí*, gen, *ríg*, Early Welsh *rhí*, meaning King).

In a prose introduction to the poem Rig is identified with the god Heimdall, watchman of the Æsir and father of all mankind. I said there were Celtic undertones. With ears that could hear the wool growing on a sheep's back, eyes that could see a hundred leagues into the dark, lungs that could blow a blast that might be heard throughout the worlds; with no fewer than nine mothers—and strength and endurance and will enough to sire the major and minor, the greater and lesser, the higher and lower, the entire three-ways divided original Patriarchal Scions of Humankind—if ever these eyes beheld a Welsh Helping Companion on loan from Arthur's Culhwch-court to Valhalla, Heimdall-Rig is he.

I wish I could convey to you in full measure the assurance, the sense of everlastingness with which our poet, gold-collared and warm-kennelled himself, puts the top-dog at the top, the middle-dog in the middle, and the bottom-dog at the bottom of the heap. One day, the story goes (and for it our unknown poet invokes a long and ancient tradition), this traveller-god came to a poorish habitation where dwelt an ancient couple Ai and Edda, Great-Grandfather and Great-Grandmother. He entered and introduced himself as Rig, and for three nights he lay down in bed between them. Then, as gods do, he departed. Nine months later Edda bore a son, black-skinned and ugly. They called him Thrall, and in time he mated with the bandy-legged, sunburnt Slavey. Between them, Thrall, Slavey, and their unlovely brood do the world's dirty work, and from them are descended the race and varieties of thralls. Of the three chief self-inflicted curses of mankind, so early do we meet the most loathsome, Slavery.

Meantime Rig had gone his ways and reached a second, more commodious home, where dwelt another couple, Afi and Amma, Grandfather and Grandmother. Rig gave them good advice, and for three nights lay down in bed between them. Then he departed. Nine months later Amma bore a son, ruddy, fresh-faced, and with sparkling eyes. They called him Freeman or Peasant (Karl) and in time he married Daughter-in-law (Snör), and by her had many children. They build houses, make wagons, handle the plough, carry keys at the belt; they have the right to bear arms, and from them are descended the race and varieties of free man.

Once more Rig had gone his ways, this time to reach a splen-did hall where dwelt a third couple, Father and Mother (Faðir and Móðir). Rig gave them good advice, and three nights he lay down in bed between them. Then he departed. Nine months later Mother bore a son, fair-haired, bright of cheek, his eye piercing as a snake's. They called him Warrior or Earl (Jarl), and he grew up to use bow and arrow, shield and spear, and hunt with horse and hound. In course of time Rig returned to greet this special son of his, gave him his own divine name, taught him the magic art of runes, urged him to take possession of all that was owing to him. So Jarl went out into the world and stirred up strife: he rode furiously, slew foes, reddened pastures, brought woe to earth. And thus early did the second chief self-inflicted curse of mankind enter the world: Warfare between Men. He came to own many dwellings, and in true lord's fashion dealt out treasure to his friends and followers. He married a lady as well-born as himself, Lively (Erna), daughter of Lord (Hersir), and among their sons, by false etymology, was King (Kon Ungr, *konungr*, Kon the Young, *king*), who mastered runes and read the mysteries and had power and understanding beyond other men. In brief, who was godlike because god-descended, god-acknowledged, and god-instructed, and whose descendants throughout a hundred generations would retain that aura of otherness and more-ness, and be distinguished thereby from all lesser great ones not grown of the divine seed. King knew the language of birds, and hunted and slew them in the copses till one day a crow reproved him thus: 'Young Kon, why should you silence birds? Better for you to bestride steed, draw sword, fell a host. You should go viking, let them feel your blade, deal wounds . . .' On which bloodthirsty advice both crow and poem fall silent for evermore.

So warfare too, like the three orders of mankind, was born of divine injunction, and suited the precept and practice of a ruling warrior-élite no whit less well. That is to say, in the long centuries we are speaking of (and it is by a powerful self-denying ordinance that I am holding as close as I can to the four and a half hundred years between the slaughter at Catraeth and the still heavier slaughters at Stiklastathir and Stamford Bridge)—in those baffling and turbulent times it suited the scores of petty kings, the hundreds of petty princelings, and the thousands of reivers and roughnecks, with all their sons and sons-in-law, their regent-uncles and disgruntled brothers, those brothers' sons and those sons' mothers, in contention for the divided and sub-divided kingdoms, earldoms, lordships and marches; provinces, hundreds, commots and cantrefs, forever starred like cowpads over the northern and western fringes of the Indo-European political killing-ground and cultural arena. To read Saxo Grammaticus on Dark Age Denmark, the *Old English Chronicle* on eight- and ninth-century England, *Heimskringla*, the Lives of the Kings of Norway, on ninth- and tenth-century Scandinavia, the *Chronicles of the Princes* on eleventh- and twelfth-century Wales, and by way of nightcap *Sturlunga Saga* for thirteenth-century Iceland (some of which are self-confessedly very unheroic ages, but on my reading of self-confessedly very heroic ages they were all equally cruel and base)—to read these and their like is to feel one's brain grow numbed by the uncompromising iron-fistedness and unalleviable pig-headedness of man as quarreller and wager of war. The 'old grey widow-makers' of the heroic North and West were ever the sunlit sword and the sunless sea.

Greed, pride, lust, fear, envy, and wrath, accident as well as design, muddle as much as malevolence, justified resentment and swollen revenge, the dream of dominion, the rank that went with territory and the territory that went with rank, and the wealth that went with both, the hankering after green grass and tall timber, fat cattle and nodding corn, tribute of gold and sea-ivory, furs, falcons, and the bowbacked captive, folk-migrations, wanderings uncharted and odysseys beyond the mariner's rose, planned sallies and expelled factions, the beckoning trade-routes by river, land, and sea, the very ideals of union and cohesion, everything made war endemic. And it was the business of the fighting man to fight it, the chronicler to record it, of the poet to glorify it.

Beirdd byd barnant wyr o galon: 'The bards of the world', says the *Gododdin*-poet, 'pass judgement on men of valour.' It was the privilege of the *bardd teulu*, bard of the war-band, to sing them into battle. Also, 'Thou without me,' cried Cynddelw Brydydd Mawr, Cynddelw the Great Poet, to the Lord Rhys, 'Thou

without me, thou hast no voice. I without thee, no voice have
I.' A great many court poets everywhere, from Trondheim to
Dyfed, from the Baltic to Galway Bay, were by prescribed function versifying public-relations men, with a product to render
in exchange for a seat at their lord's feast and a bench by his fire,
a scarlet cloak and a gilded cloak-pin—and I don't mean just
their poetic compositions, which vary from the workmanlike
to the incantatory, and took in all stations between. No, they
were salesmen for the concept of kingship, lordship, the god-
descended and god-invested rights, privileges, and duties of the
Age.

Arising out of all this, or at least contingent upon it, there
would appear to be no particular reason for supposing that a
Heroic Age with Capital Letters was likewise a heroic age in
lower case, or even for most people an age of outstanding much
less unparalleled heroism. Early wisdom literature is against
the notion, and so are the patterns of human motivation and
behaviour. Even so, we might say, first, that in respect of its art
and ethos a term like the Heroic Age (with Capitals) is no less
true, and no less misleading, than terms like the Age of the
Saints, the Renaissance, or the Enlightenment, or for that matter the Permissive Society of the Pop Age, on which we are all
authorities. And, second, with all its imperfections the term is
too useful a piece of shorthand to be discarded. The two essential
characteristics of a Heroic Age, as these are revealed by its artefacts and memorials, are that it shall be warlike and hierarchical:
in other words, that society is controlled by a king, lord, chieftain, and under him a military aristocracy whose highest good
is war and the warrior's code. Today for most of us war is something we are forced to take part in, either through the authority
of a state, especially an authoritarian state, or through the
agonized exercise of our judgement and conscience. But in a
Heroic Age, 'War', says the Norse *Bjarkamál*, 'springs from the
nobly born. For the perilous deeds which leaders attempt are not
to be done by the ventures of common men.' In the same spirit
Saxo Grammaticus, enumerating the noble dead after the
holocaust at Bravellir, declined to 'name the slaughter of the
commons', adding for good measure, 'I have felt no desire to

include the multitude.' In the same lofty spirit Aneirin left it to David Jones to speak up for Dai Greatcoat. True, one peasant-freeman, the good Dunnere, received separate and honourable mention in the *Battle of Maldon*; but in general the lower deck and PBI are neither named nor noted. Their corpses served not to deck, but to dung, the fields of glory.

Military service, some of it enforced, was the duty and obligation, even the right and pleasure, of every freeborn man. But in the nature of things the poets loved a lord. Churls could deal out clouts enow, but for style choose a lord every time. So our fellow-countryman Isag in the *Gododdin*:

Isag the distinguished man from the region of the South, his manners were like the sea-flood for graciousness and liberality and pleasant mead-drinking. Where his weapons gouged no counter-stroke might follow . . . His sword echoed in the heads of mothers. The rampart of fury, he was renowned, the son of Gwyddnau.

Fighting was Isag's business because it was his pleasure, the thing he wanted to do; and his duty, the thing he was conditioned to do. I could illustrate this dual compulsion from half-a-dozen literatures: better men might illustrate it from a score. Who does not know the witness of Tacitus respecting the Germans in the first century AD, and of Strabo and Posidonius respecting the Celts a hundred years earlier? If there is an obol of difference between them, it's that Tacitus says that among the Germans the leader fights for victory and his followers fight for the leader—which sounds very Third Reich—whereas classical testimony to the Celts records that they will fight anyone, anytime, anywhere, for any reason, or for no reason at all, which sounds no less frenetically familiar. I repeat (and I am now quoting from myself), human nature changes very little, if at all, and it may well be that in any more meaningful sense than this what we distinguish as a heroic age is merely our modern endorsement of the cherished illusion of a self-regarding ruling caste and its creative artists. The reality, no doubt, if we were better acquainted with it, would show more squalid than fine, more brutal than brave, a smirched ornament on a dunghill of human misery and oppression. Even so, nothing in our lives is more powerful than our illusions, and nothing more shapes our art. For art is not the ultimate reality, but the ultimate illusion. So we know exactly where we are, and what we are dealing with, when we hear poetry like this:

Wearing a brooch, in the front rank, armed in the battle-shout, a mighty man in combat before his deathday, a leader charging forward before armies. There fell five times fifty before his blades; of the men of Deira and Bernicia there fell a hundred score; they were annihilated in one hour. He would sooner be flesh for wolves than go to a wedding, he would sooner be prey for the raven than go to the altar, he would sooner his blood flowed to the ground than that he should get due burial, in return for mead in the hall among the hosts. Hyfaidd the Tall shall be honoured as long as there is a minstrel.

Or this:

Sweet is it to repay the gifts received from our lord, to grip the swords, and devote the steel to glory. Behold, each man's courage tells him loyally to follow a king of such deserts, and to guard our captain with fitting earnestness. Let the Teuton swords, the helmets, the shining armlets, the mailcoats that reach the heel, which Hrolf of old bestowed upon his men, let these sharpen our mindful hearts to the fray. The time requires, and it is just, that in time of war we should earn whatsoever we have gotten in the deep idleness of peace. My master is the greatest of the Danes: let each man, as he is valorous, stand by him; far, far hence be all cowards!

Or yet again, this:

Byrhtwold spoke, raised his shield on high; he was a liegeman of long standing, brandished his ash-spear, full bravely he exhorted the warriors. 'Thought shall be harder, heart the keener, courage the greater, as our strength lessens. Here lies our lord all hewn down, a good man in the dust. Ever may he feel sorrow who thinks now to turn from this war-play. I am old in years, and will not leave this place. I reckon to lie at my lord's side, that man so dear to me.'

War, valour, service, reward, loyalty, contempt of death, and love of fame: these are the constants of truly heroic verse; and for the moment we may rest on them. If I add that my first passage was Welsh, from the *Gododdin*; my second Scandinavian, from the *Bjarkamál*; and my third English, from the *Battle of*

Maldon, this is only to indicate that mankind not only holds cherished illusions, but holds them by common assumption, here, there, and everywhere.

But we must not lose ourselves in the whole wide world of heroic poetry, starting as it does, in its recorded form in our selected area, very late, strengthening greatly between the years 600 and 850, and continuing in Norway and Wales to the eleventh and twelfth centuries. Instead, we will stay with the three poems I have just quoted from. All three are about the lordly man's pattern of obligation in life, and no less in death, in a heroic society. For remember, when a man joins the heroes' trade union he contracts to *die* as well as *live* a hero. You don't just peacock it and fan your tail-feathers on parade. You must fight like an eagle, beak foremost, till you fall in red ruin from a black sky. The more a poem confines itself to the basic assumptions just enumerated—war, valour, loyalty, and reward, and the sale of life for fame—and the more resolutely it eschews such contaminatory motifs as greed for gold and treasure, the distractions of human or, still worse, divine love, the challenge of private revenge, even a pause for thought or reflection, the more truly heroic it will be. So now to the *Battle of Maldon*, which is English, the *Gododdin*, which is Welsh, and if we have time to the *Bjarkamál*, which is Norse. All three accept the heroic ethos without question or reservation, all three are exalted utterances telling of a man's duty to his lord and of the excellence of that lord. All three deal with a single situation, whose disaster is its glory, and whose glory its disaster. All three are about men in a narrow place—the defence of a ford (*Maldon*), the assault on a strong position (the *Gododdin*), the beleaguering of a royal residence (*Bjarkamál*)—where brave men cannot go forward and will not go back, but will die where they stand, and choose so to die.

The three poems are notably different in their style of composition. *Maldon* is a narrative poem, a heroic lay, and after the fashion of a miniature epic tells a story in chronological order. The *Gododdin* is commemoration poetry; each of its verses celebrates with praise an army or a member of that army; the 'story' we must supply for ourselves. *Bjarkamál* is *exhortacionum series*, and what story there is emerges from the rhetorical harangues of those participant in the action. It is true that there are elements of narrative, panegyrical commemoration, and exhortation in each and every one of the poems, but the classification is, even so, just and true. *Maldon* tells of a well-known historical event; the *Gododdin* of an event less well known but unquestionably historical; and *Bjarkamál* of an event so lost in the mists of time what we cannot accord it a firmer status than that of heroic legend.

Maldon is an unquestionably and quintessentially English poem. The *Gododdin*, preserved in a manuscript of the mid-thirteenth century, and attributed to the poet Aneirin, who according to tradition lived in the second half of the sixth century, and to judge from his poem was a court poet, and more particularly bard of the royal war-band (*bardd teulu*) at Edinburgh (Din Eidin), and fought in the battle his poem extols—the *Gododdin* is just as unmistakably an un-English poem, even apart from the language it is written in. It is a Celtic, and more specifically a British and Northern British, and by the accident of language a Welsh poem. When I say the *Gododdin* I mean of course the poem we have, in the shape in which we have it, and not the *Gododdin*, if such there was, that we do not have, of shape debatable and provenance unknown, but the familiar congeries, or at best series, of something approaching a hundred commemorative stanzas, elegiac and panegyric, held together by a common occasion, purpose, and manuscript repository. Where recognizable sequences occur, they tend to be of two, three, or four stanzas, and the longest of all, the 'Men (or man) went to Catraeth' sequence, has but nine, a matter of under a hundred lines. This deliberate or accidental concept of 'unity' is crucial.

Early Welsh literature has many heroic or heroic-elegiac poems, but no epic, or even sustained verse-narrative, because the bards, or poets, were not concerned with a long sustained mode of composition, beginning more or less at the beginning, and proceeding more or less tidily to a more or less defined end. They were less narrators than celebrants, memorialists. The 'story', the event, was known to the poet and by him assumed to be known to his hearers. It was not for him to cater for the ignorant or heedless, any more than it was for his audience to expect him to compose a poem in a fashion contrary to the canons of his art. What he has been trained to do is to commemorate the heroes who fell at Catraeth; and what we must do today, when through no fault of our own we *are* ignorant, is to piece together what happened at Catraeth from an assemblage of elegies and panegyrics.

What emerges, on the whole, is this. Mynyddog, king of the Gododdin, a North British people, had good reason to resent the northern encroachment of the English, the Anglo-Saxons, and more precisely the men of Deira and Bernicia. By way of counterstroke, he began by summoning to his royal hall at Edinburgh three hundred gold-torqued warriors from every part of Britain. For a year—and the year was approximately the year 600 AD—he feasted them there. In the language of the poets they drank his mead. In the language of ordinary men they pledged themselves—which means their lives—to his cause. And so, when the year's drinking and boasting was over (boasting, as the old Welsh proverb reminds us, being half of the feast), they rode out, all three hundred, in the cold light of dawn, on their small white shaggy-maned horses, with a stamping of hooves and champing of bits, a jingle of arm-rings and keening of spears. Old-style, new-style commando, they were to attack the combined or combining armies of two kingdoms at Catraeth, probably Richmond near the modern Catterick in Yorkshire. And attack they did, against what proved to be hopeless odds, and 'after the uproar there was silence'. One man, or maybe the survivors were three, escaped bloodstained and reeling. The rest sold their lives for the mention of glory. 'It would be wrong to leave him unremembered . . . the generous wyvern, dragon in bloodshed after the wine-feast, Gwenabwy son of Gwen, in the conflict at Catraeth.' The son of Nwython, Clydno's son, and Sywno's son (the soothsayer knew it)—these are the men whose valour, loyalty, and swift obliteration from all save a nation's memory, were celebrated in a century of stanzas preserved in the *Gododdin* manuscript.

Of two of the slain we have already heard tell: Hyfaidd the

Tall who preferred battles to bridals, and Isag whose good manners were a thing to marvel at, but whose other-mannerly sword echoed, rang, pealed in the heads of mothers. Here is a third, Bleiddig son of Eli:

Bold in battle, mighty when hard-pressed; in conflict there was no truce that he would make; in the day of wrath he would not shirk the fight. Bleiddig son of Eli was a wild boar for fierceness; he drank off wine from brimming glass vessels; and on the day of combat he would do feats of arms, riding his white steed. Before he died he left behind him bloodstained corpses.

Half of me loves it: half of me hates it. And it is not so simple a division as heart and head. I admire its panache and gallantry, its transmission of the sharp image, its stock phrases and stylistic counters so freshly yet conventionally assembled, its skill and expertise, even as I am rebuffed by its sterile doctrine and deadly ethic. Still, let us end not with the fell deeds of one, but rather with the poet's panegyric upon all three hundred of Mynyddog's war-band:

Three hundred men hastened forth, wearing gold torques, defending the land—and there was slaughter. Though they were slain they slew, and they shall be honoured till the end of the world. But of all us kinsmen who set forth, alas, save for one man, none escaped.

Half a millennium later the same ethos and a similar rhetoric persisted in Wales, and it would be surprising if this were not so. The Poets of the Welsh Princes, the Gogynfeirdd, were by design the preservers and transmitters of tradition, no less than their predecessors the Cynfeirdd. Indeed, in the very nature of things they had more tradition to transmit. As their names confirm, the Earliest Poets were followed by the Next Earliest Poets, conservative in so much of their practice, exponents of an approved rhetoric and technique, practitioners who saw poetry as a skill, a craft, whose requirements were measurable and must be learned, and once learned must be met not flouted. The most consummate performer of the second half of the twelfth century was Cynddelw Brydydd Mawr, the Big Poet who by pre-emptive claim (including his own) became the Great Poet. In his varied *œuvre* we shall find just about everything we

have been calling the heroic-heroical: a stated recognition of
the poet–patron relationship; a stated awareness of the bard's
function as panegyrist and memorialist, and a stated claim that
the bard is both recorder and assessor, and therefore the guard-
ian before posterity of a lord's excellence and a warrior's
worth. One of the lords he addressed was Owain, Gwynedd's
warrior-king:

> I praise a patron high-hearted in strife,
> Wolf of warfare, challenging, charging,
> Singing the pleasure of his presence,
> Singing his power, mead-nourished worth,
> Singing his fervour, swift-winged falcon,
> Singing a lofty soul's lofty thoughts,
> Singing daring deeds, lord of war-hounds,
> Singing of one who inspires high praise,
> Singing a song for my lavish lord,
> Singing words of praise to praise Owain.

And here is part of the song:

> At Aberteifi they cut through falling spears,
> As at Badon Fawr, valiant war-cry.
> I saw war-stags and stiff red corpses,
> It was left to the wolves, their burial;
> I saw them routed, without their hands,
> Beneath birds' claws, men mighty in war;
> I saw their ruin, three hundred dead,
> I saw, battle done, bowels on thorns;
> I saw strife cause a dreadful uproar,
> Troops contending, a rout collapsing.[1]

And as there were generous wyverns and dragons in bloodshed
at Catraeth, so there were war-wolves and war-stags and
dragons of battle at Tal-y-Moelfre:

> In arms against Angles, in Tegeingl's lands,
> Blood spilling in streams, blood pouring forth,
> Dragons encountered, rulers of Rome,

---

[1] Parts of this and the following passage from Cynddelw have been quoted in a
differing context on p. 153 above.

> A prince's heir, red their precious wine.
> In strife with the Dragon of the East,
> Fair western Dragon, the best was his.

For where were they not, the noble war-beasts, fallen in their hundreds, wide hosts who (in Taliesin's phrase) sleep with the light in their eyes?

Pursuant of the same deadly theme at the same murderous time were Owain's poet-son, 'Tall Hywel, hawk of war', destined to be killed by his half-brothers Dafydd and Rhodri, and Gwalchmai ap Meilyr, who each wrote in celebration of Owain's famous victory over an Anglo-Norman-Welsh land-and-seaborne assault upon North Wales. The battle of Tal-y-Moelfre took place in 1157, and what could be more familiar than Hywel's:

> When crows made merry, when blood ran freely,
> When men's blood was poured out,
> When war came, when houses burned red,
> When shore was red, when courts burned red—

Or Gwalchmai's:

> At Tal-y-Moelfre a thousand war-cries,
> Shaft on shining shaft, spear upon spear,
> Fear on deep fear, drowning on drowning,
> And no ebb in Menai from tides of blood,
> And the stain of men's blood in the brine,
> And grey armour and ruin's anguish,
> And corpses heaped by a red-speared lord,
> And England's horde and engagement with it,
> And them demolished in the shambles.
> And the fame raised of a savage sword
> In seven-score tongues to praise him long.

So there it is, the heroic-heroical—pure gold, true grit, mead without waste or water. Dr Johnson said of the ancient epic poets that they were 'very unskilful teachers of virtue. Their principal characters may be great, but they are not amiable. The reader may rise from their works with a greater degree of active or passive fortitude, and sometimes of prudence; but he will be able to carry away few precepts of justice, and none of mercy.' Much the same may be said of the ancient heroic poets, Celtic and Germanic. How easy we find it under the spell of their words to quell our sensibilities, and yield up pity and judgement alike to their gallantly pictorial catalogues of horror. Always the hero on his white steed, the unfeeling heart, the unfelt wound, and the decorative crimson of an enemy's blood. And if you want to sleep of nights, don't contemplate the fate of the steed.

II

And what now of the promised postscript? It is modern, and comes by way of amelioration, even of comfort; for not the most mayhem-minded of military heroes can conjure up so much as the ghost of a heroic-heroical lay today. Who could exult in Passchendaele and the Somme, in Rotterdam and Hiroshima? The Battle of Britain and its fighter-pilots would seem a better bet—it's not that there aren't any heroes any more, but we know too much, the appropriate rhetoric is out of fashion, and the *heldenlied* with it. Consider Major J. H. Marshall of the Irish Guards, who on 1 June 1918 was transferred to the 2nd Manchesters as second-in-command. In more peaceful times the Major had been an all-round sportsman and breeder of thoroughbreds. In 1914, spoiling for a fight, he disposed of his bloodstock and joined the Belgian Army as a lieutenant of artillery, and before the end of that year had received two out of the ten wounds he would have received by September 1918. One of the two was a bayonet-thrust in the face—like Hyfaidd, like Beowulf, like Cuchulainn, the Major was a man who liked to get in close. By September 1918 he had likewise received five decorations for gallantry in action. When Lieutenant Wilfred Owen of the 2nd Manchesters first sighted him and christened him, *Mabinogion*-wise and *Morte Darthur*-fashion, 'Marshall of the Ten Wounds', they both had less than three months to live.

'Major Marshall of the Ten Wounds', wrote Owen on 28 September, 'is the most arrant utterly soldierly soldier I ever came across . . . Bold, robust, dashing, unscrupulous, cruel, jovial, immoral, vast-chested, handsome-headed, of free, coarse speech.' Five days later Owen, the hater and contemner of war

('Was it for this the clay grew tall?'), wrote to his mother that he had been continually in action for some days. 'I can find no word to qualify my experience except the word SHEER . . . It passed the limits of my Abhorrence. I lost all my earthly faculties, and fought like an angel.' He told her too that he had been recommended for the Military Cross. Four days later, on 8 October, he told her why. 'You will understand I could not write—when you think of us for days all but surrounded by the enemy. All one day (after the battle) we could not move from a small trench, though hour by hour the wounded were groaning just outside. Three stretcher-bearers who got up were hit, one after one. I had to order no one to show himself after that, but remembering my own duty, and remembering also my fore-fathers the agile Welshmen of the Mountains, I scrambled out myself and felt an exhilaration in baffling the Machine Guns by quick bounds from cover to cover. After the shells we had been through, and the gas, bullets were like the gentle rain from heaven.'

His citation puts it less poetically. 'For conspicuous gallantry and devotion to duty in the attack on the Fonsomme Line on 1st/2nd October 1918. On the Company Commander becoming a casualty, he assumed command and showed fine leadership and resisted a heavy counter-attack. He personally captured an enemy Machine Gun in an isolated position and took a number of prisoners. Throughout he behaved most gallantly.'

I interrupt what is in my intention a requiem only to say that between Owen the author of 'The Show' and 'Disabled', and Owen who fought like an angel and won the Military Cross, there is no discrepancy. Owen wasn't a 'hero' in inverted commas and neon lights, as Marshall of the Ten Wounds, Officier de l'ordre de Leopold, Chevalier de l'ordre de Leopold, Croix de Guerre and Medaille Militaire, Military Cross and Bar, Victoria Cross, pretty certainly was (and none the less hero for that— and who on God's earth would one wish for in a fight more than he?), but a man of deep thought and sensitivity who did his soldier's duty bravely, conscientiously, and in the hope that good would come out of it. 'I came out to help these boys [letter of 4th/5th October, Owen then being 25 years old]—directly by leading them as well as an officer can; indirectly by watching their sufferings that I may speak of them as well as a pleader can. I have done the first.' And we now know that with his poems he did the second; and he did it superbly, because he not only watched men's sufferings but shared them.

On 4 November he shared them to the full. The 2nd Manchesters were among the British troops seeking to force the Ors Canal, determinedly defended by the retreating Germans. Everyone on both sides save glory-hunting generals, advantage-seeking politicians, and vermin like the publicist Horatio Bottomley, knew the war was decided and the fighting should stop. But the fighting continued, for Marshall who loved it, and Owen who loathed it. Crossing the Canal was a bloody business. The classic heroic situation all over again: I'm here, you are there, a bridge to put across, a bridge to destroy. Casualties were heavy. Marshall (the soothsayer knew it) crossed at the head of his men, but on the far bank, on enemy ground, fell dead of his eleventh wound. 'Through this hurricane the small figure of Wilfred Owen walked backwards and forwards between his men, patting them on the shoulder, saying "Well done" and "You're doing very well, my boy." He was at the water's edge, giving a hand with some duckboards, when he was hit and killed.' The news of his death reached his father and mother in Shrewsbury seven days later, on Armistice Day.

So there they were, dead together, Marshall of the Ten Wounds who would have drunk Mynyddog's mead as readily as he chewed King George's bully-beef, and would have led an attack at Catraeth as determinedly as he led one at the Ors Canal; and Wilfred Owen who might have done both things too, were he convinced of their rightness and justice. As no doubt most (why not all?) of the Three Hundred were convinced. For them, as for their bard, honour and fame were a man's best possessions, here, now, and forever, not for parley, not for barter, exempt from mortal trafficking. Many things that look simple and sure can suddenly appear a Merlin-web of doubts and possibilities. I set the two men together, Marshall and Owen, with the same meed of honour and regard, and a common note of irony. Marshall died almost a thousand years too late for a verse panegyric, and Owen was no less tardy and time-hung as the poet who by now could no longer write it for him.

They say that inside every Dane, Norwegian, and Swede there's a Viking trying to get out. Inside every Welshman there's a preacher trying to get out—or in my case trying to get back in. Man, we all know, is an animal uniquely magnificent and uniquely dreadful, and in either manifestation endlessly concerned to display, justify, or glorify himself. In the full exercise of the heroic code he may be seen, by a quite small shift of focus, as either or both. One of the passages that would best lend itself to the purposes of a heroic poet in the whole range of modern literature is Lawrence of Arabia's account in chapter 117 of *Seven Pillars of Wisdom* of the engagement between the Turks and Germans on the one side, and the British, Australians, and Arabs on the other, at the raped village of Tafas. There is the sublimely heroic picture of one man on his horse—the village headman who could not live on, because to do so would be shameful—charging an army of two thousand men; there is the heroic promise to exact his price; there is Lawrence's tribute to the trapped German detachments who knew they had to fight on to the inescapable end and die, and by the way they did so wrung a tribute of admiration from those who most hated them. Nothing in early poetry is or can be more heroic than this.

Tafas—where is Tafas? Seek ye below Damascus! God knows a man would have to look long and far for a more useless place to die in than Tafas. But it was here that the Allies caught up with the retreating Turks and Germans. The year was 1918. It was clear that the most hideous massacre had been carried out there. I shall read to you the 'heroic' paragraphs. Like the *Gododdin* and Cynddelw's Aberteifi-verses, Lawrence's account owes much to the shaping skills of an author.

Tallal [he was the chieftain or headman of Tafas]—Tallal had seen what we had seen. He gave one moan like a hurt animal; then rode to the upper ground and sat there a while on his mare, shivering and looking fixedly after the Turks. I moved near to speak to him, but Auda caught my rein and stayed me. Very slowly Tallal drew his headcloth about his face; and then he seemed suddenly to take hold of himself; for he dashed his stirrups into the mare's flanks and galloped headlong, bending low and swaying in the saddle, right at the main body of the enemy.

It was a long ride down a gentle slope and across a hollow. We sat there like stone while he rushed forward, the drumming of his hoofs unnaturally loud in our ears, for we had stopped shooting, and the Turks had stopped. Both armies waited for him; and he rocked on in the hushed evening till only a few lengths from the enemy. Then he sat up in the saddle, and cried his war-cry, 'Tallal, Tallal!' twice in a tremendous shout. Instantly their rifles and machine-guns crashed out, and he and his mare, riddled through and through with bullets, fell dead among the lance points.

Auda looked very cold and grim. 'God give him mercy; we will take his price.'

The price was taken. Of the two thousand enemy not one survived the horror and confusion of a scattered field. Most died in great fear.

Exceptions were the German detachments; and here, for the first time, I grew proud of the enemy who had killed my brothers. They were two thousand miles from home, without hope and without guides, in conditions mad enough to break the strongest nerves. Yet their sections held together, in firm rank, sheering through the wrack of Turk and Arab like armoured ships, high-faced and silent. When attacked they halted, took position, fired to order. There was no haste, no crying, no hesitation. They were glorious.

Maldon, the *Gododdin*, and *Bjarkamál* have nothing on this. *The Finnsburg Fragment*, *Tal-y-Moelfre*, and *Hamthismál* have nothing on this. But Lawrence gives us the other side of the picture too.

At Tafas the women had been outraged, then obscenely murdered; the children, the tiniest babies, had been speared and bayoneted; the old people beaten and cut to pieces; captured Arab soldiers had been tortured and staked out to die. And for the first and only time in his career Lawrence gave orders to take no prisoners. 'I said, "The best of you brings me most Turkish dead."' They killed the Turks and they killed the Germans, they killed the wounded and they killed the animals. And when all was over they went out and killed the dead a second time.

Was the reality, I wonder, always a bit like that? Those magnificent and terrible warriors of the Island of Britain who rode to Catraeth and slew and were slain. And those magnificent and less terrible warriors of the kingdom of Wessex who for over-pride slew and were slain at the causeway by Maldon. And those magnificent and terrible northern champions who made cairns of their foes' corpses and themselves perished at Leire. Were they like this? Believing as I do, that human nature changes little or not at all, I judge they were; and if so, then the heroes of old require the divine charity just as much as the Three Disloyal War-bands of the Island of Britain, and the cowards who ran for their lives in *Beowulf* and *Maldon* are presumed to require mankind's. So to conclude: by those of us who know we are not heroes, and hope we are not cowards—perhaps the heroes and cowards of old, equally with ourselves, should be granted the god-enjoined benefit of the man-inspired doubt.

And their dragonfly poets, everlastingly trapped and displayed in the revealing amber of verse, what of them? We must admit, they did what their time required of them, and did it at their best superbly, and it is presumptuous to judge, and unjust to censure, because new times have new requirements. But it is proper to note those requirements. Here are some sentences from Wilfred Owen's Preface to the volume of his war poems published in 1920. No man had a better right to speak, and nothing can be more antithetical to the old heroic poetry of glorious deeds and deed-won glory.

This book is not about heroes. English poetry is not yet fit to speak them.

Nor is it about deeds, or lands, nor anything about glory, honour, might, majesty, dominion or power, except war.

Above all I am not concerned with Poetry.

My subject is War, and the pity of War.

The Poetry is in the pity.

Yet these elegies are to this generation in no sense consolatory. They may be to the next. All a poet can do today is warn. That is why the true Poets must be truthful.

Owen didn't recall the cadences of Sermon and Prayer

because he had no words of his own. The most affecting and convincing war poems ever written are proof of that. He was a doomed young man talking in great earnest and some haste. If it was right for the poet to warn in 1918, how much more he must warn today, when Armageddon and Ragnarok are words restored to the vocabulary of human fear. The heroic poet of old was true to his particular truth: Wilfred Owen, the war-poet of today, was true to his; and his is the better, and the only truth for a world as fraught as ours with the means and the will to its own dismemberment and destruction. I have already expressed my opinion that Heroic Poetry as a literary kind belongs to the past, is dead, and cannot be restored. We must be happy to think that Wilfred Owen, writing in a language which makes him apprehended of half the world and more, a soldier-poet who in the shock and sheerness of battle remembered his forefathers, the agile Welshmen of the Mountains, pronounced its final epitaph. Even as Dylan Thomas's 'A Refusal to Mourn' is a threnody and epitaph not only for a Child killed, by Fire, in London, but for all the innocents and helpless ones slain on the world's great killing-grounds in a crescendo of murder from Guernica to Hiroshima, a Lamentation at once private and public, all-human yet sacral, for 'the majesty and burning of the child's death'. So, too, Wilfred Owen had spoken, as by the conventions of his age and art no heroic-heroical poet could speak, for man and Mankind caught up in war. The poetry is in the pity, and the pity is for all men, all front-line fighters of all nations, ours and theirs, friend and foe. Thanks to him and his First World War peers, the bards of the world still pass judgement on men of valour and those who share their suffering. This is not a new sun risen on a brave new world. It may be a candle that helps light a way out of the heroic old one.

⚹10⚹

The Legendary History of Olaf Tryggvason

I AM very conscious of the privilege the University of Glasgow has conferred on me this evening, by inviting me to deliver the W. P. Ker lecture for 1967–8. Few students are more indebted to Ker's writings than I; many of the subjects he liked and wrote about, I like too; and he held my present Chair at Cardiff for a period of six years. I am aware too that I follow in the footsteps not only of W. P. Ker himself, but also of his memorial lecturers, and I am gratified that your ancient and famous University has thought me worthy of so honourable a succession. And finally, I have never felt more proud of the Scottish blood in my veins than I feel now, a Welshman facing his fellow Scots.

From one of the severest criticisms of modern scholarship, that its practitioners are coming to know more and more about less and less, I hold myself exempt. Quite the contrary: day by day I find myself coming to know less and less about more and more. There was a time when I would have said that I knew just about everything there is to be known about Olaf Tryggvason. By now I am clear that I know next to nothing—for the very good reason that there is next to nothing to know. Even so, there are three sufficient reasons why we should concern ourself with this obscurely illustrious figure. The written sources are of compelling interest for their own sake; our acceptance, part-acceptance, or rejection of them must affect our view of northern history over many centuries; and they raise some awkward questions about the nature of historical writing and literary excellence. If after regarding Olaf Tryggvason as a

The twenty-second W. P. Ker Memorial Lecture, delivered in the University of Glasgow, 6 March 1968.

central pillar of Scandinavian history we find him a broken reed, we must wonder how many similar pillars from Gorm the Old and Harald Fairhair to Svein Forkbeard and Harald Hardrada are reeds in need of breaking; if we grow doubtful of his hymned share in the conversion of the Northlands to Christianity, then clearly we know less about that intricate process than we thought, especially in respect of Norway, Iceland, and Greenland; and if we can reach valid conclusions about his kingdom and kingship we may find ourselves compelled to a similar exercise in respect of other northern kings and realms. As for literature: the *Anglo-Saxon Chronicle* is a great and justly celebrated piece of historical literature, but it is not a great work of literature *per se*, whereas Snorri Sturluson's *Heimskringla* most decidedly is. It has also been esteemed as a great piece of historical literature, in that it dealt with the making of Norway in an authentic and trustworthy way. What then happens to our opinion of *Heimskringla* if we find significant areas of it merely masquerading as history, or, worse still, making nonsense of history? Fortunately I do not now have to answer this question, but it may help explain why I am talking not about Olaf Tryggvason's history, which is exiguous, but about his legendary history, which is branched and leafy as a midsummer oak.

Yet, in darkness as in light, and not least because of this chiaroscuro, Olaf Tryggvason is one of the most spectacular figures of the Viking Age. Born under threat, sold into slavery, ransomed and raised in exile, blooded in piracy in the Baltic, a feeder of ravens and gorger of wolves throughout the British Isles, with Frisia, France, and Jutland thrown in for good measure, he made a strong mark on northern historiography. He may have commanded part of the Viking host at the battle of Maldon in 991; he certainly fought in England alongside king Svein Forkbeard of Denmark in 994. In the year 995 he sailed with his fleet to Norway, tumbled the formidable Jarl Hakon out of his high-seat, and ruled a kingdom there till the millennial year 1000, when he perished in one of the most celebrated battles of northern history or legend, the sea-fight off Svold. Before making his bid for Norway he had reneged on Odinn and sworn fealty to Christ. Ever since, he has stood before posterity as one who in his day and place was Christ's best hatchet-man, and posterity has approved the role.

That is the bare outline of the life-story, history and legend, which I want to fill in this evening. But first I must advance two preliminaries, the one relating to the written sources of knowledge about our hero, the other to the milieu, political, economic, and geographical, in which he lived his thirty-two years of life as a man and achieved his thousand years of fame as a legend.

If I say we know next to nothing about Olaf Tryggvason, this is not the fault of medieval historians and poets. He was one of their darling topics, and treated by such founding fathers of Scandinavian history as Adam of Bremen (*Gesta Hammaburgensis Ecclesiæ Pontificum*, *c*.1075), Ari Thorgilsson (*Íslendingabók*, *c*.1125), and that consummate genius Snorri Sturluson himself (*Heimskringla*, *c*.1230). The monk Theodoricus wrote of him in his *Historia de antiquitate regum Norwagensium*, *c*.1180, as did the anonymous author of the *Historia Norwegiæ*, sometime before 1211. The 'Summary of the History of the Kings of Norway' whose brief title is *Ágrip* found room and verge for him. Two sagas were composed about him at the Benedictine monastery at Thingeyrar in northern Iceland, the first by Odd Snorrason in Latin (*c*.1190), but surviving only in translation, the second by Gunnlaug Leifsson, of uncertain but later date, also in Latin and surviving only partly in translation, though we judge we know its contents with some accuracy. Also there was a third saga, indeed a kind of encyclopaedia, compiled about him in Iceland, the so-called 'Great (or even Greatest) Saga of Olaf Tryggvason', written probably in the fourteenth century, and preserved in *Flateyjarbók*. Olaf figures prominently in many of the Icelandic sagas; indeed any family saga or historical work which refers to the conversion of Iceland to Christianity in the year 999–1000 must refer to Olaf, because he was early given the credit for it. *Hallfreðar Saga Vandræðaskalds* is a good example of the one kind, *Kristni Saga* of the other. Further, he was the patron and subject of poets, those skalds who in return for favours shown were a kind of versifying public-relations officers for the great men who befriended them. The well-known

Hallfred, nicknamed Troublesomeskald, wrote a *drápa* or encomium on him, and various of his exploits are referred to by poets whose primary concern was with some other patron. Finally, and not least important, he appears in the *Anglo-Saxon Chronicle*. Between them these sources give us an extraordinarily full account of everything that happened in the life of Olaf from his folk-tale birth to his epic death. If his life-story may be established from the writings of the unctuous yet atrabilious Adam, who detested him, the pragmatic Snorri, who admired him, the severe and scholarly Ari, who took him as he came, and the *Anglo-Saxon Chronicle*, which preferred him as he went, why should we feel ourselves a prey to ignorance and uncertainty?

The answer must be either very brief or very long, so I shall make it brief. We have during the last half-century very significantly changed our minds about the reliability of a great many written sources of information for medieval history. I judge it possible that in Great Britain we are still less than fully aware of the devastating examination of northern historical sources, not initiated but driven hard and deep by the brothers Curt and Lauritz Weibull in Sweden, and by Halvdan Koht in Norway, though we are reasonably well informed as to the parallel researches of the scholars of Iceland in respect of the sagas.[1] By now vast quantities of historical tradition, or perhaps we should say, unhistorical tradition have been excised from northern history and can never be reinstated. Obviously, archaeology and numismatics have made their valuable and distinctive contributions to our understanding of the Viking and pre-Viking ages of the north, but it is this reconsideration of the written sources which has most decisively affected our thinking. In a sentence, our confidence in saga and chronicle, poem and inscription, has been much diminished. Well-trusted

---

[1] L. Weibull's writings on northern history, the earliest of them published shortly before the First World War, have been brought together in *Nordisk Historia, Forskningar och undersökningar, I, Forntid och Vikingatid* (Stockholm, 1948). So with Curt Weibull, in *Källkritik och historia* (Stockholm, 1964). Koht forced much rethinking with his *Inhogg og utsyn i norsk historie* (Christiania, 1921). I am also much indebted to more recent writers, and notably to Bjarni Aðalbjarnarson, *Heimskringla, I* (Reykjavík, 1941).

narratives, long-cherished beliefs, familiar personages, and celebrated events have been re-examined, re-assessed, and not infrequently discarded. We place far less reliance than we did on the faithfulness of oral transmission, and are increasingly conscious of the limited or partisan aims of the writers of chronicles. In particular we have come to distrust the historicity of the sagas. In their day they have been seen as the sacred repositories of truth, but that was a long time ago. There was also a day when it seemed reasonable to trust to anything in a saga which could not be disproved, but nowadays even that won't do. Everything which is unsupported by independent evidence must be treated with extreme scepticism. And if it is supported by independent evidence, the value of that in its turn must be the subject of rigorous enquiry. Olaf Tryggvason died in the year 1000. Almost two hundred years were to pass before Odd Snorrason compiled a saga about him, and another forty before Snorri Sturluson did the same. This was a Yawning Gap indeed, and neither oral nor written tradition provides a bridge back to its farther shore.

And now my second preliminary. Olaf Tryggvason was from 995 to the year 1000 a king, and ruled over a kingdom. At first sight that kingdom was Norway, and thereafter Olaf Tryggvason was king of Norway. But was this really the case? How could he be king of Norway? For what was Norway in the years 995 to 1000?

Let us go back a little in time. Norway, as its name suggests (*Norðr-vegr, Nor-vegr*), was the North Way, or more specifically, it was the way north from Denmark and the rest of Europe, if your business or inclination took you in that direction. It was the way to the fisheries and whaling grounds of the Lofotens and the northern fjords, to the habitat of the Lapps who yielded a tribute of furs and hides, reindeer and down, and to the wealth of the Arctic-fronting Varangerfjord and the White Sea. For hundreds of years the Frisians had sailed up past Jutland and the Skagerrak, past the pirate breeding-grounds of the south-west provinces, Jaeren, Rogaland, Hordaland, and Sogn, and northwards still through the long leads of the west coast, protected as they are from the worst Atlantic weather by a strong fence of skerries and islands, and from the bite of ice by the Gulf Stream. Sixteen hundred miles of coast as the crow flies, this was the North Way, and except in the south there was very little except coast.

Today, inevitably, we think of Norway as a national unit, an entity both political and geographical. But in the remote times we are now speaking of it was nothing of the sort. In the sixth, seventh, and eighth centuries, it was an agglomeration of petty states, controlled by an assortment of kings, kinglings, jarls, and chieftains otherwise entitled. There were dozens, maybe scores, of these. But in the ninth and early tenth centuries Norway underwent appreciable change. Three regions grew particularly important: Vestfold with its neighbours in the Oslofjord; Vestland, the Viking south-west; and the Trondelag, the region centred on the Trondheimsfjord. The god-descended Ynglings, progeny of Yngi-Frey, lord of the Swedes and god of the World, became supreme in Vestfold and conquered the Vestland. The jarls of Hladir came down from their northern fastness by the Malangenfjord in latitude 69° north, and in time controlled the Trondelag. Both the Vestfold kings and the Trondelag jarls were forward-looking, energetic, and wealthy, and their wealth was based on farming and trade, as well as war. The turbulent seagoing aristocracy of the south-west was not much given to farming, because of a shortage of farming land; and they had elastic notions of trade, for they often found piracy more profitable. That they were well placed to prey on traffic up and down the Norwegian coast may well have brought a confusion into their ideas as to which of them was which. The goods had to pass their front doors—if we may so characterize the mouths of the fjords from Stavanger to Sogn. A toll was clearly in order—sometimes in the order of 100 per cent. Just as clearly it was in the interest of both Vestfold, south-east of them, and the Trondelag, north of them, to put an end to such harassment and loss. The decisive step was taken by Harald Fairhair shortly before 900, when he conquered parts of the Vestland and established a personal and admittedly loose-knit kingdom more extensive than anything Norway had known before. Harald Fairhair is often called by English historians king of Norway. In fact he was a king *in* Norway, and a remarkable one, whose achievement I have no wish to diminish or enshroud. But that achievement did not include the unification of Norway.

The point I am making about the nature of king and kingdom in Norway is of full relevance to Olaf Tryggvason. Harald Fairhair established a personal kingdom in Vestfold and its adjacent provinces, and in the Vestland. North of him the strong man was Jarl Sigurd of Hladir, lord of the Trondelag—a family with so good an opinion of itself that its head never demeaned himself with the title of king. North of the Trondelag was the long, narrow eel-stripe of Halogaland, where the Jarl's writ and war-arrow ran, and north of that the half-known region described by the Norwegian Ottar to his lord king Alfred as being *eal weste*, all empty, except where a few hunters dwelt, and fishers and fowlers, and they were all Lapps. Who was king in Vestfold was of little consequence up there. Then there was a second substantial region of Norway which kept very much to itself to the end of the Viking Age—the central provinces to the east, mountainous, isolated, conservative, sometimes with self-styled kings, sometimes farmer communities. But even when we have excised the Trondelag, the Lapp-haunted plateaux of Finnmark, and the surly independent eastern uplands from Harald's 'kingdom of Norway', we have still not told the whole of the story. The Danish kings had for centuries pressed their territorial claims in southern Norway, and at times ruled large areas there direct or by proxy.

In other words the Norwegian kingdom of Harald Fairhair, and in course of time that of Olaf Tryggvason, was not coextensive with what we now call Norway; it was not a nation, had no awareness of itself as a national unit, and had no national institutions. The kingdom of Olaf Tryggvason was that part of Norway which Olaf conquered and owned and failed to keep. It was a personal aggrandisement of territory and wealth, limited in scope, unstable in nature, and uncertain of duration. It was gained by sea-power, dependent on sea-power, and doomed without sea-power.

This said, we can at last approach our subject, the legendary history of Olaf Tryggvason. Properly, we begin at the beginning, with his birth and early years, but always we should be remembering that this is a man who will become one of the most famous Norwegians of all time, one of the most celebrated of Vikings, and the very pattern and sample of the heroic life and the still more heroic death.

Olaf's father Tryggvi was of the blood of Harald Fairhair and therefore divinely descended. He was a petty king down in the Vik, the Oslofjord. When Harald's son, Hakon the Good, won the fight for supremacy in Norway he confirmed Tryggvi in his privileges; but when Hakon was killed by his warlike nephews, the sons of Eirik Bloodaxe, Tryggvi's days were numbered. He was soon betrayed and killed, and his realm sequestrated. His wife Astrid like some fair distressed heroine of folk-tale, escaped the massacre and fled for safety to a small island in a lake where she gave birth to a son, in a year traditionally reckoned to be 968-9. The boy was named Olaf, after his grandfather, and this circumstance, together with the testimony of *Ágrip* that Olaf was three years old when his father was killed, casts doubt on Olaf's island-nativity. Astrid was most furiously pursued by another well-known but improbable northern lady, Gunnhild styled Mother of Kings, the widow of Eirik Bloodaxe; but she managed to get away, and with her infant son, her foster-father Thorolf Lousebeard, and a couple of her women she found various hiding places in eastern Norway and Sweden till the boy was three years old—if, so to speak, he was not three years old already. Astrid's brother Sigurd was a man of rank at the court of Valdimar 'king of Holmgard', Novgorod in Russia, that is, that Valdimar or Vladimir who achieved power at Novgorod in 972, and in 980 became Grand Duke (Great Prince) of Kiev and of all Russia. Astrid and her fellow-fugitives set off to find him, but as they sailed across the Baltic were captured by pirates from Esthonia, and sold into slavery. Olaf's price was a modest one: he went for half a goat. Thorolf Lousebeard they killed because he looked too old for work. Six years later Sigurd, in Esthonia on his royal master's business, saw a handsome young foreigner in a market place, enquired who he was, ransomed him, and took him back to Novgorod. Here he had the good fortune one day to recognize the man who had killed his foster-father, and promptly sank his hand-axe into the slaver's brain, a deed which secured him the brief displeasure of a populace inclined to fair trade and the lasting favour of a queen inclined to fair men. Snorri, relying on Odd, gives her name as Allogia, but Vladimir's household arrangements were almost as complicated as Solomon's. Anyhow, the story goes that Allogia and Sigurd brought Olaf into Vladimir's good books, he throve in all manly accomplishments, and was prominent in the king's battles. However the king's counsellors whispered in his ear that this gallant young foreigner was himself whispering into the queen's ear. 'Nor, for that matter, do we know what he and the queen are always talking about together.' It was enough, the king grew cool, the queen grew prudent, Olaf grew homesick for the north, and an impossible situation was resolved by Olaf's departure for the Baltic. Here he harried Bornholm and was storm-driven to Wendland, the Slav kingdom on the south Baltic coast, where he engaged the favourable attention of another royal lady, Geira the daughter of Burizlaf, better known as king Boleslav I of Poland. Chronology, never a strong point with the Icelandic synoptic historians, is by now all at sixes and sevens, and one could demonstrate that Olaf had now reached the age of 25, 18, or 6. But we should not press this last too hard, for he seems hereabouts to have married the princess Geira and set up in the world as an accomplished young brigand by land and water.

How much should we believe of his story so far? I am sure that we should not believe in his birth on an island during his mother's flight, which is folk-tale; his slavery and ransom, which is exemplum; his special relationship with a foreign queen, which is saga commonplace. We cannot believe in Allogia at all, for every circumstance recorded of her by Snorri Sturluson is incredible, her position, her authority, her independence, even her place of residence. The seat of Vladimir's power was at Kiev not Novgorod. But we can believe in his father's slaying, and that his mother and other kinsmen took him to Russia for safe-keeping. The origins of the ruling house there were Swedish, and the northern connection, though become tenuous, still held. Thus the three famed kings who achieved power in Norway after Olaf's time all sought refuge in Russia:

that other Olaf who in life was dubbed the Fat and in death the
Saint, Magnus the Good, and the great Harald Hardrada, the
'thunderbolt of the North', as Adam of Bremen called him,
victor at the Nissa and a loser at Stamford Bridge. Also, while
in Russia Olaf would not be sitting on his hands. By temperament, training, and obligation, for glory and reward, he would
be fighting in Vladimir's endless wars against Slavs, Poles,
Bulgars, and Petchenegs. Nor need we wonder that at last he
would be drawn back north. Saint Olaf, Magnus, and Harald
would experience the same compulsion. That he would live by
war and plunder was natural: what else would a king's son do?
But he assuredly did not marry a daughter of king Boleslav,
because it was Boleslav's father Miesco who ruled over the relevant areas of Wendland at this time; and as assuredly he took
no part, though Snorri assures that he did, in the emperor Otto
II's assault on the Danevirke and the Danish and Norwegian
forces that defended it. He may, of course, have fought in the
general area of southern Jutland on some other occasion. His
soldier-poet Hallfred Troublesomeskald tells us that he parted
various Danes from their battle-sarks south of Hedeby.

    Three years after their marriage, if there was a marriage, the
Princess Geira, if she was a princess, and if her name was Geira,
died, if she ever lived. Olaf sought to alleviate his private griefs
with public mischiefs, procured himself warships and raided, we
are told, in Frisia, then in Saxony, and even in Flanders, before
directing his attention to our own distraught and divided realm.
He began with Northumbria, went on to Scotland, where he
harried far and wide, fought battles in the Hebrides, reached
Man and Ireland, where he harried far and wide, went on to
Wales, where he harried far and wide, kept his hand in by
attacking Cumberland, and then proceeded to France, where
he harried, though not, apparently, far and wide. Snorri next
directs him to the Scillies, where he was converted to Christianity by a hermit in circumstances which would be less than
credible even had they not been lifted from a dialogue of Pope
Gregory concerning the revelations made to Totila king of the
Goths by the holy Benedict of Nurcia. Readers of the *Dialogues*
will remember that Totila sent a resplendent courtier in the

guise of a king to test Benedict, but the holy man was not
deceived. Nor was our own unnamed hermit in the Scillies. He
said to the retainer sent to him in royal guise: 'You are not the
king. The advice I give you is, be faithful to your king.'
Whereupon Olaf, like Totila before him, went in person to the
hermit, and asked him to prophesy, and in particular to tell him
whether he, Olaf, would ever win a kingdom or be comparably
fortunate. He would indeed win a kingdom, the hermit assured
him, and do famous deeds, and he would bring many men to
the true Faith. He gave Olaf an imminent token of truth,
whereupon he submitted to baptism with all his men.

Having provided Olaf with a faith out of Gregory the Great's
Dialogues, which they had almost certainly read, Odd Snorrason
and Snorri Sturluson now found him a wife out of the *Ocean of
Story*, and a dog out of the Stith-Thompson *Motif-Index of Folk
Literature* which they almost certainly had not. The wife was a
queen named Gyda, improbably identified as a sister of the
famous Irish-Norseman Olaf Kvaran, or Sandal, who held the
kingdom of Dublin lengthily, that of York intermittently, and
shortly after 980 died a straw-death in Christian Iona. So either
Olaf Kvaran had a very young sister or Olaf Tryggvason had
a very old bride. Gyda had married an English earl, he was
dead, and she was on the marriage market in a purposeful way.
She called a meeting of her prospective suitors, put them in line,
and walked around assessing what the latest translator of the
Heimskringla calls their 'manly deportment'. This was a commodity Olaf Tryggvason kept in good supply and steady repair.
The queen demanded, Who are you? and he gave his name as
Ola, and said he was a foreigner. 'If you would like to marry
me, then I will choose you,' said the queen. 'I'll not refuse that,'
said Olaf gallantly, and asked after her name and quality. He
made short work of a jealous champion, married Gyda, and they
lived part of the time in England and part in Ireland. Gyda
thereupon disappears from the written record for forty years.

It was in Ireland that Olaf acquired his dog. He was on an
unpeaceful outing, and made a raid ashore to secure provisions.
His men rounded up all the cattle in the neighbourhood and
drove them down to the ships. 'Then a farmer followed after

them and begged Olaf to let him have the cows he owned. Olaf told him to take his cows if he could recognize them. "But don't hold us up." The farmer had a big herd-dog with him. He pointed the dog into the herd of cows, and there were many hundreds of them being driven there. The dog went round the entire herd and drove out as many cows as the farmer said he owned, and they were all marked the one way. They could tell then that the dog must have known them for sure, and they thought the dog extraordinarily clever. Then Olaf asked if the farmer would give him the dog. "Gladly," said the farmer. Olaf at once gave him a gold ring in return. That dog was called Vigi, or Scrapper, and of all dogs he was the best. Olaf had him for a long time thereafter.'

Some years later when Olaf was spreading Christianity, death, and destruction up in Saltfjord, somewhat south of the Lofotens, the good dog Vigi was still with him. One of Olaf's most determined enemies was Thorir, nicknamed Hart, because of his fleetness. There was a sea-fight, Olaf won it, and Thorir got ashore and ran for his life, closely pursued by Olaf. 'He sighted Thorir Hart where he fled. Thorir was the fleetest of all men. The king ran after him, and Vigi his dog ran with him. Said the king, "Vigi, get the hart!" Vigi raced after Thorir and jumped him. Thorir stopped, and then the king hurled his spear at Thorir. Thorir thrust at the dog with his sword, and gave him a great wound, but that very instant the king's spear pierced Thorir under the arm, so that it came out the other side of him. Thorir lost his life there, and Vigi was carried wounded to the ship.'

Picturesque though this story is, it appears to be a rationalization by Snorri of something more picturesque still. This is what Odd Snorrason had made of it thirty or forty years earlier. As Thorir ran away, one of king Olaf's men sped a missile in between his shoulders, so that it came out from under his breast-bone, and he fell down. 'And at that moment a great hart went bounding furiously away from his body. And when the king's dog Vigi saw that, he ran after the hart and gave cruel chase. And when king Olaf saw what was happening he ran far up a-land after them ahead of his men. And he saw how they came together, the dog and the hart, and it was a hard encounter. The dog bit the hart, and the hart gored the dog, and it ended so that they both fell. Then the king came up and found the hart dead of his many wounds. The dog too was badly hurt below his shoulders.'

Snorri has no more to tell of Vigi, but Odd has. It may, however, be remitted to its proper place in Olaf's story, and that is after Olaf's death.

Clearly the Scandinavian recorders of Olaf's affairs in Britain, and more specifically in England, were little inconvenienced by a shortage of verifiable facts. But the *Anglo-Saxon Chronicle* is more prosaic. The Parker Chronicle (Ā) talks of Olaf being in England in 991; and that he was there in 994 is not to be doubted. There is no mention of Gyda and none of Vigi. Instead, in the Parker Chronicle, there is a mention of Olaf at the battle of Maldon. Curiously, Maldon passed unnoticed in northern verse and saga. Byrhtnoth's brave but foolhardy stand against overwhelming odds, his promise to glut the heathen host with spear and sword and hard battle-play instead of the gold they demanded, found no remembrancer among the victors— and few imitators among the vanquished. The Parker Chronicle under 993 *recte* 991 says this. 'In this year came Anlaf with ninety-three ships to Folkestone, and harried outside, and sailed thence to Sandwich, and thence to Ipswich, overrunning all the countryside, and so on to Maldon. Ealdorman Byrhtnoth came to meet them with his levies and fought them, but they slew the ealdorman there [this was 10 August] and had possession of the place of slaughter. Afterwards peace was made with them and the king stood sponsor for him [Olaf, that is] at confirmation: and this was done on the advice of Sigeric, archbishop of Canterbury, and Ælfeah, bishop of Winchester.' The other versions of the *Chronicle* do not mention Olaf. Instead they mention him under 994. 'In this year on the Nativity of St Mary [8 September] came Anlaf and Swegen [Olaf Tryggvason and Svein Forkbeard of Denmark] to London with ninety-four ships, and kept up an unceasing attack on the city, and they purposed moreover to set it on fire. But there, God be thanked, they came off worse than they ever thought possible; so they went away thence, doing as much harm as any host was capable of, in all kinds of ways wherever they went. Then the king and his councillors decided to offer them tribute: this was done and they accepted it, together with provisions which were given to them from the whole of the West Saxon kingdom, the sum amounting to sixteen thousand pounds. Then the king sent bishop Ælfeah and ealdorman Æthelweard to seek king Anlaf, hostages being sent meanwhile to the ships; and king Anlaf was conducted with great ceremony to the king at Andover. The king stood sponsor for him at confirmation, and gave him royal gifts; and Anlaf then promised, and also kept his word, that he would never come again to England with warlike intent.'

Finally, we have the text of a treaty concluded either after the Viking campaigns of 991, or in 994, between king Ethelred and Olaf Tryggvason and other Viking leaders.[1] It had something to say about mercantile and shipping practice, laid down rules for settling quarrels between Englishmen and Vikings, and draws a line under all past offences. Expectedly the first entry on the new page was that the English must pay 22,000 pounds of gold and silver for a peace.

In general then the northern historians waft Olaf into the blue empyrean of legend, while the *Anglo-Saxon Chronicle*, whether he was at Maldon or not, anchors him in the roadstead of history. And, not least, anchors him to two huge Danegelds. For his next exploit would require a lot of money. He was about to return home and win a kingdom in Norway.

We can sail a tide or two ahead of him and see what made this possible. We have noted the three main regions of geographical Norway at the beginning of the Viking Age: the area adjacent to Vestfold, the Viking heartland of the south-west, and the territories of the Trondelag jarls. For long years now the most important man in Norway had been one of these same jarls: Jarl Jakon of Hladir. His rule ran north from the modern Trondheim to beyond the Arctic Circle, and southwards to some undeterminable point in the Viking south-west. Elsewhere in the south, and particularly in the Oslofjord, the Danish king was

---

[1] It is to be found in Liebermann, *Die Gesetze der Angelsachsen* (1898 etc.), i. 220 ff.

the main incumbent. And the Danish king in 995 was Svein Forkbeard. In whose company Olaf Tryggvason had been campaigning in England in 994.

Jarl Hakon, of whom Snorri Sturluson presents a highly finished picture, is brought before us as a northern Machiavelli, a dangerous fighting-man, and a worshipper of Odinn and women. He cleared the Norwegian field of rivals, including those sons of Eirik Bloodaxe and Gunnhild Mother of Kings who had driven Olaf Tryggvason and his mother Astrid into exile. He had for a time been an ally of Harald Bluetooth of Denmark, even his vassal; but was skilful enough to extricate himself from the Danish bond, and usurped real as well as visible power in parts of Norway. He was an indomitable heathen, and for a long time the gods were good to him. They eased his early years by sending shoals of herrings everywhere along his coasts; they helped him win his naval battle with the Danes and Wends at Hjorungavag by directing into his enemies' faces a shower of hail so heavy that each hailstone weighed an ounce; but Odinn was a fickle deity and by 995 Hakon's luck had run out. *Heimskringla*'s explanation of this is both simple and naïve. The Jarl's appetite for women, by monkish reckoning always excessive, was now grown inordinate, which was bad, and discriminating, which was worse. His jarldom, we understand, was a-bristle with husbands sharpening their hatchets and fathers honing their spears. 'And now,' says Snorri, in his splendid way, 'things took an ill turn for the Jarl, in that a great leader arrived in the land just as the farmers fell out with him.'

This was Olaf Tryggvason, rich, successful, and popular, with his fleet of war-hardened veterans, and a complement of English-trained priests. Clearly, we must find a better explanation than Hakon's athletic lechery for the ease with which Olaf overthrew him. I imagine that this is accounted for by the hard facts of Norwegian tenth-century history. The rise of Olaf and the fall of Hakon was one more round in the long fight between the northern jarls and the Ynglings down south, and one more example of the constant will to independence of the Vestland and the Vik. Hakon received no help from any quarter against Olaf's bid for power. Even the Danes were his enemies. A second hard fact was that Olaf was a true Viking, whose strength lay in his fleet and crews, plus the money to pay them. With ships and control of the seaways a northern king had everything, and without them he had nothing. This is the true explanation of the otherwise bewildering reversals attendant upon the three northern kingdoms throughout the Viking Age.

Hakon appears to have been taken completely by surprise. Late sources record that Hakon and his thrall Kark sought refuge in Gaulardal with his mistress Thora of Rimul. A pit was dug in the farm pigsty, Hakon and his thrall Kark hid themselves therein, and muck and earth were spread to conceal the entrance. Olaf came to the farm, and made proclamation there that he would heap with wealth and honours any that wrought harm to Hakon. 'They heard this speech, the Jarl and Kark. They had a light with them. Said the Jarl: "Why are you so pale, and the next moment black as earth? Is it not the case that you wish to betray me?" "Not so," said Kark. "For we were born in the space of a night, we two," said the Jarl, "and there will be but a short while between our deaths." Towards evening Olaf took himself off. With the coming of night the Jarl forced himself to stay awake, but Kark slept—and slept horribly ill. The Jarl woke him up and asked him his dream. "I was but now in Hladir," said Kark, "where Olaf Tryggvason was laying a gold necklace round my neck." Said the Jarl: "Olaf will draw a blood-red ring round your neck there, if you encounter him. Watch out for yourself then! From me you will receive good, as has been the case hitherto. So do not betray me." After that they both stayed awake, as if each was keeping watch on the other; but towards day the Jarl fell asleep and was at once in grievous case, so much so that he drew in his heels and the nape of his neck under him, as though he would rear himself up, and cried out loudly and horribly. Kark was terrified, and out of his wits with fear. He drew a big knife from his belt, stuck it in the Jarl's throat, and cut it right across. That was the death of Jarl Hakon. Next Kark cut off the Jarl's head, burst out and away, to come later in the day to Hladir, where he presented the head to king Olaf. He gave him too this account of the wanderings of himself and the Jarl, as has already been written. Whereupon king Olaf had him led away and his head cut off.' Northern sources vary the details of this night of horror. Odd and *Ágrip* and the two Norwegian histories have Kark dream that Olaf promised him a great big horse, and in the event hanged him on Odinn's horse, the gallows. But I shall not deface Snorri's terrifying vignette with a cautionary notice, however well deserved. Hakon was out, and Olaf was in, and the Ynglings had taken over from the northern jarls.

Olaf would hold power for five years. But this was no golden age for Norway. Olaf was immediately caught up in the problems of his time and place. With some simplification we may distinguish these as the religious and the political problems. In 994 Olaf had accepted Christianity and an immense Danegeld. He was now a Christian king over a predominantly heathen kingdom, and this helped bring him to grief. Or so we think, for in fact we know hardly anything about him as a king in Norway. We are freely informed as to his handsome person, gallant spirit, physical strength, and bodily feats; his labours for Norway and achievements for the Faith are copiously expounded; and his changing fortunes have been brilliantly recorded. But primarily he is a legend, not a man.

Even in the matter of his Christianity there is a head-on clash between Adam of Bremen writing *c.*1070 (that is, only seventy years after Olaf's death) and the Icelandic historians who wrote roughly a century and a half thereafter. Adam, who had a grievance against Olaf because he preferred an English-flavoured Christianity to that dispensed by Hamburg-Bremen, has this to say: 'Some relate that Olaf had been a Christian, some that he had forsaken Christianity; all, however, affirm that he was skilled in divination, was an observer of the lots, and had placed all his hope in the prognostication of birds. Wherefore, also, did he receive a byname, so that he was called Craccaben (Crowbone). In fact, as they say, he was also given to the practice of the magic art and supported as his household companions all the magicians with whom that land was overrun, and, deceived by their error, perished.' Norwegian and Icelandic sources say the exact opposite, though Snorri describes a personal visit to Olaf by the one-eyed Odinn. He had travelled about the world and observed at first hand the dignity, wealth, and ceremonial of the Christian Church. He had noticed what strong support Church and King could lend each other. In any case the future belonged to the new Faith: heathendom was in decline, and for half a century a degree of Christianization had been taking place in the Oslofjord. The Trondelag, admittedly, was hardly affected, and the north and east of Norway stayed benighted. According to everyone except Adam of Bremen he now approached these recalcitrant regions with the Cross in one hand and the Sword in the other. Were he not by reputation ambidextrous, one might wonder which hand carried which, as he killed, maimed, drowned, burned, and tortured the length and breadth of his ungrateful realm. No doubt his Christian admirers exaggerated his zeal at home, as they inflated his achievements abroad. For in course of time he was given credit not only for the conversion of Norway (which is an exaggeration), but of the Shetlands and Faroes (about which little is known), Iceland (which is over-generous), and Greenland (which is wrong). But these curtailments still leave him a long way short of Adam's apostate-necromancer and picker-over of dead birds' bones.

The resentment felt by many at an enforced change of religion was reinforced by the strong separatism of Norway. The Trondelag never had any use for him; the Viking south-west stayed unfriendly and self-seeking; the inland provinces, where there were many still calling themselves kings, were inaccessible and uncooperative; and foreign influence was strong in the Oslofjord. Soon, in conformity with the unchanging realities of northern politics, three strong enemies were closing in on him. These were his former comrade-in-arms Svein Forkbeard of Denmark, covetous not only of the Danish-claimed provinces in the Oslofjord, but of as much more of Norway as he could get his hands on; Olaf Sköttkonung, Scat-king, of central Sweden, the first Swedish king named as king of the Gauts also, and greedy to develop realm and trade in a westward direction; and the dispossessed son of Jarl Hakon, the clever and valiant Jarl Eirik, well known in England later as an ally of Svein and his son Knut. Olaf stood alone, and had to find allies.

But where? This had been Jarl Hakon's problem, and Harald Greycloak's, and Eirik Bloodaxe's before them. Overwhelming strength could convert to irremediable weakness in a bewilderingly short time. With a kingdom which a little over-picturesquely may be described as coast, more coast, and all coast, Olaf now presented the classic northern picture of impending catastrophe: he was a sea-king without sea-power. He had lost the means of attack, defence, and control. In this desperate plight he looked south to Wendland, and in particular to king Boleslav of the Poles.

By now, we are told, he had married again. His wife was Thyri, sister of king Svein Forkbeard of Denmark. He had earlier gone courting a lady who according to some of the sources later became king Svein's wife. Her name was Sigrid, and she was nicknamed the Haughty. In mid course, so to speak, Olaf changed his mind, and slapped her face on the curious afterthought: 'And why should I want to marry you, you heathen bitch?' A good question—and Sigrid had a good answer. It is a pity that the episode is a fiction, and Sigrid almost certainly another. Some time later Snorri lets him marry Gudrun, the daughter of an obdurate heathen named Jarnskeggi, whom he had had killed up in the Trondelag. We need not, I judge, take Gudrun too seriously. She is a Judith, a Rosamund, who on their marriage night drew a knife on the sleeping king and aimed to avenge her father. Olaf got off without a scratch, and necessarily without a wife, and we move forward again to king Svein's sister Thyri. This was a lady all too well versed in the pains and vicissitudes of the married state. After the death of her first husband Styrbjorn the Strong, who died invading Sweden (if we can trust to some rather perilous sources), she had been married off in a dynastic way to our friend Boleslav the Pole, king of Wendland, whom she detested, first because he was a heathen and second because he was old. In her distress she fled to Norway and married Olaf Tryggvason who was neither. According to Snorri Sturluson, the purpose of Olaf Tryggvason's visit to Boleslav was to recover Thyri's dowry; and this may be the place to offer two observations on Snorri himself. He was a greedy and acquisitive man, and to recover a recoverable dowry would be second nature to him. Second, while in life he was understandably fond of complaisant and yielding women, in literature he loved to portray them masterful, and lordly: Gunnhild Mother of Kings, Sigrid the Haughty, and Thyri among them. So not only should we now be wary of the events he describes but also of their motivation.

It is altogether more likely that Olaf was seeking an ally. Thietmar of Merseburg speaks of bad feeling between Boleslav and Svein, and this might well be the case; Adam of Bremen suggests that Svein had acute problems *vis-à-vis* the Baltic Vikings, but much of what Adam says about Svein is propagandist nonsense; if we believe in the Jomsborg Vikings we might believe that Olaf would find swords for sale in their ranks, but why should we believe in a fiction?; and as for Snorri's narrative, Lauritz Weibull has reduced this part of *Heimskringla* to ruins. We shall probably do best to believe in little save the reality of sea-power and the dire consequences of losing it.

We can, I think, be sure that Olaf left Norway and sailed south. According to *Heimskringla*, he sailed with sixty ships, including the famed *Long Serpent*, crossed the Kattegat, then entered the Øresund, passed the island of Hven, and with the low green shores of Zealand and Skåne temptingly in view held south for the opening Baltic, and came by way of the island of Rügen to the mouth of the Oder. He completed his business with Boleslav, and set off on his way home. His allies betrayed him, and with a handful of ships he sailed into an ambush laid by the kings of Denmark and Sweden and Jarl Eirik of Norway off the island of Svold by Rügen. Scorning flight, though flight was possible, he sailed straight at his enemies, furiously engaged them, and fought to the end against overwhelming odds, when, to avoid the humiliation of capture, he leapt overboard in his gold helm and scarlet cloak, and so vanished from the sight of men. But Adam of Bremen has a different tale to tell. According to him, Olaf Tryggvason heard that the kings of Denmark and Sweden had formed an alliance to propagate Christianity in many realms. Of Jarl Eirik there is no mention whatsoever, and in the battle itself no mention of Swedes. Olaf's ready anger was fomented by his wife Thyri, he assembled a fleet with which to chastise the Danes, and sailed down into the Øresund. There, just south of today's Danish Helsingør and Swedish Hälsingborg, 'where Zealand is in sight from Skåne', he was attacked and routed by the Danes. Olaf, who was almost the only survivor, threw himself into the sea, 'and met the death his life deserved'. In other words, Adam was as concerned to denigrate Olaf as Snorri to glorify him. His praise was for the Danes, exclusively, and Snorri's for the Norwegians. Which is a well-tried way of writing history.

Into further detail I have no time to enter. Olaf Tryggvason died heroically, a glorious Christian king, or he died like a rat in a well, a ruffianly backslider. He died at Svold, an island or a river, in the Øresund or off Rügen. He was on his way south or north, and was fighting the Danes alone or a confederacy of Danes, Swedes, and Norwegians. He had eleven, seventeen, sixty, or seventy-one ships—and whichever he had, he had too few. He was betrayed or just deserted.

Fortunately, my subject is the legendary history of Olaf Tryggvason, and in respect of Svold what I should now do is pay my compliments to Odd Snorrason, who is responsible for so much of its detail, and to Snorri Sturluson, for his brilliantly compulsive set-piece on the theme of a beleaguered hero's death. His account of Svold is a masterpiece, and its devaluation as history gives it new currency as literature. It is fascinating to see what he does with his material. Thus the long-sustained crescendo of interest and suspense as the two kings and Jarl Eirik stand on their island and watch ship after ship of Olaf's come into sight, and the kings think each one is Olaf's famed (and I am afraid legendary) *Long Serpent* till Jarl Eirik identifies it differently, was taken immediately from Odd Snorrason and ultimately from the late ninth-century *De Gestis Karoli Magni* of the Monk of St Gall, who tells how Desiderius king of the Langobards stood with Otkar on a high tower in Pavia, watching the approach of Charlemagne's army, thought each newcomer the emperor, and was rhetorically corrected by Otkar. Likewise, Olaf resorts to a well-tried device of epic and saga to establish the identity of his adversaries, the cowardly Danes in the centre, the bowl-licking heathen Swedes on their right, and the valiant Norwegians under Jarl Eirik in the big ships to port: 'We can expect a sharp clash with that force. They are Norwegians like us.' And the most famous incident of all, Olaf's dialogue with his archer Einar Thambarskelfir, belongs not to history, but with similar laconicisms to heroic convention. Olaf had beaten off the Danes, and was not over-troubled by the Swedes, but the battle went ill as Eirik and his Norwegians cleared ship after ship till only the *Long Serpent* maintained the fight.

'Einar Thambarskelfir was on the *Serpent*, in the third compartment from the stern. He shot with his bow, and was the strongest bowman alive. Einar shot at Jarl Eirik and hit the top piece of the rudder above the Jarl's head, penetrating it to where the arrowhead was bound to its shaft. The Jarl looked at it and asked if they knew who shot it; that same moment there came another, so close to the Jarl that it whipped between his side and his arm, and so into the headboard till its point came clear out on the far side. Then the Jarl commanded a man whom some call Finn, but some say was a Finn—he was a fine bowman: 'Shoot that big man in the compartment aft.' Finn shot, and the arrow struck the middle of Einar's bow just as he was drawing it the third time. The bow broke in two. Said king Olaf: 'What broke there so loudly?' Einar answered: 'Norway from your hand, king.' 'Not such a big break as that,' said the king. 'Take my bow and shoot with that'—and flung the bow to him. Einar took the bow, and promptly overdrew the head of the arrow, and said: 'Too weak, too weak, the great lord's bow'—and flung the bow back, took up his shield and sword, and fought.'

Einar came by his nickname Thambarskelfir late, and there are few sadder discards in the legendary history of Olaf Tryggvason than to learn that it has nothing to do with *þömb*, a bowstring, but derives from a word of the same spelling meaning a fat and wobbly belly. It follows that he was not Einar Bowstring-shaker, so named for his feats of archery at Svold; but Einar Wobble-guts, for reasons unknown and best left that way.

So in a welter of blood and legend Olaf Tryggvason leapt from the *Long Serpent*'s gunwale and perished. Not that the legends were over. He was a mighty swimmer, and there were tales that he shed his mail-shirt and was borne ashore by a Wendish ship. Thereafter he was seen in many lands, the Holy Land among them, but Snorri, though he swallowed much, could not swallow this. 'Be that as it may,' he concluded, in one of the few sentences in the entire *Heimskringla* which has escaped the correction of his critics, 'king Olaf never again returned to his kingdom in Norway.'

And Thyri his widow? What of her? She died, says the *Historia Norwegiae*, of an immoderate grief at her husband's death. That unpleasant man Adam of Bremen sees it otherwise. 'After the death of her husband, his wife spent her life miserably, in hunger and want, as she deserved.'

And Vigi the good Scrapper? What of him? Sources older than Snorri, and Odd Snorrason in particular, keep track of him to the end. 'Listen, Vigi,' a faithful retainer tells him, 'we are lordless now.' The dog cried out sharply, went up on to a mound, where he laid himself down and neither ate nor drank till he died. A sad end, but at least he was spared any comment by Adam.

With the death of Vigi the legendary history of Olaf is at an end—but for one thing. We may be pardoned by now for forgetting that Olaf ever married, or was later thought to have married, a lady named Gyda, Olaf Kvaran's improbable sister. Time went by, thirty-three years of it, and the Norwegian realm was as unstable as ever. Its rulers now were Svein son of Knut and Knut's well-beloved and well-cared-for consort Ælgifu of Northampton. It was an arrangement which would not last long. Soon Magnus the son of St Olaf would be on his way home from Russia, and from England there was sailing one more fleet-enabled venturer to try for a high-seat in Norway. His name was Tryggvi, and he described himself as the son of Olaf Tryggvason and Gyda. He sounds very much a creature of folk-tale, but is also described as an impostor and son of a priest. Olaf, we have said, was ambidextrous. So was Tryggvi. In the battle which proved fatal to his hopes he hurled spears with both hands at once, shouting: 'Thus my father taught me to say Mass!' Then, having provided us with a suitably bizarre colophon to Olaf's story, he was killed. And when some time after 1050 Harald

Hard-Counsel made fat Einar kiss the thin lips of the axe, none was left who had known Olaf Tryggvason the man, and if they had not already done so, the legend-makers were free to take over. And take over they did for almost a thousand years, so that only now is their work, which has troubled a handful of historians and brought delight to untold thousands of readers, being ruthlessly and for my part regretfully undone.

⚜11⚜

The Viking World

I

WITH your permission, and maybe to your surprise, I shall start my brief discourse on the Viking World not back in the Viking Age, but a thousand years after its termination, and not in Scandinavia (where I ought to start) but in the Western Isles of Scotland, where a certain Captain Sandford, a severely wounded soldier, was doing a little fishing to get away from it all. With the Army's permission he was in civvies. An old boatman, of little conversation and even less curiosity, used to row him out on the loch. But one day the old fellow asked him a strange question. 'Tell me, sorr, is it true what they are saying in these parrts, that there's a warr on?' This epochal inquiry can be dated to the last week of August 1943. Captain Sandford eased his left leg. 'Yes, it's true: there is a war on.' A long silence. Then: 'Ah weel, sorr, I suppose it'll be those bloody Danes again.'

That my story is not just an unrelated joke will, I hope, become clear if I now quote in its entirety the entry in the *Anglo-Saxon Chronicle* for the year 789—almost exactly twelve hundred years ago. Thus: 'In this year Beorhtric [king of the West Saxons] took to wife Eadburh, daughter of king Offa. And in his days came for the first time three ships of the Norwegians from Hördaland; and then the reeve rode thither and tried to compel them to go to the royal manor, for he did not know what they were; and then they killed him. These were the first ships of the Danes to come to England.'

Delivered with the appropriate adjustments before the 'Norse of the North Atlantic Conference' at Bowdoin College, Maine, in April 1988; thereafter to a Norse Studies audience in Reykjavík in July of the same year; and to the Anglo-Saxon, Norse, and Celtic School in the University of Cambridge in 1989. This is the Cambridge version.

Danes or Norwegians (and the *Chronicle* often makes no distinction between them), these newcomers to England are among the most significant of all Vikings. The reeve evidently thought they were traders come within the jurisdiction of Dorchester, but their deed was the deed of lawless piratical men, and a presage of the entry for 793 which records how 'the harrying of the heathen miserably destroyed God's church in Lindisfarne with rapine and slaughter'.

Whatever is impressive enough to become embedded in the folk-tale memory deserves our close attention and study. So with those bloody Danes and the Norwegians with whom in the British Isles, Ireland, and western Europe they were so endlessly confused. The Swedes took their differing paths east and southeast, but to the peoples they so mistreated they were all the same scourge and affliction out of the North. No wonder that their northern heyday would become known as the Viking Age, and their exploits abroad as the Viking Movement.

The Viking Age is the name bestowed by modern historians on the three centuries which start rather indeterminately almost anywhere between the years 760 and 780, and close according to one's sense of propriety and drama, and no doubt one's nationality too, anywhere between the death of Harald Hardrada in battle at Stamford Bridge in 1066 and the murder of the second Knud or Canute in church at Odense in Denmark in 1086. Throughout this substantial period of time the peoples to whom the name 'Viking' is generally applied, that is, the peoples we now know as Danes, Swedes, and Norwegians, were hammering out the rough shape and texture of the kingdoms we now know as Denmark, Sweden, and Norway; making a powerful and often brutal impact on their European neighbours; and essaying trade and colonization not only within a reasonable distance of home, but southwards to the river-mouths of Spain and *c.*860 to the Central Mediterranean (this last a particularly hideous interlude of outrage and destruction); eastwards as far as the Volga and Caspian; and west to the Atlantic Isles, Iceland, Greenland, and the eastern shores of North America. In every sense of the word, literal and metaphorical, theirs was a tremendous story.

But why the name 'Viking'? Our modern noun and adjective we have taken from two Old Norse words, *víking*, which means piracy or a pirate raid, as in *fara í víking*, to go viking, to make a raid for gain and plunder; and *víkingr*, one who goes on such raids. This association with piracy makes it something of a misnomer to call an entire period of Scandinavian history and culture 'The Viking Age', but it has proved too convenient and is by now too well established to be abandoned. And no one has effectively demurred at the title 'Viking Movement' to cover Danish, Swedish, and Norwegian activity outside Scandinavia.

The start of that activity in England we have already noted, and marked too the *Anglo-Saxon Chronicle*'s gasp of outrage at its murderous nature. An equal consternation was registered by Alcuin, then resident at Charlemagne's court. And these were but the prelude to a symphony of complaint and indignation that tells of Viking misdeeds in Frisia, the Western Kingdom of the Franks, and the divided realms of England and Ireland. I would illustrate all this, were it not that we have had Professor Page's lecture on Early English Historians on the Vikings, which says it all. Let the bare title suffice: 'A Most Vile People'. *Plebs spurcissima.*

But to demonstrate, or illustrate, the Viking presence in Western Europe and the British Isles is no part of our programme tonight, for it is altogether more germane to our purpose to explore the Viking Movement overseas to more distant regions in less violent guises. For throughout the Viking Age the Scandinavians were notably active in the east and west. In the East it was the Swedes who won fame and profit; in the West it was chiefly the Norwegians. The Swedish acquaintance with the lands and peoples east of the Baltic is early if vaguely attested. Their progress into Gotland and along the south Baltic coast was the prologue to their entry into Russia not later than the 830s. The earliest significant archaeological evidence for their presence there comes from the southern end of Lake Ladoga, where they seem to have persisted from the ninth to the eleventh century. These Swedes were not settlers in the sense that they farmed or cultivated the land. Rather they were merchants, which in their day and condition meant they were soldiers—I had almost said *pirates*—too.

From Staraya Ladoga they would make their way past Novgorod to Smolensk, and so down the Dnieper to Kiev, and thereafter the whole way to the Black Sea. From Lake Onega they sought trade in Rostov and Murom, names unexpectedly familiar to us from the Second World War. Other waterways bore them to the important mart of Bulgar on the Volga Bend, where in the company of an observant Arab we are about to make their acquaintance—and beyond Bulgar to the Caspian Sea. From the Black Sea they would be constant visitors to Byzantium, a city with maybe as many inhabitants as the three Scandinavian countries put together. From Bulgar they had contacts with the silks and spices of India and China. From the Muslims everywhere they acquired the great bulk of the tens of thousands of silver coins which arrived in the North before 970–80, and the raw material of much silver ornamentation. The importance of the Swedish (Rus) contribution to the development of the Russian state and empire to which it gave its name can be easily exaggerated, but is not on that account to be doubted. That a small Viking élite would eventually be submerged in a predominantly Slav environment was to be expected. It was, after all, *pari passu*, the course of events in England, Ireland, and France too. The Vikings, for all their fearsome individualism, were assimilable.

But it is time to meet our observant Arab. He is none other than Ibn Fadlan, author of the *Risala*, who during the years 921–2 served as secretary from the Khalif of Baghdad to the Bulgars of the Middle Volga. At their camp and trading-post he met the Rus or Swedish traders who brought their wares to market there. Among these wares would be sables and foxes; arrows and swords; wax, honey, amber, and fish-lime; goatskins, horse-hides, hawks, and acorns; cattle, horses, and— hateful to add—an unhappy convoy of Slavonic slaves.

'I have seen the Rus as they came on their merchant journeys and encamped by the river Volga. I have never seen more perfectly made human beings, tall as date palms, blond and ruddy. They wear neither tunics nor caftans, but the men wear a cloak flung back over the shoulder, leaving an arm free. Each man has an axe, a sword, and a knife, and keeps them with him at all times . . .' From their sexual and sanitary habits our polite Arab thought them as filthy as donkeys. But prudential. Thus 'The Rus prostrates himself before a big carving with a face like a man's, and says: "O my lord, I have come from a far land, and have with me such and such a number of girls, and such and such a number of sables", and so on. Then he says, "I have brought you these gifts", and lays down what he has brought with him, and continues, "I wish you would send me a merchant with many dinars and dirhems, who will buy from me whatever I wish, and won't get haggling over things with me." '

With that familiar sentiment sounding in our ears, we leave the eastern arc of the Viking Movement. Now, clearly, it is time to call in the New World to redress the balance of the Old. We shall do this, succinctly, with a paragraph from the *Íslendingabók*, or 'Book of the Icelanders', of the so-called Father of Icelandic History, the revered Ari Thorgilsson, attempting in the 1120s a condensed sketch of his country's discovery, settlement, colonization, and early history. The passage in question is part of his sixth section: 'Of the Settlement of Greenland'.

'The land which is called Greenland was discovered and settled from Iceland. Eirik the Red was the name of a Breidarfjord man who went out there from here, and took land in settlement at the place which has ever since been called Eiriksfjord. He gave the land a name and called it Greenland, arguing that men would be drawn to go there if the land had a good name. Both east and west in the country they found the habitations of men, fragments of boats(?), and stone artefacts, from which it may be seen that the same kind of people had passed that way as those that inhabited Vinland, whom the Greenlanders call Skraelings. When he began to settle the land, that was fourteen or fifteen years before Christianity was introduced into Iceland [which means 985 or 986].'

II

So much for our pocket-guide to the Viking World at the time of the Norse Atlantic voyages, with its sketchy illustrations of the Danish and Norwegian irruption into a disunited England and Ireland, the Norse rampage through the dismembered Western Kingdom of the Franks, and the Swedish political and trading progress along the great Russian rivers, and their making contact with the Greek and Muslim worlds. Our next concern is with the Atlantic Voyages themselves, and for these I propose to start with a flourish which sets pride above modesty, and truth above both. For we are most assuredly not assembled here together to count the small change of history. The sequence of voyages across the North Atlantic Ocean which carried the Norsemen, or Vikings, from their Scandinavian homelands by way of the British Isles and the Faeroes to the discovery of Iceland by 860–70, to south-west Greenland *c*.986, and to the discovery and attempted colonization of some part of the east coast of North America about the millennial year AD 1000, was of immediate and practical consequence to the peoples of Scandinavia, of major though at the time unrealized significance to the course of European history, and as we now know, a meridian point in the history of mankind.

But before we discuss the voyages themselves we must dispose, however briefly, of (as I see it) three helpful preliminaries. The first of these is that important events can usually be traced back to compelling causes. Sure enough, this is the case with the Atlantic voyages, as with the Viking Movement overseas in general. A number of needs, pressures, and desires had to come together at the right time: political compulsions and economic dissatisfactions, personal ambitions, and our human desire for the good things of life. By the second half of the eighth century all three Scandinavian peoples were in search of betterment by means of trade and piracy, the seizure of goods and territory in wealthier lands, and the discovery of new and undefended pastures, hunting-grounds, and fisheries. Land-shortage played its part, especially in south-west Norway by *c*.800. The Viking lands are in the north of Europe. Their physical axis lies north-east by south-west; but in terms of human geography it lies north-south, with most of the fertile and level areas in the south. The northern half of the peninsula is largely mountainous, often inhospitable, and cold. Distances are formidable. The coastline of Norway, not counting its well-nigh countless indentations, is sixteen hundred miles long—and if that leaves an American or Canadian unmoved, it astounds me in small Great Britain, and stuns me in tiny Wales.

The retardive effect of high latitude, long winters, severing distances, and a barriered landscape upon the emergence and development of the northern kingdoms and their society was considerable. Harsh mountains, dense forests, and sundering waterways ensured the persistence of the old enclosed farmer communities and the Viking aristocracy, blest with estates, privileges, weapons of war and too many clamant sons, and stiff-necked in its pride. The felt shortage of cultivable land, the search for tribute, and the never-ending need for fighting men to defend one's own goods and rights and usurp those of other people were powerfully contributory to the strife-torn internal and external history of the Viking Age. As was its tripartite social system of rulers, free-born men, and slaves. While the Norse gods and the heroic poets did little for the cause of peaceful living. So for many, 'Out they must!', and for Norwegians the outlets lay west, within the 500 km belt of ocean *c*.58°–63° N, which gave access to the Orkneys, Shetlands, and Faeroes, Iceland, south-west Greenland, and the North American coast from southern Baffin Island to northern Newfoundland.

Second comes our recognition that whatever the compulsions the Scandinavians could not undertake transatlantic voyages until they had the right kind of ship or ships to do so. It is by now generally agreed that the Gokstad ship, so proudly on display in the Ship Hall in Oslo, is a true representative of the vessels that carried the first Viking raiders to the British Isles *c*.790 and made possible the voyages to the Faeroes *c*.825 and to Iceland *c*.860–70. She could transport 30–35 men, and though furnished with 16 pairs of oars was essentially a sailing ship, with a tall mast of *c*.55 ft., and a big square sail. Her overall dimensions were 76½ × 17½ ft. Modern replicas have amply confirmed her notable reputation for performance at sea. A later development was the true ocean-farer, the ship of all work, the *hafskip* or *knörr*, whose best exemplar is Wreck One in the Roskilde Ship Museum, her dimensions 54 × 15 ft. with an open carrying-space or hold amidships estimated to carry a cargo of 15–20 tons. It was her like, we think, which eventually maintained the Norway–Iceland–Greenland routes. With her good design, sound construction, tractable sail, ready steering, and shallow draught, this northern type clinker-built, double-ended keel boat could carry her cargo to all marts, and put it safely ashore.

And now, third, what can be said of the world, that only part-realized geographical entity within whose bounds the Atlantic voyages took place? What of the Viking world-picture? We are at once confronted by practice and theory, by tested knowledge, reasonably conceived misconceptions, and a fascinating hang-over of heathen mythology, classical learning, Dark Age encyclopaedics, and, in time for the sagas, biblical reminiscence and Christian colouring. From these we learn that the world was round, and either flat or saucer-shaped. The Viking world-picture was of an Inner Sea (the North Atlantic and its contiguous waters) enclosed within a 'land-ring' or 'land-bridge' extending from east of the White Sea over and above Scandinavia westward to Greenland whence it continued southward until (and we are by now around the year 1200)— until it reached Africa, a well-attested place brooking no contradiction. Where else *could* it go? For outside the land-ring lay the mythical Mare Oceanum, equated with Ginnungagap, the Phantasmal Void, utterly inimical to human life as we know it. In the then state of knowledge the land-ring was not only a reasonable belief: it was a comforting one. It completed the totality of Earth, and supplied the navigator with a framework. Wherever he touched the land-ring he could turn round and hope to make his way back. Whether his hope was realized, that is another matter. But the northern mariner had two things on his side: he confined his ocean voyages to the summer season, with its milder weather and enhanced hours of daylight, and his Age of Discovery fell within the Climatic Optimum of *c*.800–1200. Even so, in northern latitudes the beds of roses and bowers of bliss were few and far between.

This is a very brief summary of a very complicated subject, and I would like to add two simple illustrations—if they *are* simple—of the mixture of sober truth and learned fantasy in the geographical record. The first relates to that admirable Norwegian Ottar, better known to students of Anglo-Saxon as Ohthere—a man who in his own words 'dwelt farthest north of all Norwegians', and came to King Alfred's court towards the end of the ninth century and substantially extended his knowledge of both the physical and the human geography of the North. On a given occasion, Ohthere tells us, he decided to find out how far Norway extended to the north. For three days he sailed due north and reached the northern limit of the walrus-hunt. He was now facing Terra Incognita, but kept going and after a second three days reached what we now know as the North Cape. Here the sea veered due east, or the sea in on the land, he knew not which. Here he waited for a wind from the west and a little from the north and in four days' sailing reached what we now know as the White Sea. Here he waited for a wind from the north and with it sailed south for five days, and so reached the entrance to what we now know as Kandalaks Bay. He gives us a sober account of his own farming and hunting economy, and that of his Lapp neighbours. In short, this admirable man sets himself, and us, firmly on the map. No lies, no inventions, just the facts. Would that there were more like him!

Second, let us spare a minute or two for the *einfætingr*, the uniped, the one-legged quasi-inhabitant of Vinland-America. It was a uniped, you will remember, who hopped down to take a closer look at the Norse explorers, shot a fatal arrow into Thorvald Eiriksson the Greenlander, and then hopped off to safety. Inevitably there have been many attempts to explain away or rationalize this curious creature. He was an Eskimo dancing on one foot; he was a genuine one-legged American Indian; while to Professor Howlett of the Newfoundland Archaelogical Survey (I quote): 'This uniped was undoubtedly an Eskimo woman of short stature; and dressed in the conventional Eskimo woman's attire with a long tail coat, she would undoubtedly look to the men who chased her as if she had only one leg.' Ah, lucky Professor Howlett! For my own part I have lived a very sheltered life and never chased a short Eskimo woman dressed in her long tail coat, so my opinion is completely useless. And in any case, in my opinion, there is no need to see our uniped as anything save a uniped. Icelandic scholars, *fræðimenn* like Hauk Erlendsson, were well-informed and highly intelligent men. They knew that Vinland-America was a northward extension of Africa, and they knew on the authority of such encyclopaedists as the seventh-century Isidore of Seville that there were unipeds in Africa—so why not in Vinland too? As Mark Twain said of History: 'Many great historical events did not take place as they are said to have taken place. Most great historical events did not take place at all. It is the business of the serious historian to repair these omissions.' And so with Geography. It was a wise old bird, admittedly mistaken, who supplied *Eiríks Saga Rauða* with its missing uniped, and who among today's wise old birds will cast the first stone?

And so at last—at long last, some of you may be thinking—we come to the voyages themselves—the voyages which brought the Island Countries of the North into the Known World of Men. A very early sailor in northern waters was Pytheas the Massalote who pressed on north of Britain in the third century BC, went ashore somewhere, but certainly not in Iceland. We must dismiss too the skimpy case for a Roman presence in the third century AD. But it is quite otherwise with the Irish claim, for Irish *peregrini*, or pilgrims, better described as hermits or anchorites, who in their search for a solitude to be shared only with their God, rounded in their wicker-and-hide curraghs the north of Scotland, and in due succession discovered the Orkneys, Shetlands, and in the 720s and 200 miles further on reached the Faeroes, Faeringjar, or Sheep Islands. And from the Faeroes, 240 miles over the gulf of ocean they came to Iceland.

Our authority here is the Irish monk Dicuil, in his work *Liber de Mensura Orbis Terræ*, written *c*.823. Here is his witness with regard to the Faeroes:

There are many other islands in the ocean to the north of Britain which can be reached from the northernmost British Isles in two days' and

nights' direct sailing, with full sails and an undropping fair wind . . .
On these islands hermits who have sailed from our Scotia [i.e. Ireland]
have lived for roughly a hundred years. But, even as they have been
constantly uninhabited since the world's beginning, so now, because
of Norse pirates, they are empty of anchorites, but full of innumerable
sheep and a great many kinds of seafowl. I have never found these
islands mentioned in the books of scholars.

Here you may well feel is where our narrative, as opposed to
our exposition, begins. For here are the Norsemen, the Vikings,
pirates and robbers to boot, with their feet set firmly on their
first Atlantic stepping-stone. The first settler and dispossessor
is said elsewhere to have been a Norwegian chieftain with the
Norse name Grim (*Grímr*), and the Irish nickname Kamban
(*camm*, bent or crooked, or maybe Bandy Grim), and we think
he got there by way of Ireland or the Hebrides. Certainly we
think he got there by virtue of the intelligence he had gathered
about the voyages and whereabouts of the *peregrini*.
Of Iceland, which not unnaturally he calls Thule, he has
equally crisp news:

It is now thirty years since priests (*clerici*) who lived on that island from
the first day of February to the first day of August told me that not only
at the summer solstice, but in the days on either side of it, the setting
sun hides itself at the evening hour as if behind a little hill, so that no
darkness occurs during that very brief period of time, but whatever task
a man wishes to perform, even to picking the lice out of his shirt, he
can manage it precisely as in broad daylight. And had they been on
a high mountain, the sun would at no time have been hidden from
them . . .

Dicuil then goes on to correct those who aver that Iceland's
year consists of a six-months' night followed by a six-months'
day. And echoing Pytheas and Strabo on Thule, he says that one
day's sail to the north you will find the frozen sea.
At this point, with Dicuil's avouchment of the presence of
Irish priests domiciled in Iceland since roughly the beginning
of the ninth century, we leave the Irish evidence, and turn
to Northern sources. Of these the most important are Ari
Thorgilsson's *Íslendingabók*, 'The Book of the Icelanders', written in the 1120s, and *Landnámabók*, 'The Book of the Settle-

ments', as it is preserved in the thirteenth-century version of the Icelandic historian, Sturla Thordarson. Both record that there were Irish *papar* dwelling in south-eastern Iceland when the Norsemen arrived, but that 'later they went away', and the whole land was occupied by men and women of Norse or sometimes part-Norse descent.

A resumé then of our progress so far: Iceland, like the Faeroes, was discovered, or rediscovered, by the holy men of Ireland. This information was readily available to the Vikings who irrupted into the Celtic countries towards the end of the eighth century; and in the light of it they dispossessed them of both island-refuges. This happened in respect of Iceland *c.*860–70, and might well have happened earlier but for the lure of easy gain which drew large numbers of Vikings to the British Isles and western Europe after 830.

To Icelandic eyes 250 years later things looked a little different. This is what 'The Book of the Icelanders' has to say:

A Norwegian named Ingolf is the man of whom it is reliably reported that he was the first to leave there for Iceland, when Harald Fairhair was sixteen years old, and a second time a few years later. He settled south in Reykjavik . . . .

The discovery Ari mentions not at all, and the rest of the Settlement, including the *papar*, he disposes of in some 200 words. By way of compensation 'The Book of the Settlements' has no fewer than three discoverers, all of them different, in its several redactions, in addition to the good Ingolf and *his* additional foster-brother Hjorleif. The result is a proliferation of motifs and happenings: storm-driven mariners, tow-parted castaways; three voyages, three land-namings, Gardarsholm, Snowland, Iceland (*Ísland*); three hallowed ravens, true love triumphant, murder most foul; supernatural intrusions, onomastic inventions—in brief, the all-too-familiar apparatus of saga, folk-tale, and romance, where we start with recognition, proceed to caution, and arrive at a tolerant and moderately regretful disbelief. We shall encounter similar problems when we come to consider Greenland and Vinland. Still, whatever we conclude about the reliability of this or that piece of the written

sources that tell of Iceland *and* Greenland—whatever person
converts from history to legend, and whatever event from fact
to fiction—the histories of both are well charted, and confirmed
by an abundant and eloquent archaeological witness. The
Greenland colonies were to survive for five centuries, and after
eleven hundred years the Icelanders still hold their ancient
patrimony.

Despite the *papar* found in the south-east of Iceland, and
despite the presence of Celtic slaves and concubines brought in
during the first hundred and fifty years in particular, and despite
the honourable alliances between Norsemen and high-born
women in Ireland and the Western Isles, and despite the claims
now being made for Irish influence on early Icelandic prose
and verse, and despite the increasingly enthusiastic awareness expressed by Icelanders today of their Celtic inheritance—
despite all these legitimate reservations, the colonization of
Iceland was essentially a Norse undertaking, with the men of
south-west Norway decidedly the strongest contributors. They
came to an empty land, only about one-sixth of which was
suitable for human habitation. They at once set about exploring
it and taking it into private ownership. Because the land had no
king and no hereditary nobility, and because it quickly established a National Assembly for law and legislation, the Althing
at Thingvellir in south-west Iceland, and evolved a national
Constitution, the Icelandic Commonwealth has sometimes been
seen as a democracy; but all power, local and national, lay in
the hands of 36 chieftains or *goðar* (lit. godly ones), a number
later increased to 39, and finally in 1005 to 48. Their authority
rested unshakeably on both a secular and a religious foundation.
The country was fairly well off for natural resources: sea mam-
mals and fish, bird-life, grass and berries, hot springs—and also
in volcanoes, glaciers, powerful rivers, and lava-deserts. Farming and fishing were the staples of life.

The Norsemen, we may here remind ourselves, were traders
as well as plunderers. For export Iceland had wool and woollens,
dressed sheepskins and hides, fats in forms as diverse as cheese
and tallow, and such indigenous novelties as falcons for the sport
of kings, and stallions for horse-fighting, and after the Third

Crusade, 1187–92, the country did its bit for Christianity (to which it had been converted from heathendom *c.*1000) by the export of sulphur for the manufacture of 'Greek Fire'. Oddly enough, during the Commonwealth period Iceland seems not to have exported stockfish to Europe, though of all Icelandic exports this would later become the best known. In return for these goods Iceland received timber (always a prime necessity in a more or less tree-less country), tar, tools, weapons and metals in general, grain and flour, salt and honey, wine and church vestments, and fine linen. These would prove the staple imports of Greenland too.

The Commonwealth thus established lasted until 1262–4, when it was so undone by a worsening climate and other natural hardships and disasters, a weakening of communications, civil unrest amounting almost to civil wars, and political pressure from abroad, that it acknowledged the sovereignty of the Norwegian king. It is a troubling story, alleviated for posterity by two spectacular and world-famous triumphs. The first (though not in point of time) was the development of the art of prose narrative whose richest flowering is seen in the family sagas and kings' sagas in the thirteenth century, but would also deploy an assortment of historical (with and without inverted commas) and geographical treatises, bishops' lives, and sets of annals too. It is to these that we owe our knowledge of the other wondrous feat of the Icelanders, the European discovery of Greenland and the first European acquaintance with North America some 450 years before the voyages of Columbus. And it is they that tell us still that it is wiser to look for the visible evidence of that acquaintance in Newfoundland rather than New Mexico, and—not a promise, mind—in Maine rather than Minnesota. For it was the Icelanders—a Celt is speaking—and not the Irish or the Welsh, who added these new dimensions to what the Greeks called the *Oikumene*, the known World of Men. It is in their direction that we now turn.

But let no one tremble. Just a thumbnail sketch, and I promise it shall be a very small thumb. Greenland was first sighted, reputedly by accident, in the 930s, first explored in the 980s, and that same decade saw the arrival of its first settlers, under the leadership of Eirik the Red. There were two main areas of settlement, the Eastern Settlement near the modern Julianahaab, and the Western Settlement some 400 miles to the north, near the modern Godthaab. The entire subcontinent—which in effect means the western coastal areas—was uninhabited. The native Eskimo population had withdrawn. The Norse population would eventually be of the order of 3,000–4,000 souls. The colonies survived by a mainly animal husbandry, by fishing, hunting walrus, seal, and caribou, and by a limited trade with Norway. But by the mid-thirteenth century things were going wrong. The climate deteriorated cruelly, communication with Scandinavia became increasingly difficult, and the Eskimo returned, at first up north, but then pushing his way down the western coastal scrip. The economy, never very firm-based, collapsed, the Western Settlement was extinguished in the 1340s, and the Eastern Settlement perished in macabre and gruesome fashion *c*.1500. Even for the professional student it is a rending story. And, of course, it carries us far beyond the Viking Age.

So much—and so little—of Greenland. What of *Vinland hit Góða*, Wineland the Good? What of North America? True to pattern. It was first sighted by a storm-swept Iceland skipper named Bjarni Herjolfsson, looking for his father, who had departed for Greenland with Eirik the Red's land-takers the summer before. He didn't put ashore at his first landfall (in Labrador south of the tree-line), but coasted northwards for five days, saw the rock-slabs and glaciers of southern Baffin Island, took a poor view of them, and got safely across to Greenland and duly found his father. Several voyages of exploration followed, across the Denmark Strait and thereafter southwards, and it is now established beyond all doubt that there was a short-lived Norse settlement, almost certainly a ship-repair and survey-base at L'Anse-aux-Meadows on the northern tip of Newfoundland. All the known voyages were associated in saga tradition with the family of Eirik the Red, and were over and done with by *c*.1025. There is slight but acceptable evidence of later trading contacts with the native populations further north, i.e. in Canada. It is reasonable to assume that Norse sailors reached the Gulf of St Lawrence, but it is worth emphasizing that there is no trustworthy evidence for a Norse Viking presence anywhere (and I repeat *anywhere*) in the United States. The quick withdrawal of the Norsemen was due to their long and difficult lines of communication (later made worse by climatic change), no decisive superiority of weapons, a lack of manpower sufficient to defeat the determined resistance of the Indian and Eskimo peoples already in possession of the country.

III

And now, before I conclude my brief account of what I began by calling a tremendous story, a final question intrudes itself. How do we know about these things? I promise a thumbnail answer.

Briefly, our sources of knowledge are three: (1) the written sources, or documents; (2) what in a probably old-fashioned way I would call that traditional archaeology and its ancillary sciences which in part confirmed, in part modified the documents by revealing the visible evidence of Viking society, culture, and civilization—farms, churches, cemeteries, weapons and ornaments, ships, art, utensils, for example; and (3) the evidence and its interpretation now being proffered by the palaeo-scientists.

Myself I am a student of literature and history, a reader and (I trust) assessor of documents, who has been fortunate enough to enjoy the friendship and support of archaeologists and palaeo-scientists for some 35 years. I am also a Welsh Viking: I have pillaged the learning of these admirable men and women without shame or mercy—and mean to do so for the rest of my working-life. The Icelandic sagas and related documents which tell of the northern voyages are precious and irreplaceable by any other source of knowledge, but they have little, or maybe nothing, more to tell us, whereas on what I will call the applied sciences side—palaeo-ecology, -economy, -entomology, -ethnology—all the *e*'s in the world, and the rest of the alphabet from *Anthro* to *Zoo-o* for good measure—we are witnessing a mighty accumulation of new and scientifically determinable information only now made possible by the instruments and techniques of what I will a shade vulgarly call our New High-Tech Age.

To stay with the Western Voyages, the patterns of settlement, the patterns of life—and death—are now being revealed as never before. Supposition and approximation are on their way out; demonstration and exactitude are on their way in; and the artificers of change are busy on just about every site from the west of Greenland to the east of Iceland, and from Newfoundland to the Viking Kingdom of York. Bones, teeth, slag, fibres, and lice, and all the discards and droppings of the human and animal creation, have never spoken so eloquently. Shakespeare, who said everything, spoke of Sermons in stones, books in the running brooks. And so today: Manuscripts in middens, tomes in the chromosomes. One shining example from my own very limited experience: one vellum core the size of a pinhead destroyed the claims to authenticity of the Vinland Map, which all the learning, expertise, arguments, and doubts of half-a-hundred savants at the Smithsonian Vinland Map Conference in 1966 had failed to do. And finally, the new sciences are deep-rooted in humanity and our human story.

Good luck and gratitude to them all! And gratitude too to the authors, scribes, and preservers of the written sources. Nothing is easier than to find faults in them. Read the classical historians and geographers, the Vulgate Bible, Germanic (especially North Germanic) religion, mythology, and heroic literature, Germanic and Celtic legend and folk-tale, the Dark Age encyclopaedists—read all these and you become a kind of sniffer-dog for unipeds, grape-clusters, perilous maidens, furry-gloved sybils and seeresses, and all things that happen in threes. There are so many of these in the written sources that nobody any longer gives you a biscuit for finding one.

But with all these imperfections—if in thirteenth-century works they *are* imperfections—which in my opinion they most emphatically are not—I would be more worried if they were *not* present—anyhow, along with all these imperfections the Norse documents give you a remarkably coherent account of the northern voyages and discoveries, and in the most spectacular area of all, which is Vinland-America, they offer the enquirer a set of sailing directions which will take you from southwest Greenland to the North American (which here means Canadian) coast, and so down to the Strait of Belle Isle, and so to L'Anse-aux-Meadows, where the visible and assessable evidence of the Norse discovery of *c*.1000 awaits you.

And so my hour's tale is done. But long habit compels me to end with a threnody and a concluding flourish. Thus, of the three major Atlantic ventures, Iceland, Greenland, Vinland-America, only the settlement in Iceland took deep root and continues to bear fruit. The Greenland colonies perished miserably, and in Wineland the Good the fabled grapes soon withered on the vine. And yet all the voyages stand high among the more peaceful Viking battle-honours, and we must mark them and praise them as an unforgettable contribution to our common European–American heritage, and more widely to the spirit of human endeavour.

⚜12⚜

Address To My Friends
24 May 1987

Mr Principal Sir, Your Excellency, Professor Slay, Distinguished Guests and Colleagues, Ladies and Gentlemen—all of whom I would gladly subsume under the heartfelt title, *Gyfeillion Annwyl*, my dear and treasured friends:

This is one of the supreme occasions of my long and ever-lengthening professional and private life, and with your permission I would wish to mark it not by rhetoric or hyperbole, but by a resort to the unadorned simplicities of nature and folk-wisdom. And first: by one simple and all-embracing expression of gratitude and affection to each and every one of you for the honour you do me and the kindness you show me. And to you, Mr Ambassador and your gracious Lady—Ambassador as you are of my second homeland—my warmest thanks of all. Like the western voyages from Norway to Iceland, from Iceland to Greenland, and from Greenland to God's Own Country and the Land that God gave Cain—I refer, of course, to Vesturheimur, the eastern seaboard of North America, which candour compels me to admit your ancestors discovered somewhat ahead of mine—like those great seaways, the Road to West Wales is long and arduous. But you have made it—and made it in good company—and you will find, Sir, that the natives—not Karlsefni's Skraelings, but Prince Madoc's Welsh-speaking Indians, are friendly.

And so to my first simplicity. I owe it to no less a man than

Spoken before a gathering of friends, colleagues, and distinguished Norse scholars at a dinner given by the University College of Wales, Aberystwyth, to mark my eightieth birthday and the conferring upon me by His Excellency the Ambassador of Iceland of the Commander's Cross of the Icelandic Order of the Falcon (*Stórriddarakross hinnar íslensku falkaorðu*).

Sigurður Nordal. On an appropriate occasion, long, long ago, he confided to me this great truth: 'It is very pleasant to be a little drunk, on a little pony, in a little rain.' What a beautiful sentiment! Folk-wisdom on the high heights—or as we preferred to pronounce it in South Wales, on the 'igh 'ights. The ingredients, need I say, are not mandatory. Myself I have come to prefer: 'It is very pleasant to be a bit above oneself, on a falcon's wing, in a downpour of goodwill.' The soft spring rain of praise was ever grateful to an autumnal head.

My mention of Professor Nordal reminds me that he was part of the history of Icelandic Studies at the University College of Wales, begun by Norman Garmonsway, and now so powerfully upheld by Professor Slay. Sigurður came here in the mid-fifties and delivered three lectures on the Icelandic Sagas, to match my own feat at the University of Iceland in 1951, when I delivered three lectures on our Welsh medieval collection of stories and romances, *The Mabinogion*. There is a copy of the superb Golden Cockerel edition of that work in your University Library, as well as the diplomatic editions of the *White Book of Rhydderch* and the *Red Book of Hergest*. Einar Ólafur Sveinsson was another great scholar who came here and lectured on the Celtic (which in this context means Irish) influence on early Icelandic literature. Nor must I forget that a third, much younger, Icelandic scholar came to North Wales and so mastered the Welsh language that he delivered a short address in Chapel on his travels and adventures. By a pardonable error he temporarily confused the two Welsh words, *cyfaill*, friend, and *ceffyl*, horse, so that his 'Conversations with my *Ceffyl*' became as prized a connoisseur's piece in Gwynedd as Robert Louis Stevenson's 'Travels with a Donkey' in less cultured climes. (I would not have retailed this last little story, did not that splendid man and scholar concerned delight in telling it himself.)

I shall not allow any consideration of merit or desert to intrude on my happiness this evening. My first acquaintance with Icelandic literature and the language that enshrines it took place back in—hold it!—1926, which surprises me even more than it can surprise you—and I have stayed with it ever since. My first visit to Iceland was in 1948, and that too I have stayed with ever since. I have followed in the footsteps (or do I mean the hoofprints?) of Ingólf the first settler from Ingólfshöfði to Reykjavík; and in the wake of Garðar the first circumnavigator, though unlike him not from the Eastern Horn back to the Eastern Horn, but from Reykjavík harbour right around and back to Reykjavík, with a change of boat at Ísafjörður, where I stayed at the Temperance Hotel, said to be much favoured by honeymooners, but whose notice-board displayed the most stringent list of prohibitions and barriers to joy since Leviticus. Just like West Wales, I thought: Dame Wales to the T! And indeed the resemblances between Ynys y Kedern and Ynys yr Ia, the Island of the Mighty and the Island of Ice, are both many and compelling, shaped as we are by our political history, the thinness of our soil, our count of sheep and mountains, our fish and poachers (you may have more of the one, but we have more of the others), our attachment to place, our love of our literary heritage.

The people too. I can think of so many Icelanders without whom my life and labours would be the poorer. But as with you, my friends here present, if I list even their names, much less their distinctions and achievements, and all they mean to me, there would be no time for anything else. So let one name suffice for all—a name, Mr Ambassador, held in the highest regard by many of our guests as well as myself: Kristján Eldjárn, archaeologist, university teacher, Director of your National Museum, and finally your President, and to such old Icelandic hands as Peter Foote and David Wilson the same friend and sustainer as he was to his own countrymen. He *was* our fellow-countryman, as we felt ourselves to be his. And here it is with pride I recall the tribute of that lovely man Vilhjálmur Bjarnar, curator of the Icelandic Collection at Cornell until his death in 1985. 'You two Welsh ones,' he said to Mair and me at our parting. 'You are just like two of us.'

Why, I wonder, this affinity, this sense of kinship between the Icelanders and me? But speculation is always dangerous. Arthur Machen was once asked by an earnest reader of *Titbits*, 'Who was the grandfather of Alfred the Great?' Said Arthur—and he said it in print too—'That, sir, is the kind of question no gentleman would dream of asking.' It cost him his job, and I can't afford to lose mine, so no more of affinities. And yet . . .

And now I have just two things more to say. The first will confirm what my friends know: the nineteen-eighties have been good years for me. In 1982 came the beautiful new edition of *The Mabinogion*, already revised in 1974 by the scholarly care of our friend Bryn Roberts, now our National Librarian. It was published—appositely enough—by Dragon's Dream. In 1984 came the extensively revised *History of the Vikings*, and last year in 1986 the considerably expanded and revised *Norse Atlantic Saga*. Northern studies are advancing very rapidly, and will continue to do so. I judged it a better service to the subject to bring those two books up-to-date than to branch off anew. That I have been able to complete this programme is due in large measure to the strong support, the editorial expertise, and scholarly practice of Mair, my wife. If there were any justice in marriage, her name would be on the title-page with mine. But we do not marry for justice. We marry for love.

Which brings me to my closing sentences. I have already said that my mind is not for the time being distracted by any consideration of merit or desert. Both heart and head are taken up with the affection of friends and the approval of my fellow-students and teachers. My gratitude I cannot hope to express. But my modesty I will furnish out with my second piece of nature and folk-wisdom. In fact, Welsh poetic wisdom, freely translated. 'When God gave the nightingale a voice, he didn't tell the crow he shouldn't sing.' Or as Hans Andersen put it: 'When the hooves of the Emperor's warhorse were shod with gold, the little dung-beetle held his leg out too.' Well, Nightingale or Crow, Beetle or Warhorse, boys and girls bach, am I happy! Thank you. And God bless you.

INDEX

This short selection of personal names and assorted subject-matter is primarily intended to amplify and particularize the broad directives of the List of Contents.